New Theology No. 6

New Theology No. 6

Edited by
Martin E. Marty
and Dean G. Peerman

The Macmillan Company
Collier-Macmillan, Ltd., London

Library of Congress Catalog Card Number: 64-3132

SECOND PRINTING 1969

The Macmillan Company
Collier-Macmillan Canada Ltd., Toronto, Ontario

Printed in the United States of America

ACKNOWLEDGMENT

"Toward a Political Hermeneutics of the Gospel" (Copyright © 1968 Jürgen Moltmann) is from the book by Jürgen Moltmann titled *Religion, Revolution and the Future,* soon to be published by Charles Scribner's Sons. Used by permission of the author and Charles Scribner's Sons.

Contents

5

III: THE PRACTICE OF REVOLUTION: THEOLOGICAL
     REFLECTION

Theology and Revolution

No one can accuse editors of theological journals—on whose decisions these annual books depend—of having turned their backs on the world. Whatever happened to the ivory tower, the thick seminary wall, the stained-glass filter? True, responsible editors keep on monitoring developments in the disciplines of biblical studies, church history, and dogmatic theology. Many journals are committed to specialties that screen them from overexposure to the mundane scene. The best editors do not worry about the relevance of every change in the theological disciplines: they care about the quality of research and the value of discovery. But most journals do not any longer prevent their editors from seeking to relate theology to the public world. Last year most editors featured revolution in that world.

The Visible Revolutions

No one can accuse that world of failing to offer evidences of revolutionary unrest. In the Old World, in a climate of renewed hope for East-West and Marxist-Christian entente and dialogue, the Soviets invaded liberalizing Czechoslovakia. In university centers like Paris, Berlin, and New York, names like Daniel Cohn-Bendit, Rudi Dutschke, and Mark Rudd alerted the world to the measure of student discontent and the precariousness of intellectual and academic establishments.

The United States saw the most unsettling year in living memory and perhaps in a century. Protests against the war in Vietnam led to what amounted to abdication by a President who three and a half years earlier had received a virtually unprecedented mandate not to enlarge that war. He had been toppled by a band of students and peace advocates gathered around the banner of a relatively unknown senator who broke all the rules of campaigning but stood on a side that received overwhelming support in the majority party's primaries. Certainly, something revolutionary was going on inside American politics. But an assassination took the life of another candidate, and his and the other senator's young followers were thwarted by party leadership and their ranks dispersed after considerable head-knocking by Chicago police in August.

The more radical elements of American youth, like their counterparts in Latin America and in the Eastern hemisphere, began to make heroes of Ché Guevara, Ho Chi Minh, Mao Tse-tung, Régis Debray, Frantz Fanon, and other symbols of the violent anti-colonial and anti-Western spirit. The world became aware of student revolt. Because of the racial policies of certain participating nations, athletes threatened boycotts of the Olympics and other athletic events. The dropout hippies of 1967 dropped back in as a new "New Left" in 1968–69. Counterrevolutionaries reacted with compulsive calls for repression, for law and order.

In the churches revolution proceeded apace. Pope Paul VI went to Bogotá in the summer of 1968, ostensibly to grace in sanctuary style events of the Eucharistic Congress. Actually, he was engrossed with a mission of another kind: to persuade Latin American elites to yield power, and to advise Roman Catholic revolutionaries to keep fighting for social justice but to eschew violence. Meanwhile he met revolution in his own church after issuing *Humanae Vitae*, an encyclical condemning birth control, though the majority of Western theologians had declared themselves for it. The World Council of Churches in its meeting at Uppsala, Sweden, tried to talk about things ecumenical, but constantly came back to the subject of revolution. And the recognized world leader of nonviolent revolutionary forces, one who worked out of specifically religious motivations, lay dead in Memphis. His death was observed by rioting in the streets.

One hesitates to begin the catalog of evidences because he cannot end it, and one knows that after he lays down his pen and submits his writing for publication, many new events of revolt, rebellion, revolution—and certainly reaction and repression—will have begun to make his listings out of date. Here they have been introduced almost as incantations and for liturgical effect, to make a simple point: the world to which theologians address themselves at the moment is not a world of subtle political shifts, quiet and respectful dialogue, or nuanced adjustments.

The Risks of Theology

Theology exists in such a world to help people interpret, to inspire them, and to judge their aspirations and methods. Theology, of course, speaks largely out of and to specific communities—in the instance of this book, the Christian community; so its power is limited to some extent by the limits of that community. But when that community numbers nominally hundreds of millions of people, and when these people relate to the same evocative symbols that theologians do ("Crucifixion," "Resurrection," "All Things New"), there is considerable power potential. Apathetes and repressors in the churches and in the surrounding world have learned to pay attention to certain kinds of theologians and ecclesiastical leaders as they have not for decades.

Such attention can lead to temptations, and theologians have not always been able to resist. Many have dealt with revolution obsessively; that is, at the expense of other legitimate Christian themes. Some have done so without definition; the result is confusion. Many have exploited the theme of revolution in order to become relevant or to assert their virility or to satisfy egos; often there has been thoughtless chatter on the part of comfortable academics who have not counted the cost of revolution because they were located where they did not have to count that cost.

These hazards accounted for and these failures repented, the theological community has had to take the risks and to speak of revolution. The theologians live in a world wherein, as Robert McAfee Brown put it, people live who hold four aces and are not asking for a new deal. In that world of abundance, most are hungry; in that world of affluence, most are unsheltered; in that world of technological mastery, few live by promise or share hope; in that world of potency, few have freedom. How are the many going to get it?

The conservative nonrevolutionary, Christian or not, has his answers. Some say simply: They are not going to get it, and it is immoral to build up rising expectations toward revolution. We have to live with the way the cards have been dealt. The poor you have always with you. Assure freedom for the already free, and do not risk its extension.

If they are Christian, these conservatives will add two points. One, Christianity is not of this world, so the churches should not be compromised over concerns about material things or about meddling in politics. Two, if there is to be political involvement, it must be on the side of orders and Order—status quo and established order; Pauline and Petrine writings in the New Testament say so.

Their antagonists—and every theologian in this book is one, no matter how they differ among themselves—reply: Such views abandon the world to the demonic. They lead to stagnation and death. They line up the churches on the side of violence in the status quo as assuredly as if the churches were to side with revolutionaries and their violence against the status quo. Christianity is a material religion; read the parables of Judgment Day with their concrete tests about material goods and services. Christians may respond to an eternal vision, but it is tested in time; they may not have a political program, but they have an impetus toward the needs of people and a pull from the future. They are born in the context of a community that witnesses to change, to the new. Thus the lines are drawn.

The Motifs of Revolution

Defining revolution is as difficult as defining "religion" or "secularity"—words focal in many debates in the previous volumes in this series. Most of the authors represented here give at least functional definitions appropriate to their arguments, and some of them (like George Celestin) at least begin to be systematic in their attempts. Here it is important to note only some common threads running throughout these essays. For the Christian, revolution is born not merely in response to the empirical world but in the effort to follow the "eschatological" note imparted by biblical witness. Is the world as we now find it the Kingdom of God? Is its way congruent with the way of the Kingdom? Of course not; inside history it never will be. But the mandate is there: to respond, to move with God's momentum in history, to accept Christ's gift of newness, to live "as if" (and actually) experiencing the new creation, to change, to preach, to heal, to serve, to love.

The second motif is based on discontent with the world as it is, with the tradition that has been handed down. For Christians this involves acceptance of the churches' guilt in establishing the no longer humanizing status quo. There must be tearing down, sundering, and shattering. Thereupon people who participate in revolution must follow up not with a specific program for a new order but at least with some vision and some practical and strategic concerns, so that they help build institutions that extend freedom and permit access to goods and means.

That leaves one big question, and in some sense or other all the essays in this book deal with it: *how* bring about change? As Christians or simply as men? Violently or nonviolently? As political Christians or as Christian people who happen to be citizens inside autonomous political orders? By verbal witness or direct action? With utopian or more ambiguous promises? Out of sectarian or catholic motives?

The Movement of Theology

If we edit these volumes many more years, we may, despite ourselves, begin to become Hegelians. We keep seeing how last year's syntheses contain elements that lead to new theses. (Being accumulators and not repudiators, junk collectors and not garbage burners, curators and not only inventors, we also find it difficult to throw away positive contributions from earlier theses, and like to think that at worst and at best *New Theology* Nos. 1 through 5 provide a record of continuities worth reconsulting!) In the earlier volumes we noted the obsession with the secular in theological circles. By the time of *New Theology No. 3* the secular became the formal theme. But themes like "beyond the secular" and "the new religiousness," while not full-fledged antitheses, were at least partial counters to the secular preoccupation. They preempted the attention of the theologians in *No. 4*, who argued that mere secularity meant accepting the world on its own terms and that theology must be discontented, must come at the world from a different approach.

That approach, according to the authors in *No. 5*, was eschatological, from the future, respondent to the not-yet, guided by Christian symbols like promise and hope. It was clear that the futurism and hope implied in last year's cluster was not concentrated on the solitary individual's extrication from the temporal and material world into the transtemporal realm of salvation. No, the essays had also temporal, social, and political implications; most of them (Weissman, Fackenheim, Keen, Braaten, Metz, Cox, Novak, and Garaudy, to cite some) were on tiptoe toward this year's topic, revolution. By the time last year's collection was put to bed at the presses, this year's theme was already clear to us. A summer of visits to libraries and systematic surveys and content analyses confirmed all the hunches. From Christian promise and hope to theology and revolution—that is the direction of the thesis born out of a disquieting yet promising synthesis.

"Theology of Hope" was not a movement so much as an emphasis, and the editors hope that "Theology and Revolution" will also be no more than that. Motifs like hope or revolution can indeed be prisms through which all theology may be viewed or can cast shadows on all theological reflection, but that does not mean they become the only theme, the whole substance. Not all "new theology" was about revolution in recent months, nor—we hasten to stress!—was all talk about revolution "new theology."

Common Problems, Critical Stance

Certain common problems come up in the following essays. "Theology and Revolution" deals with people and not only with individual persons. Inevitably, this means that these essays are churchly in a way that secular theology, with its interest in world-blending and its accommodation to things as they are, was not. That they are not churchly in the conventional or static sense will be clear to every reader and needs no elaboration. *How* they are churchly, what the church is to which these authors relate, and what it is to become: in such questions lies much of the drama of this book.

Again and again, readers will note that the authors have to deal with another revolutionary force in the world, Marxism. Like some forms of Christianity, Marxism has become established, dehumanizing, and oppressive—as demonstrated now by events in Czechoslovakia or not many years ago by Stalinism. But no Christian theologian can talk long about change without recognizing that for a hundred years Marxism has been on the scene with its alternative interpretation of the industrial order, technology, mass man, and the status quo. (Alasdair MacIntyre's *Marxism and Christianity* [New York: Scribner's, 1968] is a succinct statement of the reasons why Christianity and Marxism so often clash and so often coincide.) The reappraisals of Marxism in these essays are often positive but just as often negative. That they can be made at all is evidence of a revolutionary spirit; that reappraisals may not long be accepted is a legitimate fear in a time of promised (if disguised by slogans) repression and suppression, at least in American society.

Do the editors agree with all the essays? The question is important not because we must assume that all readers have intrinsic curiosities about the editors' psyches or positions, but because the editors' commitments may have a bearing on how they determine which articles should be included and which should be rejected. One answer is easy: How could they agree, since dramatically opposing views appear here, as they have within each volume and between the volumes. But it is true that we have not found it worthwhile to try to track down right-wing reactionary essays from politically fundamentalist journals, a few of which operate also in the theological world. The theology represented here does come from the mainline Catholic universities and seminaries, from representative Protestant denominations and schools of thought. We beg readers to notice that one of the most revolutionary documents in the book was written by Catholic bishops; ten years ago not many would have thought that writing by bishops could be classed as "new theology"!

The editors are not uncritical of all the talk about revolution in the churches. Often that talk is mindless and sloganizing itself; often it underestimates riches in Christian tradition and minimizes the role of reason and political evolution; a utopian tinge sometimes blights its promise and a nihilist shadow falls over its failures; not always does it hold to the Protestant principle of self-criticism (what if we *win* a revolution, and our establishment runs the show?) or the Catholic substance, which demands support of cultural formations; it often fails to calculate the cost and to measure the terror that follows lost revolutions (who, after all, has the guns and bombs in our societies?). Needless to say, we have tried not to presume upon the reader's good will or disappoint him by including writings that overdo any of these traits or manifest these faults.

Anticipating the Plot

Now, to anticipate but not to summarize, we present the thread of the essays as we see it, so readers can discern the rationale behind the choice of articles along with our hopes for their effects. *New Theology No. 6* opens with three "disciplined" theoretical statements from the fields of biblical, historical, and systematic theology. They are to provide a foundation for what follows and to indicate that revolution-in-theology is not a motif that can be isolated from the Christian past and responsible work in various fields of study.

J. Christiaan Beker gives expression to the world of basic scholars who are supposed to feel left out by the passion for novelty or, worse, to market Instant Relevance of a kind that would be uncongenial to their research and inquiry. How do biblical scholars, who deal with millenniums-old materials, have anything to say to the world of change and the new? Beker's answer includes what looks conventional and staid, but when he describes what exegetes do, especially because of the character of the book they are interpreting, one can see how apropos biblical studies are to this theme. He calls for a "theological assessment of revolution" and begins to show that the Bible speaks not only to the world of Freud but also to that of Marx.

The second essay blends recent history with theological formulation. *Thomas W. Ogletree* further develops Beker's themes, though his code words change from *Freud and Marx* to *Anxiety and Responsibility*. Like Beker—and this we find appealing—he does not try to throw anything away that might be valid and helpful now. So while he is critical of the "anxiety" generation, which stressed theology and the limits of man (Barth, Heidegger, Bultmann, Tillich), he wants to appropriate its findings into a richer view of those who are working on "responsibility" and the potential of man. Such concerns take him into the realm where power must be discussed; power takes him back to God-talk and church-change.

Jürgen Moltmann, much discussed but not represented in last year's volume devoted to the Theology of Hope motif that is so much associated with his name (see: we did not want to be cultic!), makes an overdue but very much in place appearance in this year's annual. Moltmann's major book on hope, along with his other writings, accented the sociopolitical implications of eschatology; here he has the opportunity to set forth the connection explicitly. To no one's surprise, he builds on the Resurrection of Christ as the basis for Christian revolutionary talk and, after some critical appraisal of

Marxist contributions, shows why the Bible and the church cannot "fit in" to support established order.

The second part of the book is a head-on discussion of the way revolution comes to twentieth-century man: across lines of East-West, Developed Nations-Third World, Colonial-Anticolonial, Marxist-Christian distinctions.

Because his brief essay audaciously attempts six definitions of revolution along with numerous illustrations of theological and historical motifs associated with these definitions, we have placed *George Celestin*'s piece next; it may be rather familiar material for people who have read much in the field. For newcomers it should be particularly helpful. Everybody should appreciate the bonus thrown in: a brief introduction to the "Bonhoeffer of the Christian revolutionaries" (as we might call him), Father Camilo Torres. And we hope they will keep in mind the last ten words of Celestin's piece as they take the plunge.

Plunge they will, into the thick of things, with *J. M. Lochman*'s summary of ecumenical talk on revolution. If it were only summary, it would have no business here, for Lochman's take-off point is a report on a conference held two and one-half years before our publication date. But that "Geneva Conference of 1966" remains a live issue; it first made many in the churches aware of discontent in the Third World and of the many kinds of Christian expression moving beyond that discontent. And Lochman (who was also in *New Theology No. 1*, by the way) does more than summarize. He takes sides and faces some of the main issues of force and strategy.

The reappearance of Professor Lochman gives us the opportunity to make amends for our introductory remarks on him in the 1964 volume. Out of stupid automatic reflex we then called him "an Iron Curtain theologian," so conditioned are we by the parlance of Western media. Well, since then we have been privileged to meet Lochman, and he asked us with the proper mixture of Christian brotherliness, pain, and twitting spirit, "Why do you call me an Iron Curtain theologian? Would not Christian, or Protestant, or Reformed, or Czech do as well? Do I call you imperialist theologians? Why so much judgment in your adjectives?" He forgave us our thoughtlessness, and promised to write an East-West Ecumenical Glossary for *The Christian Century* (we are still waiting). Meanwhile we have learned a good deal about the world, about Czechoslovakia, about Lochman—and, alas, about imperial America and *its* presuppositions for politics and theology.

Lochman makes much of *Richard Shaull*'s presentation at Geneva. Shaull has consistently developed his revolutionary views, based on long experience in Latin America, and has assumed a leadership role on the topic of revolution in developing nations in American Protestantism. Lochman sets the stage for Shaull, in his story about Helmut Gollwitzer's rueful remark that "understanding for Christian pacifism and for 'nonviolence as the most appropriate form of Christian witness'" was growing at the same moment that "we hear from our brethren in the underdeveloped countries (where the situation is a revolutionary one) that they consider it incumbent upon them to participate in national and social revolutionary struggles which involve the use of force." Shaull deals directly with the issues of force and comes out more explicitly for its possible use than do most contributors.

A young Jesuit, *Rolland F. Smith*, is no less interested than Shaull in radical social change. Curiously, however, by taking up a different aspect of the problem, he is more "Protestant" about revolutionary movements than Shaull. For that reason he chooses to speak of "rebellion," suggesting that Christianity is in the world to help bring about continual upheaval inside establishments rather than to live and die for a specific program which could become entrenched in the hands of unself-critical victorious revolutionaries. He wants to ward off revolutionaries' presumptuousness and their despair. His essay complements and does not necessarily contradict Shaull's.

Finally, for this section, because of the inevitable implications for Marxist-Christian conversation in the preceding essays, we have included *Louis Dupré*'s strictures against the romantic idea that Marxism as now constituted could begin to find religion acceptable. But Dupré, neither a romantic nor a reactionary, moves on and boldly sketches some things that could happen to Marxian thought so that it could be reconstituted, reopened to religion, and thus reformed.

The final section is quite concrete, community-oriented, and full of case studies. For revolutionary talk is not always abstract and general. It appears in the experience of specific groups of people with particular languages, methods, and goals. A sample follows. The first two deal with the most vivid (but by no means the only or all-encompassing) revolution that affects the American readers of this book: the black revolt. Coming from a "peace tradition" in the churches, *Vincent Harding*, an eloquent spokesman for black Americans, constantly has to wrestle with the issues of force versus nonviolence in times of change. His approach is basically historical—naturally, for Harding is a historian. But it is also theological, for it shows us something of what theology was to the ancient people of God, to later Jews, and to American blacks: the reflection on a history, the interpretation of an experience. Harding's main theme is the concept of "chosenness," and he does novel and fresh things to it.

The other article growing out of the black revolution is *Herbert W. Richardson*'s piece insisting that the late Martin Luther King, Jr., is underestimated if he is taken only as a charismatic political leader. Dr. King was a theologian, *the* theologian for our times—so says Richardson, who is himself no mere enthusiast for "the movement" but a highly innovative thinker.

Then follow three pieces on the urgent issue of war and peace. *Hans-Werner Bartsch* has written what is to us the most consistent and disturbing essay in the book. It states the case for Christian pacifism so clearly and eloquently that we find we can wriggle past it only by blinking at much biblical witness. A surprising counterpart to Bartsch is *R. W. Tucker*'s words out of and to Quakerism. We assume that Friends make up only a small minority of our readers, even as they do of world Christianity. Therefore, at first glance, some of Tucker's intradenominational concerns may make the rest of us feel like kibitzers. But most thoughtful Christians (and many others, too) are intensely curious about the weight of Quaker witness to peace and its transformations in our time. When he calls for participation in "the Lamb's War" Rob Tucker proves that there are transformations.

The third of the peace articles deals specifically with the war that has done more than anything else to awaken the developed industrial nations to the power of revolutionary nationalism in other cultures: the Vietnam war. *Robert McAfee Brown*, born to be a moderate, has been forced into revolutionary expression on at least one subject, because of what he sees to be (as we do) an immoral, unjust, unwise, and unjustifiable American military intervention. In this article and elsewhere, Brown has been saying consistently that, however intrinsically horrible Vietnam realities are, they only or also serve to point to other horrors—unless men of good will counteract. Here is a responsible Christian reflection on dissent, conscience, humanization, credibility, openness, and reconciliation.

We choose to be somewhat churchly in the final section of the book. In the course of the half decade since Vatican II, the largest and least revolutionary-looking of the Christian churches, the Roman Catholic, has become the object of most upheaval and the subject of most revolutionary expression. One must haul out all the "re-" words for today's Catholicism: renewal, rebellion, revolt, reformulation, reconstruction and, yes, revolution. First is the first "new theology by a committee" which we have yet published. *Sixteen Bishops* from the Third World discuss Christian faithfulness in revolution. Talk about revolution comes easily and with urgency in what is often called the "Third World." Does it have a dilettante tinge in the developed nations? *Desmond Fennell* introduces a remarkable group of British Catholic Marxists, has some good things to say, and then chides them for their Catholic inferiority complex. Finally, *Rosemary Ruether* points to the dimensions of intraecclesiastical revolution in American (and world) Catholicism. The book ends on an ecumenical note: Dr. Ruether sees one model for Catholic renewal in the free-church or sectarian Protestant movements of the sixteenth century.

We have not canvassed all the revolutions: "generation gap," "media revolution"—here we go, starting a new catalog! For these there will be other theological journals, other years and, we hope, future annuals of *New Theology*.

D.G.P. and M.E.M.

I: The Groundwork of Theologians

Biblical Theology Today

J. Christiaan Beker

In this essay J. Christiaan Beker points the finger of blame
at his own breed—the so-called biblical theologians—for
what he characterizes as the "bedlam" of contemporary theology. According to Beker, much of the confusion stems from
the fact that the biblical theologian has been unsure of the
demarcation lines of his discipline; as a consequence he has
indulged in theological speculation and "sloganitis." Beker
sees the biblical theologian as mediating between biblical research and theology, and as having a critical rather than a
systematic function. One of the issues to which he feels that
function should be applied is revolution—which is also the
general subject of this volume. Originally delivered as an address at his installation as Professor of Biblical Theology at
Princeton Theological Seminary, Dr. Beker's article appeared
in the Winter 1968 issue of *The Princeton Seminary Bulletin.**
A native of the Netherlands, Dr. Beker is the author of *The
Church Faces the World: Late New Testament Books,* and
numerous articles in journals and encyclopedias.

THERE are types of confusion. Ours is no longer
a nihilistic confusion of a Sartre-type, personal despair in the
face of death: ours is a confusion of too much rather than
too little. There are so many possibilities—too many. Indeed,
we rejoice in a new sense of freedom—freedom from all the
heteronomies which bound us in the past and to the past and
which still chain our fathers in our opinion—and we are determined to establish ourselves as men of sober integrity—
men with a new sense of autonomy—men who truly belong
to a mankind come of age. All this is possible—but our too

* Princeton Theological Seminary, Princeton, N.J. 08540.

many possibilities of explicating reality turn in on us, and they erode commitment. Possibility may be our new idol and a life of non-commitment our new "possibility." For Hegel the real was the rational, for us the real is the relative. The possibility-syndrome produces our identity-crisis, so that it becomes increasingly rare to meet students with a mature sense of vocation and commitment.

Now, theology shares the confusion of our time. We no longer know what it means to do theology or what a proper curriculum should look like or how to schematize an orderly flow of theological disciplines. And it is good that theology should share the confusion of our time. For a theology which bypasses this confusion is a timeless theology and thus irrelevant. Unless theology is contemporaneous, it is not. Therefore a quick panacea for the present confusion of possibilities is beside the point—whether of a fundamentalist, new orthodox, existentialist or sociological stripe.

A romantic yearning for the eternal verities of dogma (or an however sincere lamentation over lost values) often confuses thoughtlessness with conviction, whereas, a quick existentialist posture of commitment and decision betrays too often the desire to run away from one's actual present and to float in the boundless absurd, a *credo quia absurdum*. Our professional eagerness for proclamation is too often an exhibition of spiritual vacuity.

It is in this situation then that I am asked to do biblical theology. And in a situation of confusion, the easiest thing is to wrap oneself in an academic gown—to simply withdraw from the world to the isolation of the otherwise-so-necessary library cell.

What then shall biblical theology be in our time?

1. Among the different senses biblical theology has employed in the course of time for the interpretation of scripture —the liberal, allegorical, tropological, etc.—it too often has neglected common sense. Our time calls primarily for common sense—a common sense which, hopefully, avoids the commonplace, so that at least we may clarify our present confusion, detect its components and possible direction.

2. Common sense dictates that whatever biblical theology

may be, it is primarily and simply a reflection on the value and possibility of Bible study, intended, not for the specialist, but for the average man.

This frightfully naïve observation makes us aware of the fact that recent discussions around biblical theology and hermeneutics have become so abstract, are so loaded with germanic-linguistic niceties and incomprehensible subtleties, that it is no wonder that only phenomenal statisticians and computerized experts can untangle the verbal explosions. To everyone—but the humourless specialist—it is simply comical that the science of hermeneutics, promoted to facilitate understanding, has reached a climax of unintelligibility.

3. Common sense also recognizes that the people most responsible for this bedlam are the so-called biblical theologians. Instead of mitigating the general confusion of our times, they have greatly contributed to it. Who are they actually, and what are they about? Are they historians, exegetes theologians—philosophers—therapeutic agents—cultural analysts, or all of these? It seems that they are neither fish nor fowl.

Who amidst the knowledge-explosion of our time can less execute a responsible academic function? In the discussion around hermeneutics, for instance, who is the biblical exegete who can claim philosophical competence in the realm, let us say, of the old *versus* the new Heidegger, or in the realm of process-philosophy as adequate framework for the biblical message? Cullmann's work, for instance, as biblical theologian, shows how philosophical-theological naiveté mars his great exegetical skill. Whatever salvation-history there is in scripture, it is simply not a viable modern option. If the knowledge-explosion is our common lot, how much more does it affect the biblical theologian, who must mediate between biblical research and theology. Who has ever adequately defined biblical theology? When I, today, accept the chair of biblical theology, I am somewhat envious of the solid chair offered to my colleague, a chair of New Testament studies which has withstood the centuries. My chair, in comparison, seems a rocking chair, not finding a centre of stability, but rocking back and forth between Bible studies and theology. Biblical theology, after its initial conception by Johann Philipp Gabler in the eighteenth century—as defense against the inroads of dogmatic theology—was redefined by Wilhelm Wrede in the nineteenth century as a purely historical discipline—a definition which Krister Stendahl reaffirms today.

However, I suspect that biblical theology became really in vogue with the neo-orthodox movement, but without any clear definition. Even apart from this, although Stauffer came close to a biblical theology in his New Testament theology, and although Miller Burrows produced a book under this title, a viable biblical theology of Old and New Testament, as such, have never been produced after the work of von Hofmann in the middle of the nineteenth century. It is no small wonder then that the biblical scholar questions the academic integrity of the biblical theologian, suspects him as exegete and fears from him an intrusion, not unlike the one Gabler feared from the systematic theologian. Biblical theology in our recent past was more a popular slogan than an analytically precise concept.

4. Indeed, a lot of what has gone for biblical theology is simply theological speculation, for which the epithet "Biblical" must provide respectability. Too often an isolated text is taken out of context and unambiguously propagated as *the* central biblical motif; too often James Barr's observations on the illegitimate use of Kittel's *Dictionary* are true; too often a "Biblical doctrine of the Spirit," for instance, is artificially created by a mish-mash of statements taken from all over scripture and glued together by some fanciful idea; too often the New Testament is pressed into relevance, for instance, on social-political questions, bypassing the exegetical evidence pointing to the essential indifference of the New Testament—apocalyptic community to political and social problems. The understandable eagerness for relevance and some hidden equation of the Bible with the word of God *written* (although not so hidden in the Confession of 1967) makes some almost metaphysical entity like "the Word of God" the ever-handy, prepossessed problem-solver, whereas it simply overlooks the order of priorities, namely, that the New Testament is pri-

marily addressed to first century problems, and that to neglect this produces the fallacy of immediacy. A curious lack of historical imagination and honesty often perverts the Bible for the sake of honoring it. The result is allegorization, a gross reading into scripture what it cannot support. And so the biblical theologian has enriched the "sloganitis" of theology: words like kerygma—eschatology—the Word—*agape*—salvation-event have lost nearly all precise exegetical meaning and are tossed about to give the biblical theologian some excuse for his existence.

What can be said positively?

I

The biblical theologian is primarily an exegete. He is in no sense distinguishable from the biblical scholar except for the fact that he should be as conscious as he can be about his status as a contemporary man, as the bridge-builder of the biblical field. As such he can never forget that the written document of the text confronts—and is confronted by—the living document of the interpreter. Both documents occupy his attention and the possibility of mediating between the two is decisive for the "to be or not to be" of biblical theology. The biblical theologian is interested in dialogue. However, he cannot take the dialogue situation for granted. He must face rigorously the romantic implications of the term dialogue; kerygmatic texts tend to be apodictic rather than invitations for a pastoral counseling session. The conflict is continuous between academic historical purity and the convicting insight of faith, between the claims of rationality with their in-built suspension of judgment, their fostering of the relativity of all things and the claims of commitment to faith and action; indeed, the biblical theologian must contemplate the *possibilities* of dialogue and must *assist* in enabling a dialogue situation to occur. In other words, he must assist in providing the *occasion* for a "happening." Whether such a happening occurs —i.e., essential rejection or acceptance of the biblical message—he must leave to the freedom of God and his Spirit.

As a contemporary man who is also a Christian, he can only *hope* for a happening. In that sense the dialogue takes place in the context of the Church—in the context of the community which sponsors the hope in the happening. At this point many distortions will occur—profound tokens of unbelief. Unbelief, namely, takes the form of monologue in perverting a possible dialogue. Monologue does not allow the text to speak or it does not allow the interpreter to speak. It precludes dialogue either by securing in advance an admission of an inspired test (i.e., the "hush-up-and-swallow" technique) or because of a prepossessed conviction that no text will speak unless I amputate it or overload it with ideological weight secured from elsewhere.

How little has the possibility of dialogue shaped the execution of commentaries on scripture! How odd that the most ambitious American commentary venture—the *Interpreter's Bible*—has raised up not a distinction, but a wall between "what it meant" and "what it means," so that what was supposed to be a dialogue becomes two sometimes-clashing monologues: one, that of the historian who maintains his dubious integrity by being unconcerned about the question of why he is interested in the text; the other that of the homiletician, who at every turn must jeopardize his integrity by blowing edification into texts of questionable edifying content. At least "*Biblischer Kommentar*" is making a dialogical attempt by the exegete himself in its "*Ziel*" sections (at the end of exegetical pericopes).

Too often biblical scholars disregard the dialogue target and so prevent the conditions necessary for dialogue: honesty and text concentration. On the one hand, we have the eager theologians who are so upset by nineteenth-century conceptions of honest—so-called "dry"—scholarship that their interpretations of texts are often simply fanciful meditations on modern problems with an occasional paraphrase and reference to biblical texts or biblical language. The hermeneutical "language-events" of Ernest Fuchs and his pupils can never be a substitute for exegetical control.

The greatness of Barth's commentary on Romans, for instance, should not blind us to dismiss Julicher's complaints as those of an "outdated, nineteenth century liberal," for far too often "the strange new world" of the Bible is not as strange as Barth would have us believe. No New Testament Christian, for instance, would have understood resurrection simply to mean *"Ewigkeit im Nu!"*

On the other hand, the conditions for dialogue are frustrated by the historians. Whereas the theologians just described use the text often as a springboard to jump *away from* the text at us with their own ideologies and inspired concoctions, the historians often use the text to jump *away from* the text into the hinterland of archaeology and the mysterious ramifications of *Religions-geschichte*; in short, they play the game of what Sandmel has called "parallelomania." No one denies the necessity and revelatory character of this hinterland, but hinterland should remain hinterland and not become a welcome evasion from the demands of the text itself. The target for the biblical theologian is and remains the text itself in its context.

Biblical theologians today must honestly recognize that no viable solution has been found to the centuries-old problem of the relation of the Word of God to the words of scripture, the relation of faith and history. It is Bultmann's merit to have posed the issue: *Geschichte versus Historie*. He has *not* solved it. In the meantime dialogue, even though jeopardized, must be attempted.

II

Since the biblical theologian is primarily an exegete who is conscious of the contemporary situation, his function is not systematic—as if there is anything possible like a systematic biblical theology—but critical. Professor Hiltner mentioned once the imperialism of the psychoanalytic movement. In the theological realm it equates, I think, theology with therapy. Now, the recent past has witnessed too much imperialism by the biblical theologian. This is primarily due to the claims of Barth and Bultmann who tended to equate biblical theology with the theological enterprise as such. The critical function of biblical theology should be much more modest, namely, to determine to what extent biblical insights can function in the various fields which together constitute the theological enterprise. The function of biblical theology is correlation, not domination. The imperialism of biblical theology in the recent past has created a back-lash which now threatens to isolate the Bible from today's theological quest. Bleak days lie ahead for biblical studies unless biblical theology is willing to come to terms with its own imperialism.

III

In this context, the biblical theologian views the present academic theological divisions as anachronistic. It is beyond me why Schleiermacher's model for theological studies is still operative in the clearly inter-disciplinary situation of the future. The Bible cannot operate in an academic vacuum. The insights of Professor Loder on the learning process indicate that the unique contribution of America to theology lies not in a "death of God" theology but in a true integration of the so-called Practical and Content Fields: theology outside the living experience of man becomes merely another ideology. The biblical theologian could richly contribute to heal the often divergent tendencies of sociology and psychology by suggesting on biblical grounds that private therapy can never be separated from a therapeutic social-political and communal context.

IV

One sample of the critical function of the biblical theologian could be applied to the theological assessment of revolution. We are and will be involved in great upheavals. Technological progress seems inevitably to involve dehumanization. The question is not: should we be involved or not? We simply are and will be. The question is only how the Christian will be involved. Now with respect to models for revolution—amidst political and social strategies with respect to the Establishment and the ideological power structure of the privileged *status quo*, issues with which Professor Shaull is courageously concerned—the biblical theologian asks:

1. Is the New Testament—to put it in vulgar and probably outdated language—not essentially a more Freudian than Marxist book? Is the primary focus of the New Testament not on the enemy within the self rather than the enemy outside? Is self-transformation not prior to, although not separable from, transforming societal structures? Is it not absurd to attack society purely negatively with a desire to transform it, as long as the revolutionary nucleus is itself not transformed?

2. The so-called biblical center of reconciliation may not be as central to the New Testament as recent theology has asserted. Reconciliation must pass through the revolution of the cross; and even apart from biblical insights, reconciliation may not be a target-word in our time, since a *bourgeois* affluent Church interprets it inevitably as a sanctioning of the *status quo*. Reconciliation in the race issue has simply been translated as integration. Whereas the Church should have recognized that integration which bypasses "Black Power" demands means a resurrection without a cross.

3. Has recent Reformed theology placed so much emphasis on a realized eschatology of cosmic reconciliation that it has overlooked the dualistic components of New Testament eschatology and thus assumed the role of superior mediator without participation in the ongoing struggle, which demands Christian soldiers and martyrs?

4. Has theology not over-hastily rejected the apocalyptic component of the New Testament? Existentialist theology under Bultmann may have gnosticized the cosmic dimensions of the New Testament (i.e., individualized them) to such an extent that the "theology-is-therapy" issue and an unhealthy health-cult became—against Bultmann's intentions—inevitable.

5. Does, perhaps, the apocalyptic model of the New Testament give impetus to a model of radical transforma-

tion? Is it not to be distinguished from a prophetic theology *within* history, since the apocalyptic model lives out of a new *creatio ex nihilo*, so that apocalyptic models tend toward upheaval rather than progress *within* given structures? Does the revolutionary argue against the prophetic liberal on this basis? To what extent is this apocalyptic model blunted, however, by Jesus' rejection of Zealotism, and what are the alternatives?

V

But above all, the biblical theologian is concerned with a critical evaluation of the spirituality of scripture. Bible reading is becoming increasingly a pious wish today in a cultural ethos where a Word of God, if quested at all, is sought not in scripture, but in the self in dialogue with itself, or in a reading of societal structures and movements. A primary affirmation must be that the Bible is the book of the Church: Luther's *Sola Scriptura* must be understood *in the context of* the Church, as the reforming principle of the tradition and not apart from it. Essentially, the Bible is written for believers, not for non-believers. Its self-authenticating nature in the hand of non-believers is extremely dubious. notwithstanding the many tractates about its direct relevance, and notwithstanding the abstract principle of many Protestant interpreters that the Bible is simply one book among other books, but nevertheless authenticates itself as Word of God. The Bible is basically the document of the Christian's self-identity: within our identity-crisis, it points to the source and origin of Christian self-identity. Much of the rebellion against scripture is not due to scripture itself, but to false expectations of it, of the fallacy of immediacy, immediate relevance. Succinctly: without introduction to Biblical books, i.e., without the Church's explication as to its self-identity as located in scripture, the Bible remains a locked book. And yet, the Church lives by the authority of the Bible: it posits its own creation as its creator. Concretely: the witness of scripture to the Lord of the Church, to the risen Lord Jesus is couched in an imagery so potent and effective that no demything can displace it. Time and again the Church experiences that seemingly hopeless anthropomorphisms become the central matrix for religious truth. The post-biblical Protestant can learn here from the joyful renaissance of the Bible in Catholicism.

However, contemporary man finds dialogue with the New Testament impossible, because the dialogical situation seems so limited and the motivation to it absent. Concretely: Old and New Testament piety are concerned basically with questions of unbelief—with false gods—false metaphysical options, not with non-belief, i.e., with the profound anti-ideological consciousness of men today.

Old and New Testament piety are concerned with hostility to the God of Scripture, not with indifference and scepticism with respect to the Church's absolute claims about the God of Scripture, which it empirically denies in its practice. Unbelief today desires holy men and holy actions, not holy propaganda or the ghetto-language of the Church. And the truth in the students' confusion today is this: they are searching for true models of commitment which they have not found in our collapsing world of the mighty word and the empty deed.

And the biblical theologian must recognize that unbelief is not just out there, but as contemporary man, it is within himself. Faith is too often a form of repressed unbelief. No longer, if ever, is the biblical theologian or preacher an "answer-box"; in many ways he is unbeliever—in hope. He must recognize that the question of communication and proclamation to others—the "how"—is dependent on the prior question—the "what"—i.e., the communication of the Gospel to the self. Luther's *Simul iustus ac peccator* in our time must mean first of all the willingness to demonstrate in one's own person, not the ready answer of the biblical or theological paraphrase, but the struggle of how to become a believer in the midst of one's own unbelief.

For ultimately, the irrelevance of New Testament spirituality may be our inability to come to terms with the one central question posed to us by the Bible: "My God—My God—why hast thou forsaken me?" Through the words "My

God" shines the resurrection light, and thus the affirmation of life through death—the peculiar trust that the absence of God is the pledge for his presence. Whoever possesses this secret has perhaps found a way to overcome his identity-crisis in the midst of crisis.

From Anxiety to Responsibility: The Shifting Focus of Theological Reflection

Thomas W. Ogletree

Taking exception to the prevalent notion that contemporary theology is utterly chaotic, Thomas Ogletree discerns a fairly clear-cut trend—a movement away from the anxiety-centered theology of the earlier decades of this century and toward a responsibility-centered theology more appropriate to the new situation of man. Despite their many differences, such older-generation theologians as Barth, Bultmann, and Tillich shared a concern about man's encounter with his limits; they dealt with the "boundary situations" of life—death, guilt, meaninglessness. "In contrast, the newer thrusts in theology are increasingly concentrated on the meaning of man's power and his consequent responsibility for shaping his own life and the life of the world." For those who reflect on the Christian message are finding that it has something to say to men not only at the point of their weakness but also at the point of their strength—such as in the areas of technology and politics. Dr. Ogletree, whose essay is reproduced from the March 1968 *Chicago Theological Seminary Register*,* is Assistant Professor of Constructive Theology at Chicago Theological Seminary. He is the author of *Christian Faith and History* and *The Death of God Controversy*.

IT IS hardly a secret that a major shift is taking place in the shape and style of theological thinking. A recent seminary graduate dramatized the extent and abruptness of the shift by observing that the present situation in theology seems almost wholly different from that which prevailed dur-

* 5757 University Ave., Chicago, Ill. 60637.

35

ing his formal education. Different language is being used; different authors are cited; and most important, the questions occupying the center of attention are themselves strange and unfamiliar. As he viewed it, his own program of study apparently marked the end of an era. Shifts of this kind are always disconcerting to say the least. Yet the present changes are particularly disturbing since they are reflected in studies which do not have an obvious claim even to be legitimate forms of theological expression, let alone to be sound theology. We seem to have entered the age of an anti-theological theology where everything is permitted and where all discernible critical norms have disintegrated. Not surprisingly, persons who have become adjusted to established ways of engaging in theological reflection now speak gloomily of the chaos or even bankruptcy of contemporary theology, especially Protestant theology.

While there are unquestionably chaotic elements in the current theological scene, it would be premature to conclude that nothing of significance is happening—still less that the appropriate course is to continue following familiar lines of thought. We are facing new questions, new problems, new challenges, which require a recasting of our theological understanding. Much of contemporary theology even with its weaknesses and exaggerations represents a serious attempt to deal with these new questions and challenges. If the current mood in theology is to be adequately understood and assessed, it must be explored in relation to the distinctive features of the present historical moment.

A central conviction underlying this assertion is that authentic Christian theology is situational in character. It does not consist of the gradual elaboration and refinement of a body of truths which have eternal validity. It rather consists of the attempt to interpret the fullness of the Christian gospel in a way that can address most pertinently the concrete concerns of men in given situations. Fresh theological work must be undertaken in every generation not simply because man's frail attempts to grasp the meaning of the Christian message stand ever in need of correction and revision, but also because new situations present new challenges to faith that must be met on their own terms. There are, to be sure, common elements in the various situations of men, at least in the form of "family resemblances" or overlapping characteristics (Wittgenstein) if not of a common "essence" or core of experience. Otherwise, we could not participate so sympathetically in the understandings of other times and places. Indeed, it is perhaps possible to isolate certain structures of experience which are so elemental as to be inescapable factors in every situation. Yet even these structures do not have the same meaning in every context since their particular manifestations are conditioned in important ways by historical and cultural factors. Consequently, an understanding of the Christian message which dares to address men concretely must be situational.

The aim of this essay is to offer an interpretation of the shift currently taking place in theology in light of the issues which are at the present time bringing fresh challenges to Christian understanding.[1] Attention will first be given to the style of thinking that largely dominated the theology from the twenties through the fifties. The contention is that this

---

[1] The emphasis on the situational character of theology is in general agreement with Tillich's discussion of the "material theological norms." Cf. *Systematic Theology*, Vol. I (Chicago: University of Chicago Press, 1951), pp. 47–52. In the present usage, however, attention to the situation is not so much motivated by apologetic considerations as by the concern to deal responsibly with the basic thrust of the Christian message. Also, Tillich's rather artificial methodological distinction between the questions and the answers is not being urged. The dialogue between biblical faith and contemporary culture is integral to both of these aspects of theology. It might be added that shifts in theology are not simply a result of changes in the situation. The dialectic of thought is itself continually a factor in new theological developments. That is, new lines of exploration are formulated to overcome difficulties which have emerged in previous ways of putting theological questions. If we take ideas seriously, this second factor is also quite important for theological understanding. The focus of the present essay, however, is on the way situational factors have forced shifts in the shape and style of contemporary theological reflection.

theology focused on the finitude of man and the anxiety states which disclose man's awareness of his limits. It highlighted the possibilities the gospel offers for helping men deal creatively and courageously with their limits. In contrast, the newer thrusts in theology are increasingly concentrated on the meaning of man's power and his consequent responsibility for shaping his own life and the life of the world. No suggestion is offered that the more recent accents must now radically displace the achievements of an earlier generation of theologians. The discontinuity between the first and second halves of the twentieth century is hardly so sharp. What is being suggested is that a fundamental reordering of the basic themes of Christian faith is now required if we are to respond appropriately to the new situation of man. If the aim of this essay is realized, it will show the importance of moving steadfastly beyond the most notable conclusions of our predecessors without requiring us to belittle or ignore the contributions which they have made and can continue to make to constructive theological work.

I

Recent American introductions to the so-called "Crisis" theology have characteristically begun with the telling observation that two world wars and a great depression rendered impossible the naïve optimism of the earlier liberal theology with its belief in the essential goodness of man and the inevitable progress of the human spirit. Violent upheaval within Western civilization demanded instead a theology of tragedy, a theology which could help men deal with the disintegration of order and the collapse of moral and spiritual values. Even parts of the world relatively untouched by the full dimensions of these upheavals could no longer assume that human progress had made the threat of chaos and moral decay obsolete.

Karl Barth's *Epistle to the Romans*, particularly the celebrated second edition, set the tone for the theological re sponse to the crisis in Western civilization.[2] To be sure, the crisis which concerned Barth was not the crisis of Western civilization, but the radical, all-enveloping judgment of God upon all human achievements, even those which are ostensibly the most noble and sophisticated. In this respect he was not offering a "tract for the times," something to be used when the going was difficult only to be set aside when the situation improved; he was offering a "footnote on all theology," a fundamental qualification of every endeavor to be a theologian. The upheavals in Western civilization had significance for theology only in the sense that they dramatically disclosed the inescapable limits which bind all man's thinking and knowing and doing. Yet by helping men respond in faith to the ultimate and absolute crisis of human existence, Barth in effect reduced the crisis of Western civilization to manageable proportions.

For our purposes, the significance of Barth's commentary is that it locates the starting point for theology not in man's religious experiences nor in his struggles to realize value, but precisely in his radical confrontation with his limits. In this connection, *The Epistle to the Romans* can appropriately be seen as a rigorous and sustained analysis of what it means to be a finite being. Barth saw in the culture of his time, particularly the religious and moral features of that culture, a persistent temptation for man to obscure the distinction between the finite and the infinite, to act and plan and behave as if he somehow participated directly in what is infinite and eternal. To counter this temptation Barth vigorously drove home the point that to be finite is to be wholly bound up with the ebb and the flow, the rise and the fall, of historical reality. It is to be immersed in that which is transient, relative, and passing, indeed, in that which is finally vacuous and without substance. To be sure, if man has nothing more than

[2] Trans. from the sixth edition by Edwyn C. Hoskins (London: Oxford University Press, 1933). This edition is virtually the same as the second. From the beginning Barth was joined in his new theological venture by Friedrich Gogarten, Rudolf Bultmann, Emil Brunner, and his life-long companion Eduard Thurneysen.

his finite values and achievements, he must simply do the best he can with what he has, gloomy though his prospects may be. Barth was not concerned to condemn estimates of the human situation which took this essentially skeptical form. The issue for him was that we not make the mistake of identifying the promise of the Christian message with the questionable and ephemeral possibilities emerging out of the historical process, not even when those possibilities take on a religious or moral form. Instead, he argued, the gospel concerns the radically new possibilities of God which stand at the boundary of all human achievements, indeed, which become manifest precisely in the negation of those achievements. If Barth seemed severe in his strictures against granting any theological significance to human capacities, it was because he saw in such a concern simply a more subtle and dangerous form of the old confusion between time and eternity, and hence, a refusal fully to accept the implications of being finite.

Even the markedly affirmative tone of the *Church Dogmatics* does not fundamentally alter Barth's estimate of man's limits and possibilities. Barth does correct his earlier writing in a number of important ways. He labors to counter the notion that theology can begin with man's questions and problems, or for that matter with any starting point other than the one provided by God's gracious approach to man in Jesus Christ. He also seeks to overcome his earlier tendency to treat history as though it were utterly lacking in significance, offering instead an overwhelmingly positive word about man's life in time.[3] Still, Barth's new "humanism" does not stem from a fresh assessment of the import of human decisions and actions, but from his interpretation of Jesus Christ as the decisive disclosure and actualization of the "humanity of God."[4] It is because God has breached the limits of human

[3] For a fuller treatment of this point see my *Christian Faith and History* (New York: Abingdon Press, 1965), pp. 109–114, 119–126.

[4] See especially Barth's essay, "The Humanity of God," trans. by John Newton Thomas in a collection bearing that title (Richmond, Va.: John Knox Press, 1960), pp. 38–62.

finitude, filling all man's being and knowing and doing with content they do not of themselves possess, that we must affirm the value of human history. Though the meaning of human actions and decisions within the context of the divine initiative is not altogether ignored by Barth, it is so completely over-shadowed by his attention to God's initiative in bringing his electing love to fruition that it never receives careful develop-ment. In this respect the recognition of man's inescapable limits remains crucial for Barth's theological perspective.

Barth's work was not very warmly received in the United States in spite of the fact that it marked a revolution in con-tinental theology. It seemed too negative and pessimistic about the prospects of man—perhaps because we had not participated so profoundly in the cultural crisis which pro-vided its setting. What we did not so readily understand is that a civilization experiencing the breakdown of some of its finest achievements could receive Barth's uncompromising word not as an expression of pessimism and gloom, but as an expression of promise and hope, indeed, the one word of hope which could stand the turmoil of the times.

The thesis here being argued is that the orientation to the limits of man so sharply formulated in Barth's *Epistle to the Romans* was broadly shared by the theology of the next few decades. This orientation also gained significant support from the existentialist philosophies of the period. Karl Jaspers, for example, argues that the "boundary situations" of life—guilt, sickness, and death—provide the occasions in which man is most open to Transcendence, and hence, most genuinely human. Even more important for the purposes of theology is Martin Heidegger's celebrated "*Dasein* analytic" in which man's sense of being "thrown" into existence and of living toward death is portrayed as opening up the possibility of authentic existence.[5] Of course, Heidegger does not assert with Barth that man's authenticity derives from the possibility of God which becomes manifest at the boundary of all human possibilities. He is rather concerned to identify those situa-

[5] *Being and Time*, trans. by John Macquarrie and Edward Robinson (London: SCM Press, Ltd., 1962), especially pp. 219–225, 299–312.

tions which clearly thrust upon man his "ownmost potentiality-for-Being," his freedom to choose himself and to take hold of himself.[6] Still, it is precisely in encountering his limits that man becomes aware of this freedom.

One of Heidegger's major contributions is in picking up the category of anxiety, so powerfully analyzed by Kierkegaard over three-quarters of a century earlier, and developing its significance for the fulfillment of man's being. Anxiety is that affective state which discloses to man his own possibility for authentic or inauthentic existence, primarily by awakening him to the anticipation of his approaching death. Anxiety wrenches man loose from his immersion in the everyday affairs of life, from his unthinking participation in the commonly accepted valuations of his culture. It individualizes him and thrusts him back upon himself to decide for himself about the shape and meaning of his life. Death is particularly important in this process since it is the most completely individualized and unsurpassable possibility man confronts. Where death is brought to mind in anxiety, it functions as a call to authentic existence, to a free and resolute decision about the possibilities of life which are outstanding.[7]

Considering the power and penetration of Heidegger's analysis, it is not surprising that it quickly proved serviceable for the theologian's reflections. Rudolf Bultmann sees it as an indispensable aid for bringing to awareness the meaning of the biblical texts. It fulfills this role by enabling the theologian to clarify the questions raised by the texts. Apart from such clarification the message of the Bible cannot be grasped. In keeping with Heidegger's own focus, Bultmann highlights the theological significance of situations which disclose the transitoriness of the world, even its ultimate emptiness and unreality in the face of eternity.[8] It is in confronting the boundary of human life and the finiteness of the world that man is opened to the subject matter of the biblical texts. The real stumbling block of the gospel, Bultmann contends, is not its

---

[6] *Ibid.*, p. 232.

[7] *Ibid.*, pp. 294–295.

[8] Rudolf Bultmann, *Jesus Christ and Mythology* (New York: Charles Scribner's Sons, 1958), p. 23.

connection with a pre-scientific world-view, but its frontal assault on all man-made security, on every effort on the part of man to gain mastery over the world and over his own life.[9] It must be emphasized that man's liberation from the necessity of guaranteeing his own security does not imply his withdrawal from the world. It means his freedom to participate in the world and to enjoy it without being decisively conditioned by it or depending upon it for the meaning of existence. It is to have the world "as though not."[10] Still, the important point is that the entree into fundamental theological questions is provided by man's radical confrontation with his limits, and by the anxiety and despair that inevitably accompany his vain attempts to find security for himself.

Bultmann modifies Heidegger's thought in appropriating it into his exegetical work. Heidegger concentrates on what is distinctive about the manner of man's being in the world in order to reopen the classical quest for the meaning of being as such.[11] For Bultmann, Heidegger's analysis is significant primarily for the light it sheds on human existence itself both in its authentic and its inauthentic modes. An illumination of these possibilities and their relation to the Christian message is the matter of decisive importance to the biblical exegete. The second modification is more crucial. In Heidegger's view authentic existence is a possibility man can and must lay hold of for himself. It is a matter of resolve, a purposeful response to the call of conscience.[12] Without undercutting the necessity of decision and responsibility, Bultmann contends that authentic existence is a possibility which can be actualized only by the action of God. It is a transcendent possibility which is just as much gift as it is demand. The effect of this contention is to underscore the unsurpassability of the limits that bind human existence, and to identify faith with the new possibilities that ever stand beyond all man's being and know-

[9] *Ibid.*, pp. 39–40.

[10] Cf. *Existence and Faith: Shorter Writings of Rudolf Bultmann*, selected, translated, and introduced by Shubert M. Ogden (New York: Meridian Books, Inc., 1960), pp. 177, 181–182.

[11] Heidegger, pp. 24–35. Cf. *Jesus Christ and Mythology*, pp. 45, 53–59.

[12] Cf. Heidegger, pp. 343–348.

ing and doing. On this point, Bultmann explicitly continues the theme which dominates Barth's commentary on Romans.[13]

On the American scene, the most effective development of the general style of theology we have been examining is found in the writings of Paul Tillich. His *Courage To Be* is a succinct and brilliant example of a theology taking its starting point in man's awareness of his ultimate limits.[14] Tillich's aim is to analyze the meaning of faith in terms of the category "courage." In his usage, courage is not simply a moral term, referring to acts of valor, but an ontological term, expressing the affirmation of life in all its dimensions. In order to clarify the significance of this notion, Tillich examines the threat which demands courage if man is to affirm his life and live it in a human way. He begins his study with an analysis of anxiety. The anxiety that primarily interests Tillich is not pathological anxiety, that is, the anxiety resulting from faulty human relationships or perhaps the inability to achieve a satisfactory balance between libidinal drives and the necessities of social life. Such anxiety is largely the province of the physician. Tillich focuses on ontological anxiety, the vague sense of dread and uneasiness that stems from man's awareness of his own finitude, or better, from the inescapable tension he experiences between his freedom and his finitude. Tillich identifies three principal forms in which this anxiety comes to man: ontic anxiety (anxiety over fate and death), moral anxiety (anxiety over guilt and condemnation), and spiritual anxiety (anxiety over emptiness and meaninglessness). While these basic forms of anxiety are distinguishable, they are not separable since each involves the others. Tillich

---

[13] Bultmann has difficulty showing that the difference between Heidegger's position and his own is more than verbal. Cf. *Jesus Christ and Mythology*, p. 70. For a "humanistic" development of Bultmann's program, see Herbert Braun, "The Problem of a New Testament Theology," trans. by Jack Sanders, *Journal for Theology and Church. The Bultmann School of Biblical Interpretation: New Directions?* (New York: Harper & Row, 1965), pp. 169–183, especially p. 183.

[14] *The Courage To Be* (New Haven: Yale University Press, 1952).

suggests that man's experience of anxiety is usually dominated by one of its basic forms, ontic anxiety in the classical period, moral anxiety during the Protestant Reformation, and spiritual anxiety in the present. The key point is that ontological anxiety cannot be removed by treatment. It can only be faced and taken up into a courage that affirms life "in spite of" that which threatens it. Tillich completes his study by analyzing some of the forms man's courageous attempts to deal with his anxiety have taken. In keeping with his own conception of the situational character of theology, he gives particular attention to the courage which enables man to deal with the radical doubt that threatens his drive for meaning in the twentieth century. Clearly the assumption is that theological issues arise where man encounters his inescapable limits and is forced to deal with the threat presented by those limits whatever its particular form.

It must be kept in mind that there are important differences between the viewpoints of Barth, Bultmann, and Tillich, differences in method, style, and content. Many of these differences are linked to major issues in theological and philosophical discussion. Yet in spite of the importance of these differences, there is a common interest in the theological significance of man's limits and the anxiety which discloses his awareness of these limits.[15] In one way or another the greater part of the theology of the earlier decades of this century focused on the possibilities the Christian message offers man for dealing creatively with the boundaries which mark his being as a finite creature. Not surprisingly, this sort of focus has taken on the character of a "given" in theology, a self-evident interest in any authentic theological discourse.

---

[15] Of the men discussed, Barth fits the pattern least well. The christological focus of his thought makes his theology less "problem" oriented, for in his view theology begins at the point where the basic problems of man have already been overcome. Moreover, apart from Jesus Christ man cannot adequately grasp or face his real problem! Still, insofar as Barth does identify "signs" of God's presence in the general experience of men, he points chiefly to the mystery surrounding the limits of life, both beginning and end. *Church Dogmatics*, Vol. III, Part 3 (Edinburgh: T. & T. Clark, 1960), pp. 226–238.

If we are to grasp the significance of what is currently taking place in Christian theology, we must see that it is precisely this basic assumption that is now being called into question. The conviction guiding many of the more recent voices in theology is that the experience of basic anxiety is not the only entree into theological understanding, that in our time at least the fundamental issues must be posed in another way. The remainder of the present essay is directed to an analysis of this conviction.

II

One of the earliest expressions of a basic dissatisfaction with the prevailing style of twentieth-century theology is found in Dietrich Bonhoeffer's prison letters. Bonhoeffer raises two central objections to this theology. First, it concentrates on the weaknesses of man, largely disregarding the significance of man's strengths. Its primary interest is the man in despair, the one who is clearly up against questions that God alone can handle. Where men are apparently healthy, strong, and secure, the strategy is to "spy out" their weaknesses and convince them of the hopelessness of their condition in order that they might be open to the Christian gospel. In contrast, Bonhoeffer calls for an understanding of Christian faith that addresses man not simply at the point of his weakness, but also at the point of his strength, not simply at the boundary of life, but also at its center.[16] The second difficulty with "boundary situation" theology is that it drives man inward, linking the central issues of faith with the "interior" life. On this point, recall Heidegger's contention that death is significant precisely because it "individualizes" man and thrusts him back upon himself. Bonhoeffer sees in this emphasis a contemporary form of the pietist concern for individual salvation. In contrast, he contends that man lives

[16] Dietrich Bonhoeffer, *Letters and Papers from Prison*, ed. Eberhard Bethge, trans. Reginald Fuller (New York: Macmillan Co., 1962), pp. 191, 195–196.

as much "from outwards to inwards as from inwards to outwards," and calls for a "worldly" mode of Christian existence.[17]

Bonhoeffer's reaction to his own theological milieu has been sharpened and enlarged by younger American theologians, particularly Harvey Cox and William Hamilton. Cox states flatly that "there is something immature about existentialism," and suggests that its preoccupations have become irrelevant and uninteresting to a "world come of age." He contends that Tillich's concentration on questions of "ultimate concern" reflects the breakdown of a particular life style rather than issues inherent in human existence as such.[18] More recently he has suggested that the net effect of Heidegger's brilliant philosophical achievement is "almost wholly deleterious."[19] His call is for a freer and more positive participation in the new possibilities for humanness opened up by a secular, urban civilization. In a similar vein Hamilton reacts against the pessimism and the tragic sense of life that characterized "neo-orthodox" theology. He speaks of a "new optimism," by which he means "an increased sense of the possibilities of human action, human happiness, human decency, in this life."[20] He seeks to show that this optimism marks the sensibility of contemporary man, documenting his case by reference to positive assessments of the technology of a "post-civilized" age, to expressions of delight and life affirmation in the arts, and to the confident mood of the civil rights movement. He links the new optimism with the "death of God," calling it a "worldly optimism" rather than an "optimism of grace":

It faces despair not with the conviction that out of it God can bring hope, but with the conviction that the human conditions

[17] *Ibid.*, p. 214.

[18] Harvey Cox, *The Secular City* (New York: Macmillan Co., 1965), pp. 79–80, 253.

[19] Harvey Cox, "Afterword," *The Secular City Debate*, ed. by Daniel Callahan (New York: Macmillan Co., 1966), p. 200.

[20] William Hamilton, "The New Optimism—from Prufrock to Ringo," *Radical Theology and the Death of God* (Indianapolis, Ind.: Bobbs-Merrill Co., Inc., 1966), p. 159.

that created it can be overcome, whether those conditions be poverty, discrimination, or mental illness.[21]

In their present form none of these "reactions" to the theology of the first half of this century can stand up under critical analysis. Cox's dismissal of Tillich, Heidegger, and existentialism is much too facile; Hamilton's optimism, simplistic and uncritical. Even Bonhoeffer's more cautious call for a counterbalance to "boundary situation" theology leads him to caricature his predecessors. As long as the debate is carried on at this level, we should not be surprised by counter-reactions that also caricature. Consider, for example, Haroutunian's portrayal of the "secularists":

"See," they cried, "we are not anxious. In our secular city nobody who is up to date is anxious. There is no depth of reason and no question of being. Finitude does not trouble us; death does not dismay us; nonbeing is the bunk. This is an age of hope, not of existential despair. We shall produce more and better things. We shall tear down our little barns and build bigger and bigger barns. We shall build the Great Society, and live happily; we and all mankind ever after. We are finite, but we are capable of the infinite. Our finitude is no problem. It does not make us anxious. We are new men, mature men, in a world come of age. We have much to do. Leave us alone. *Heraus* Tillich! Away with the religious man!"[22]

Yet Haroutunian's characterization no more "wraps up" the issues being raised by Bonhoeffer, Cox, and Hamilton, than Cox's own comments demolish Tillich's theological achievement! There are deeper issues which require more careful formulation.

Bonhoeffer's comments can provide a convenient framework for identifying the shift in theological focus required by our present situation. To begin with, developments of the past two decades have made increasingly apparent the urgency of his call for an understanding of Christian faith that addresses man not at the point of his weakness, but at the point of his strength; not at the boundary of life, but in life's

21 *Ibid.*, p. 169.
22 Joseph Haroutunian, "The Question Tillich Left Us," *Religion in Life*, XXXV (Winter, 1966), 708–709.

center. In making this assertion it must be clear that man's weaknesses and "boundary" concerns have not simply dissolved in the world's "coming of age." Man is still limited and finite. He is still going to die; he must still come to terms with his attitudes toward his own moral worth; he must still find some "ultimate horizon of meaning" in terms of which he can make sense of his life. We can also say that these issues are inherent in man's being, and that they arouse a destructive anxiety if man has no means of dealing with them in courage. In this respect there is no surpassing of the achievements of our predecessors. Indeed, if contemporary man is unable to appreciate those achievements, it may mean he is less rather than more mature. The "modern way" of death is a case in point. While advances in medical science have greatly increased the possibilities of life, they have also intensified the problems of dying. They prolong the dying process, often meaninglessly; they increasingly isolate dying persons from significant human contacts; and they apparently make it more difficult for man even to accept death as a final reality. Dr. Elizabeth Ross, a physician who has become interested in the problems of the terminally ill, reports that her first efforts to make contact with dying patients met with almost total failure. Hospital personnel, especially physicians, either found it difficult to acknowledge that they had any "dying" patients, or they assumed that such patients were better off without unnecessary "disturbances." In contrast, Dr. Ross soon discovered that dying patients were generally starved for human contact, and especially for an opportunity to discuss their feelings toward the approach of death.[23] We are scarcely "spying out" men's weaknesses when we condemn the inhuman consequences resulting from modern man's inability to deal openly and personally with the fact of death! Clearly, questions of death, guilt, and meaninglessness must continue to occupy places of importance in theological discussion.

The crucial point, however, is that man's encounter with

[23] Elizabeth Ross, "The Dying Patient as Teacher: An Experiment and an Experience," *The Chicago Theological Seminary Register*, LVII (December, 1966), 1–11, especially p. 6.

his limits is not the only way in which basic theological issues can and must be raised. In our time, it is perhaps not even the most pressing way. Issues concerning man's "humanness" are now being posed more in relation to his possibilities than his limits. The enormous expansion of man's power requires him to find a human way of dealing with the new possibilities he has for shaping his own life and the life of the world. If the Christian message is to speak to contemporary man, it must learn to address him at the point of his strength, enabling him to exercise his power constructively and redemptively.

The fact of power confronts contemporary man principally in two ways: in his technology and in his politics. Christian theologians have for some time concerned themselves with the meaning of modern technology. Often their assessment has been almost wholly negative, stressing the fragmentation and depersonalization of life resulting from modern industrial society. More balanced estimates have called attention to the ambiguity of technology. Paul Tillich, for example, notes that man's technical art both increases his control over life and enslaves him by subjecting him to the demands of technical actuality. The most disturbing feature of this subjection is that in transforming the materials of nature into "things" man turns himself into a "thing" as well.[24] These judgments cannot be lightly waved aside. Particularly important is their insight into the fact that technology does not consist of tools and procedures which are neutral or external to man's selfhood. Technology is an "extension of man" (McLuhan) and as such enters into the constitution of human selfhood. Consequently, revolutions in technology involve transformations in the character of man's humanity as well. Yet we have scarcely begun to deal with the challenge of new technological developments simply by calling attention to their ambiguity. Since human society scarcely has the option to "forget" what it knows or to back away from the mode of life it has brought into being, its primary task is to find a way to utilize its skills and resources for the realization of human purposes and intentions.

[24] *Systematic Theology*, Vol. III (Chicago: University of Chicago Press, 1963), p. 74.

Hamilton has spoken of the new technological possibilities in terms of optimism. Though it needs qualification, optimism is not wholly out of place. For one thing, the emerging "electric" technology of the post-war period may not fragment and depersonalize life as much as a "machine" technology does. McLuhan in particular has called attention to this point, emphasizing the heightening of "participation" resulting from an instantaneous net-work of world-wide communications.[25] Likewise, as manufacturing processes become more sophisticated through automation and cybernation, there is a reduced need for man to function as a "cog" in a machine. While the latter developments are having an unsettling effect on the total socio-economic system, their long-range promise is that men will be able to occupy themselves in activities more compatible with what is distinctive about their humanity. In the same vein, man's hopes for overcoming some of the crucial pitfalls endangering the realization of the promise offered by technological development are not wholly visionary. There are rational grounds for believing that man *may* be able to avoid a nuclear holocaust, control the pollution of his environment, limit population growth, find stable sources of material and energy to replace the exhaustible supply from the geological past, etc. Doubtless the most critical question is whether man will be able to make the adjustments in his social institutions and value systems requisite for a viable human society based on the new technology! Still, from a theological perspective the import of the present situation can be expressed neither in terms of pessimism nor optimism. The key point is that man's increased technological power makes him answerable for the future quality of human life in a way he has never been before. In the words of Robert Theobald:

Analysis of where we are must start from the fact that man has achieved—or is achieving—the power to remake his environment in any way he chooses. One of the consequences of this is the condition which I have called abundance—which

[25] Marshall McLuhan, *Understanding Media: The Extensions of Man* (New York: New American Library, Inc., Signet Books, 1966), pp. 36 ff.

is not a condition of having everything we want, but a condition where we can, by making intelligent decisions, bring into existence what we want.[26]

It is to this kind of situation that theological reflection must now address itself. What is needed is an understanding of the Christian gospel that will illumine the meaning of man's power and will enable him to exercise that power in authentically human ways for authentically human ends. A theology which obscures the urgency of this challenge or encourages flight from it is not simply irresponsible; it is positively demonic![27]

The problem of power also confronts contemporary man with heightened intensity in a political form. Once again, problems relating to political power are not new, nor is the theological analysis of these problems. We need simply call to mind Reinhold Niebuhr's life-long insistence that responsible ethical reflection requires us to take into account the role of power in adjudicating the conflicting interests of human society. Yet the theological significance of power has more recently been reopened in a new way, primarily through persons previously excluded from the decision-making processes of society who are now showing a profound determination to seize and exercise power in their own right.

At this point the impact of the civil rights movement on current theological reflection can scarcely be overstated. It has taught us that power is not simply a political or social issue, though it is surely both of these; it is also a fundamental human matter. As early as 1960, students leading the lunch-counter sit-ins in Nashville, Tennessee, saw this point very well. In order to affirm their basic dignity as men, they found it necessary to *repent* of their "acquiescence in a system of racial discrimination." "Uncle Tomism" as they saw it is

[26] "Power and Possibility," United Church of Christ, Council for Higher Education, *Journal*, February, 1967, pp. 3-4.

[27] Doubtless, it is this danger which led Cox to judge Heidegger's achievement as "almost wholly deleterious." Yet Heidegger's work has that result only if it is made the "last word" or turned into some sort of fetish. His insights can continue to make many positive contributions provided they are incorporated into a new setting.

not simply a harmless or charming style of life that is passing away with the times. It is a sin, an abdication of one's basic humanity. Being a man means that you do not permit others —not even the benevolent white liberal—to decide who you are or what your place in society shall be or what you can appropriately expect from society. You must decide these things for yourself, and begin to behave in ways that can give actuality to what you have decided. While the civil rights movement may be losing some of the buoyancy and optimism that characterized its earlier stages, its understanding of the significance of power has, if anything, been enlarged and reinforced. As it increasingly focuses attention on the ghettoes of our cities, its concern is not simply that something be done to improve the condition of the poor and the exploited, but that these persons should themselves be equipped to participate in the process of determining their own goals and shaping their own future. A "war on poverty" that is not pre-eminently aimed at motivating persons and communities to assume responsibility for their own destiny has not yet grasped the full significance of the poverty problem. Under the impact of these developments, Christian theologians have been directed to pay fresh attention to certain neglected features of the Christian gospel—those which define man's dilemma, even his transgression, in terms of his subjection to forces beyond his control; and those which proclaim his redemption in terms of his liberation from alien powers and his elevation to a share in the power God exercises over all things. In this frame of reference, being a man—a mature man—involves the exercise of power, the act of assuming responsibility for your own life and the life of the world.

What the civil rights movement is teaching us on the domestic scene, the revolutionary mood of the so-called "third world" is teaching us on the international scene. Here too we are encountering the political awakening of masses of people who were previously acquiescent before the established powers, including the sovereignty of the Western nations. This awakening is not simply taking the form of a drive for national independence, but more fundamentally of a drive on the part of the peasantry to have a share in the wealth of the modern world, even if this requires violent revolution. To realize this goal, they are prepared to challenge the awesome power of the United States, which tragically finds itself allied more often with the exploiters than with those who represent the rising aspirations of the people. We are being forced to reflect theologically on the fact that countless numbers of people are willing to die in order to have a share in shaping their own future.

The political awakening of exploited groups is having an unsettling effect on those of us who have previously occupied positions of privilege, for it means that our own special interests can no longer be assured of favored treatment. Doubtless there is also fear of possible reprisals. It must be granted that power exercised by persons representing the peasantry of the developing nations or the racial minorities of our own land can become destructive and demonic in its own way. If the human meaning of power is to be realized, it must finally be directed toward the emergence of an interdependent human community that has regard for the legitimate interests and aspirations of all men. It must, like the power of God, be used not to dominate or exploit others, but to empower them to participate in the direction of human life. Yet in the short run, the crucial issue is that persons who have previously played only a marginal role in human society should now be liberated from their "victim image" and called to new levels of worldly responsibility.

There is some conflict in understanding between those concerned with the implications of the new technology and those preoccupied with political activation. For the former, further technological development tends to make irrelevant the ideological conflicts that have previously divided men. There are a number of factors in this judgment. For one thing, the "technologists" are dealing with problems of such overwhelming importance that the survival of human life itself depends upon their solution—matters such as overpopulation, the pollution of man's environment, the rapid exhaustion of the present sources of material and energy required for modern society. In the face of problems of this magnitude, ideological conflicts appear to be a luxury mankind can ill afford. Second, the new technology brings with it the promise of radical abundance where all necessities of life will be freely available. In this setting there can no longer be a problem of poverty, nor can there be any continuing meaning to the "class struggle." Third, even national and cultural differences are being reduced by technological development, partly through increased intercultural contact, but more fundamentally by the fact that a technology universally shared implies the emergence of a common life style. Cultures having highly developed technologies are simply becoming more similar than dissimilar, causing national differences among men to lose their serious importance. Finally, there is the recurring hope that further refinements in social scientific methods will transform political issues and ideological conflicts into problems wholly amenable for their solution to scientific analysis and prescription. In contrast, analysts concerned with political activation, especially in the context of the developing nations, continue to see the problems of our time as preeminently political. The issue for them is not so much increased scientific and technological mastery of man's environment as it is the equitable distribution of the resources of human society. Technological development as such will not settle the distribution problem. It may even heighten it, for a society based on an increasingly sophisticated technology has virtually no place for the man of limited skills and education. The primary need is for the dispossessed to discover and learn to utilize the levers of power in a way that will enable them to participate more significantly in the process of defining the goals of human society. Such participation will inevitably result in a redistribution of the resources of society.

The opposition between technological and political forms of power cannot in the long run be maintained. On the one hand, modern technology is itself a precondition of the increased political awareness of contemporary man. Degradation and poverty as such do not result in political mobilization. There must also be a rise in expectations and a realistic basis for believing that those expectations can be satisfied, both of which have been provided by technological development. On the other hand, the technological problems which have been under consideration have a crucial political dimension. It was suggested earlier that the principal question facing mankind is whether he can make the necessary changes in his social institutions and in his previously accepted values to enter into the promise of the new age. If such changes are to come about, political processes involving public debate and interaction on the appropriate means and ends of social development will have an indispensable role to play. While the analytic work of the social sciences can contribute immeasurably to these processes, it is simply naïve to assume that the crucial issues can finally be resolved through scientific understanding alone. In short, political and technological forms of power finally require each other if their significance for the fulfillment of man's being is to be realized. For our purposes, the important point is that the issues most vitally affecting man's humanity are now being raised not in terms of his weaknesses, but in terms of his strength; not in relation to his ultimate limits, but in view of his new possibilities. Theological reflection must be sensitive to this new situation if it is to unfold the meaning of the Christian message in a way that can address contemporary man with pertinence and power.

Bonhoeffer's second major objection to "boundary situation" thinking equally serves to illumine the current focus in theology. As was noted earlier, Bonhoeffer questioned theology's preoccupation with the "inner life" of man. He observed in contrast that man lives as much from outwards to inwards as from inwards to outwards. This simple observation has many ramifications. To begin with, it points to what might be termed an "incarnational" view of human selfhood, where the being of the self is understood in terms of its integral connection with its body. While such an understanding does not reduce the reality of the self to bodily actions and processes, it does underscore the fact that the self is what it is in, with, and through its body—never apart from it. The principal consequence of this insight is that significant human decisions cannot be actualized in the mode of "inwardness" alone; they necessarily involve concrete behavioral changes as well. Indeed, new ways of behaving may themselves be the pre-condition for alterations in the interior life. Bonhoeffer speaks most pointedly about the need for a reorientation of this kind in his reflections on the relation between thought and action. "We have learnt a bit too late in the day," he concedes, "that action springs not from thought, but from a readiness for responsibility."[28] Since thought is often little more than the luxury of the spectator, we can no longer assume that "everything will somehow happen automatically" if we only think matters through carefully in advance. Instead, thought must itself develop in the context of responsible action.

Consideration of the role of action in shaping thought or of behavior in molding the "inner life" leads directly to an interpretation of Christian existence as worldly responsibility. Heidegger's own contention that the self is always "self-in-world" (*In-der-Welt-Sein*) lays a foundation for unfolding the meaning of selfhood in terms of worldly responsibility. Yet Heidegger so emphasized the inauthenticity of life in the public sphere and the existential significance of those experiences which "individualize" man and thrust him back upon himself, that he was never able to explore the connection of his own insights to life in society. Bonhoeffer forces us to recognize that patterns of thought which attend simply to "private" matters, such as death, guilt, and meaninglessness, involve a flight from the realities of the world. As such they are little more than contemporary versions of the old pietistic concern for individual salvation in the world to come. In contrast, our present task is to bring to awareness the processes by which the fundamental issues of Christian existence confront us in the midst of the social and political struggles of contemporary life. The urgency of this task should be clear from what has already been said about power. The political and technological developments of the twentieth century are such that the factors which at the present time affect most decisively the quality of human life are precisely those involving social and political questions. A theology concerned with the "humanization of man" cannot disregard the promise of the gospel which comes to man in society.

Exploring the social meaning of the gospel does not imply that man can be understood wholly in terms of the social conditions which shape and mold his life. That would be as one-sided as the assumption that authentic existence is a self-contained inner attitude wholly divorced from the actualities of the world. Consequently, fresh attention to the role of social responsibility in Christian existence must not be taken as an attempt to equate Christian faith with social action. The point is rather that the pressing social questions of our day confront us with the necessity of gaining clarity about who we are and of assuming responsibility for the future quality of human life. Heidegger highlights the significance of death because it wrenches us out of our unthinking participation in the commonly accepted valuations of life and forces us to decide for ourselves about the meaning of our life. By the same token, the social ferment of contemporary life no longer permits us to be anesthetized by the constant repetition of well established routines. It requires us to make basic decisions about our own place in the contemporary struggles of men and about our own commitments to the future shape of human life. While these decisions bear most immediately on social responsibility, they finally reach to the very core of our own selfhood. Theological reflection must illumine the meaning of these developments, especially the role they play in opening us up to the possibilities of life offered by the Christian gospel. It is in response to this situation that contemporary theology is seeking to address man both at the point of his strength and in terms of the urgent need of our time for new levels of social responsibility.

III

Thus far, discussions of the new thrust in theology have revolved primarily around the category of secularity or secularization. As a theological term, secularization encompasses a variety of meanings. It points to an understanding of the nature and destiny of man which centers largely on life in this world. It accents the call which rests upon every man to assume responsibility for shaping his own life and the life of the world. It links the intellectual life of man to the struggle to find pragmatic solutions to concrete problems—in Bonhoeffer's terms, subordinating thought entirely to action. Finally, it embodies a recognition of the relativity of all institutions, values, and viewpoints held by men, and hence, the acceptance of a vital pluralism in human society. The contention is, on the one hand, that developments in Western civilization in the past three or four hundred years have made these characteristics increasingly predominant not only in the West, but throughout the whole world. On the other hand, these same characteristics are interpreted as expressions of certain essential features of biblical faith. Consequently, Christian theologians find themselves speaking of secularization as the legitimate consequence of the impact of biblical faith on Western civilization (Gogarten). As a corollary, the Christian's task is to further the secularization process where it has not yet come to completion.

The theological celebration of secularization has features which cannot go unchallenged. For one thing, an exclusive problem-solving approach to reality leads necessarily to an impoverishment of the human spirit. Along with the resolution of concrete problems, man needs the possibility of receiving life and rejoicing in it *as it is* in spite of its intractable difficulties and frustrations. He also needs the largeness of vision which results from the attempt to comprehend life as a whole. These needs assure a continuing place in man's intellectual life for both artistic creativity and metaphysical construction, even when these activities are not directly related to problem-solving concerns. By the same token, a too ready identification of secularization with biblical faith narrows unduly the many-faceted character of the biblical message and tempts us to respond too uncritically to certain dominant features of contemporary society. Nevertheless, the theology of secularity is seeking to meet the peculiar challenge confronting Christian faith at the present time.

In the present essay, the category of responsibility is being lifted up as the most decisive one for characterizing the shape of contemporary theology.[29] Responsibility is a term which is frequently abused in public usage, often meaning little more than a readiness to behave in conventional ways or at least in ways that are compatible with the smooth functioning of the established institutions of society. More carefully considered, however, it has a richness that simultaneously opens up many fruitful lines of theological reflection. To begin with, it suggests the *freedom* to deal creatively with new situations arising in human experience. Far from being reducible to conformity with established practice, it underscores man's ability to transcend his own past in order that he might meet the problems and opportunities emerging in the forward movement of history. In this sense, responsibility is essentially a historical category, indicating the possibility of moving from the accomplishments and failures of the past into an open future. Openness to the future does not mean that the hard-won values and understandings of the past can be ignored or lightly cast aside, for the past never ceases to inform and condition the life of man. It does mean that the authority of the past is continually being relativized, maintaining its power only as it proves itself anew. In this frame of reference, responsibility highlights the stimulus to creativity provided by the pressure of new possibilities.

Second, responsibility suggests the *power* man has to shape his own life and the life of the world. It underscores the fact that man is never a mere product of forces he cannot control. He is able to participate in determining the future character of human life. Indeed, not only can he make effective decisions about the utilization of new possibilities presented to him in the forward movement of history; he can also bring

[29] H. Richard Niebuhr's posthumously published volume, *The Responsible Self* (New York: Harper & Row, 1963), makes a number of helpful contributions to the exploration of the notion of responsibility. His influence on what follows should be apparent. See especially pp. 56–66. What Niebuhr has attempted in terms of "Christian moral philosophy" is here being recommended as a basic entree into fundamental theological questions.

into being new possibilities not already present in his situation.

Finally, responsibility suggests the element of *accountability*. Man must answer for what he does. Being able to answer cannot be equated with success in "measuring up" to some pre-established standard. The openness of the historical process continually erodes the authority of such standards, unless they are given a highly abstract form, e.g., "loyalty to being," or "doing what love (agape) requires." Since the abstractness of such formulations makes their applicability to concrete situations problematic, it is clear that there is no precise measuring instrument by which human behavior can be tested. Basically, man is able to answer for what he does when he acts out of the fullest possible awareness of what he is doing and why, and when he is prepared to accept the consequences of his actions. There is no way to remove the moral risk from human action, partly because no one can ever adequately grasp the nature of his situation or the possible consequences of his action, but also because the appropriate task in a given context may be to innovate, to give rise to the new possibility which cannot be comprehended in terms of previous values and understandings. There is an important social dimension to accountability. It points to a process by which each man answers to the other who questions him about what he is doing. I must answer the other, both because my own selfhood is bound up with his reality, and because what I do invariably affects him. Moreover, the other has an indispensable role to play in my determination of the fitting way to exercise my power in any particular situation. He enables me to test my understandings by setting them alongside or even against his own. He is the occasion of insight and encouragement for me in my confusion and uncertainty. He is the one who breaks open the self-enclosed circle of reasoning by which I justify the evil I would do. Even so, the notion of accountability cannot be exhausted by reference to the other. Since I can never submerge myself in the other or give myself wholly to his judgment, I cannot escape the necessity of answering to myself for what I do.

Consequently, no act can be called responsible unless in that act I am able to come to terms with myself. Though other persons necessarily participate in my decisions, the notion of accountability is one which thrusts me back upon myself to bear the risk of human action in an uncertain and rapidly changing world. Finally, accountability points to what might be called the ultimate meaning of our acts, the role they actually come to play for good or for ill in the forward movement of process. At this point the significance of our acts reaches beyond what we are able to control. Indeed, we are tempted to despair of meaningful action altogether in view of our inability to control the consequences of our actions. Yet the man of faith is sustained in the risk of action by his confidence that his acts are continually being received and transformed so as to enter constructively into the unfolding of the divine purpose in the forward movement of history.

Though we are living in a time which demands new levels of responsibility, there is no guarantee that men either can or will act responsibly. In fact, the various dimensions of responsibility—freedom, power, accountability—are often far removed from the actual behavior of men. Mere exhortations to responsible behavior are scarcely sufficient to change this situation since the failure to act responsibly is as much an indication of the paralysis of the human spirit as it is a mark of human perversity. Men cannot respond creatively to the new possibilities opening up in the historical process when their anxieties over the uncertainty of the future drive them to cling to the apparent security of the past. They cannot exercise power positively and constructively when the complacency or despair of believing that nothing can be done about the way things are seems preferable to the vulnerability that inevitably accompanies actions aimed at actualizing new possibilities for the fulfillment of human life. They cannot endure an open accounting for their acts when such an accounting exposes their impotence or brings to light the role of prejudice and narrow self-interest in determining their actions. In view of these considerations, the notion of anxiety is not likely to disappear from theological analysis. Still, it takes on a different character when its significance is not so much to indicate man's ultimate limits as to identify the barriers to the realization of his possibilities, his growth toward mature manhood. The task of theological reflection, therefore, is not only to clarify the meaning and significance of responsible existence, but also to unfold the promise the gospel offers for enabling men to be responsible and mature in a "world come of age." The gospel does empower man to take responsibility for his own life and the life of the world, for it breaks the hold of those anxieties that keep him so preoccupied with his own well being as to make him ineffectual in dealing with the critical issues of life. It does free man to move creatively into an open future, uninhibited by the limits of past and present conditions, because it continually mediates the future to him as the hope for overcoming the negativities of life in the realization of new levels of personal and social fulfillment. It does enable man to account for his life in openness because it calls him to that accounting with a word of forgiveness, forgiveness which does not simply excuse his irresponsibilities, but also transforms the distortions of his being into a new integrity and wholeness.

Undoubtedly, the new focus in theology presents serious difficulties for contemporary attempts to understand the meaning of Christian existence. Two issues in particular have gained notable public attention. First, the new situation of man has for many people resulted in the loss of God. Since reflection on the meaning of God has characteristically taken its starting point in man's encounter with his ultimate limits, a theology which gives attention to the power of man, to his possibilities for shaping his world, tends to find the notion of God superfluous. God has disappeared as a "need-fulfiller" and "problem-solver," William Hamilton observes.[30] In large measure, his contention, which expresses one facet of the "death of God" theology, simply makes explicit a judgment that is inherent in the situation of contemporary theology. If there is to be a recovery of significant speech about God, it cannot be accomplished by minimizing or obscuring the importance of the new possibilities of man, perhaps by in-

[30] *Radical Theology and the Death of God* (Indianapolis, Ind.: Bobbs-Merrill Co., 1966), pp. 40–41.

sisting that man is after all still bounded by ultimate limits he cannot surpass. While the latter is certainly true, it points at most to a recognition of the God of the boundary, and hence, to a God removed from the most pressing challenges facing man today. Instead, reflection on the meaning of God must take its starting point in those explosive happenings in the midst of life which empower man for responsible action, which open up new possibilities for the actualization of a more human future. In this frame of reference, the impact of the divine reality is not to make men more dependent, but to make them more responsible, more able to participate in shaping their own lives and the life of the world. Second, the current focus in theology raises difficult problems for the constitution of the church. Though developments in the shape and style of contemporary life have increasingly restricted the church's outreach to the private sector, no severe crisis presented itself as long as the mediation of the gospel to men centered on such matters as death, guilt and meaninglessness. Traditional forms of the church are more or less well suited for carrying out that task. However, where the challenge is to bring to light the meaning of the gospel as it confronts man in the midst of the social and political struggles of our time, the preservation of established patterns of church life amounts to a flight from responsibility, a failure to accept a ministry to the contemporary world. Consequently, an imperative now rests upon the Christian community to find modes of life which will enable it to mediate the gospel to men in the public sector, in the arena where men are called to the responsible use of power for realizing the new possibilities opening up in the present age.

The problems faced by contemporary Christian theology are by no means simple ones. However, it is a mark of the vitality of the Christian community that many persons in many different ways have been bold enough to tackle these issues head on, even when their reflections have led them to startling conclusions. It is never possible to capture the whole Christian message in any leading theme. There are always important counterthemes which cannot be safely disregarded. Our present situation is no exception to that rule.

Still, the unique challenge of our time is to explore more fully the meaning of the Christian message as it addresses men at the point of their strength in the midst of their political and social involvements. It is in the fulfillment of this task that the bearing of the gospel on the contemporary world can become manifest.

Toward a Political Hermeneutics
of the Gospel

Jürgen Moltmann

Jürgen Moltmann, author of the influential work *The Theology of Hope*, is here concerned with *kerygma* and man's struggle for freedom, as they involve man's historical consciousness, political action, and Christian faith. In particular, he advocates bringing Christian hermeneutics—inquiry into presuppositions of biblical interpretation—out of the realm of the formal and the abstract and into relationship with present social reality. "In *kerygma, koinonia,* and *diakonia,* the spirit of freedom and of the new future of God is brought into the whole present affliction." The Bible records promises of freedom; therefore, says Moltmann, we must develop a hermeneutic that deals with means and methods of practical liberation. Dr. Moltmann's essay originally appeared in the Summer 1968 issue of the *Union Seminary Quarterly Review** and will appear in *Religion, Revolution and the Future,* to be published by Charles Scribner's Sons. He is Professor of Systematic Theology at the University of Tübingen.

THE modern historical consciousness can be characterized as a crisis consciousness because, with the beginning of modern times, the traditions and the institutions which regulate life have become uncertain and insecure. New experiences of history compel critical revision of the former structures of life. And, on the other hand, historical criticism of tradition and ideological criticism of social and political institutions evoke a revolutionary freedom for the future which undermines prejudice against novelty in the future.[1]

* 3041 Broadway, New York, N.Y. 10027. Reprinted with permission.
[1] The "sole historical-empirical foundation of all these institutions and the stripping away of all of their absolute validity is

At the beginning of modern times, historical criticism was directly bound up with revolutionary criticism. It began by unmasking the authoritarian myths of the contemporary powers of Church and state. Then in the name of comprehensive and many-faceted truth, it turned its attention to the scriptures in order to undermine the Church's claim to authority. As Wilhelm Dilthey has written: "The historical consciousness breaks the last chains which philosophy and natural science could not rend asunder. Now man stands there completely free."[2] Thus, in the hands of the historical critic, history becomes a kind of judgment about every metaphysical or dogmatic claim to absolutism. Two problems which arise out of criticism and crisis will be analyzed in the following two sections.

An Enlightenment Inheritance of Freedom

When the historical basis of a tradition is subjected to criticism, a gulf develops between the past, from which it emerges and in which it belongs, and the present, in which it claims validity. In the first phase of the Enlightenment, this distance between past and present meant the liberation of man from the guardianship of tradition and from the burdens of the past. Historical reflection on a present power—be it the state, the order of society, or the Church—serves to expose one's own experience and one's own creative powers to the future.[3] This relationship of the historical critique of tradition

---

taken care of today by sciences which are thoroughly historicizing in their methods. They are therefore shaken by the most emphatic and complete of all revolutions that there could be. This is also true of all authorities and norms." Cf. F. Gogarten, "Historicism," *Zwischen den Zeiten* 2/8 (1924), p. 8.

[2] W. Dilthey, *Gesammelte Schriften*, Vol. VIII (Stuttgart, 1960), p. 225.

[3] Thus, on the contrary, in the course of the restoration in the nineteenth century, the revolutionary spirit of democrats and socialists was reproached again and again for its lack of tradition. Cf. e.g., A.F.C. Vilmar, "Kirche und Welt," *Gesammelte Aufsätze*, Vol. I, 1872, p. 17: "Of course it appears that the

and the sociological critique of institutions with the freedom
of the present for the future must be brought back vividly
into our consciousness because the notion of historical criti
cism is growing more and more hazy. Historical criticism
produces freedom and freedom manifests itself in historical
criticism of all repressive powers.

This does not yet mean that modern historical-critical
research is a child of the Protestant freedom of belief. This
"pedigree" also bears ideological traces of subsequent adop
tion.[4] For when the historical basis of one tradition is uncov
ered, other traditions simultaneously appear once more. That
which has been forgotten is retrieved, and the historical ho
rizon of the present extends backwards. History no longer
merely binds one to a tradition which one calls his own, but
it becomes the broader field of past human possibilities. When
the compulsive character of the present is broken critically
by the tradition of one's own past, this past loses its claim to
absolutism and becomes relative to other truths in history.
Historical criticism supports both the freedom *of* the Chris
tian faith and the freedom *from* the Christian faith, just as
the pluralistic society, its mirror image, functions over against
the Church.

Romantic "Organicism"

With the consciousness of the distance between the present
and a varied past, the other problem of the appropriation of
history arises. In the last phase of the Enlightenment, the ro
mantic philosophy of history took up this question. It recog
nized the peculiar character of the traditions as they are at
home in their own original place and time. The historical gui

calling of the German people for a thousand years will in the
not too distant future come to a perhaps ignominous end, be
cause. . . . For their part, a very great mass of people have
purposefully and consciously turned their backs on all former
times."

[4] This must be maintained, in all honesty, against the familiar
and oft-repeated assertions of A. Schweitzer and P. Tillich about
the "act of truthfulness" of Protestant historical criticism.

was bridged with the help of the idea of organicism. Through this idea, each epoch of history could be understood in its uniqueness. Simultaneously, as a constitutive element in world history, each epoch could assume its unique value in relation to the present.[5] For the critical consciousness of freedom in the initial period of the Enlightenment, however, the presentation of the past (with the help of the idea of organicism) was nothing more than the old heteronomy of what had been handed down dressed up in new garb. In fact, the romantic philosophy of history represents a restoration of the historical tradition opposed to the spirit of the Enlightenment and the powers of the "holy alliance," which jointly have held the field against revolution in order to conquer the terrors of freedom. It performs this function even today. Therefore, the question becomes how the past can be brought into the consciousness of the present so that the freedom of the present for the future can be maintained or increased without being limited by the prejudices of tradition or subordinated to an ideology of history.

There is a special problem for the Christian tradition and for Christian freedom: Within the framework of the free and possible understanding of the Christian tradition and proclamation, how can one come to an understanding of the necessity of this proclamation? And how can one arrive at the necessity of the understanding and appropriation of precisely *this* tradition? If the hermeneutical dialogue between Christian text and the present is opened, the question remains for the most part unheeded and unanswered: Why dialogue precisely with *these texts* and with *this past*? As long as hermeneutical theology does not answer this question, it still lives on the interest of the churchly tradition which the text presents to it. And thus, it is a continuation of traditionalism by other means. However, behind the question, how can and should one understand the Christian tradition today, is heard the even more radical question: *Why* is one compelled today to preach precisely these texts, to understand and believe them?

[5] Cf. W. Maurer, *Aufklärung, Idealismus und Restauration*, Vol. II, 1930, esp. pp. 115ff.

The Hermeneutics of Wilhelm Dilthey

From Wilhelm Dilthey comes the famous definition, "Her meneutics is the art of understanding written expressions o life."[6] Life, expression of life, and understanding of life con stitute here the nature of the historical world. They indicat both the distance and the common factor in history. Betwee the written expressions of life in the past and those who try t understand in the present, there lies the distances of history nevertheless, there also lies the common communication wit the unfathomable life itself. Dilthey calls the ground out o which all historical manifestations originate, in so far as the are *expressions of life*, "life." On the one hand, it is unfath omable and inexhaustible; while on the other, it is objectifie in ever new historical expressions of life. "Only through th idea of the objectification of life do we achieve an insight int the nature of the historical. . . . What the spirit project today of its character in its expression of life, tomorrow i history as it stands there."[7] Still, this expression of life woul be quite foreign and inaccessible if we ourselves did not par ticipate in life and did not have to form objectifications c our own lives. "We are first of all historical beings before w become observers of history and because we are the forme we become the latter."[8]

So against the obscure background of the common flow c life there is the possibility of understanding the historical ex pressions of life. A presupposition for interpretation is, there fore, the primordial relation of the interpreter to life itsel because the phenomena of history can be understood as th objectifications of life. When there are innumerable object fications of life, how then can they be understood in the individual and characteristic significance? How can they, i their incongruence and their lack of simultaneity with th

[6] W. Dilthey, *Gesammelte Schriften*, Vol. V (Stuttgart, 1957 pp. 332f.

[7] W. Dilthey, *Gesammelte Schriften*, Vol. VII (Stuttgart, 1958 p. 147.

[8] *Ibid.*, p. 278.

present, be shown to be meaningful without becoming from the outset entangled by the presupposed, obscure flow of life for which they are only indications, expressions, and manifestations? Dilthey attempted to evade the obvious pantheistic, historical relativism and struck against a deeper *aporia*: The real meaning of individual historical phenomena can only be disclosed in their associations with other such phenomena, and thus only in view of the whole of history. This totality is, however, not available and cannot be surveyed because we do not yet stand at the end of history.

One has to wait until the end of the course of his life and he can only survey the whole in the hour of his death. Only from this vantage point would his part of the relationship be ascertainable. One has to await the end of history in order to possess all of the material necessary for the determination of its meaning.[9]

This view of the individual case from the vantage point of the whole which is necessary for history, but which in practice cannot actually be carried out, would be the deductive method. But on the other hand, phenomena of the past which we remember do become quite meaningful for us in so far as they open up possibilities of the future and thereby inform the present with the responsible determination of goals. A moment of the past becomes for us

meaningful in so far as in it a connection with the future is set up by a deed or through an external event. Or to the extent that the plan of the way life is to be conducted in the future is conceived . . . What we set as the goal of our future serves the determination of the meaning of the past.[10]

The individual's view of the greater whole and his view from the past upon the future, for which he is to be responsible, is the other, more inductive side of understanding. Nevertheless, only the end of existence and the end of all things conclusively opens up history in the significance of its parts and moments.

Let us set aside here the possibility that death need not in

[9] *Ibid.*, p. 233.
[10] *Ibid.*

any way be identified with the consummation of life. Rather death is the disintegration of what cannot be consummated. Let us also set aside the possibility that the end of history may not be the consummation of the whole, but perhaps is more the conclusion of that which is not presently consummated and cannot be consummated and is therefore ambiguous. Yet, the reflections of Dilthey make it clear that hermeneutics need not end in historical relativism, but that the meaning of past expressions of life, together with the present's responsible determination of goals for the future, can be attained. For in these determinations we accept responsibility for the whole and with that, responsibility for the past.

Existentialist Hermeneutics

For the existential thinker, the actual meaning of individual historical events does not lie in the speculative association of the objectifications or manifestations of history. But as Kierkegaard said against Hegel:

Demoralized by too assiduous an absorption in world-historical considerations, people no longer have any will for anything except what is world-historically significant, no concern for anything but the accidental, the world-historical outcome, instead of concerning themselves solely with the essential, the inner spirit, the ethical, freedom.[11]

In Heidegger's existentialist analysis, history is no longer viewed as the self-development of the absolute spirit as it was with Hegel. Neither is it seen as an expression of the life of the unfathomable life, but rather as being grounded in the "historicity of existence."

And because Dasein, *and only Dasein*, is primordially historical, that which historiological thematizing presents as a possible object for research, must have the kind of Being of *Dasein which has-been-there.*[12]

11 S. Kierkegaard, *Concluding Unscientific Postscript* (Princeton, 1941), p. 121.
12 Martin Heidegger, *Being and Time* (New York, 1962) p. 445.

The summation of all individual moments and parts of history is therefore not to be sought in a future end of world history, but is to be decided in one's historical ability to be integral in the face of death. Accordingly, history is no longer questioned concerning its actual developments and tendencies, but about the possibilities of existence which have always been inherent in it.

Rudolf Bultmann also brings the texts to present-day understanding with this general presupposition. Based on the questionableness of being, they disclose possibilities of human existence. If a certain self-understanding expresses itself in the texts, then a genuine understanding must yield to the question it answers and the claim it makes, the claim which summons one to the responsible acceptance of one's own existence. This general approach, however, in so far as it has any validity at all for the understanding of texts from the past, does not yet grasp the special claim of the texts of the New Testament, for in biblical hermeneutics there is something that is unique. This unique "something" is the *kerygma*, which is not identical with the foundation of the historicity of being but constitutes something like its own history of proclamation, the history in which Christian faith flourishes.

Of course, this existential event can be understood only in the framework of existentialist analysis and existentialist interpretation. But this is not sufficient. The appeal of the existentialist interpretation of the event of word and faith lies in the intelligibility of the new existence it promises to the believer. Its limitation lies in the undemonstrable nature of the ground of kerygma and faith. Is it enough to be constantly aware of the significance of the Christian kerygma in the correlation of claim and decision in one's own being? Must not the meaning of the proclamation be perceived for its own sake, in a historical horizon of the total being? In this way, the unique Christ-event can be conveyed as the ground of the kerygma with its own goals of the kingdom of God and freedom. And the history of the proclamation, inclusive of the new existence in faith, is grasped as the means of this conveyance. This does not mean replacing faith with an idea of world history, but bringing faith to its historical self-consciousness.

Bultmann Bypasses Knowledge of the End

Here we must mention another line of Bultmann's thinking which corresponds to that emphasized by Dilthey. It is known that the modern problem of historical distance establishes certain alternatives for Bultmann: either objectifying viewing or personal encounter (and decision). In addition, Bultmann intimates a third perspective which is adapted to overcome that new form of the subject-object scheme (as Wilhelm Kamlah calls it) without suppressing it.[13] At this point, the alternative between "the historical fact in itself" and the "historical event for me" is finally bypassed and relativized in respect to "the future," for which historical events and persons are open. Therefore, to "each historical phenomenon" belongs "its future, in which it first shows itself for what it is; more exactly, in which it *increasingly* shows itself for what it is."[14] Also, one's own present is related to the future in so far as it is accepted in responsibility. With this, the relation between past and present, between event and existence, falls into a framework of the "end of history" in so far as the future which will finally reveal the significance of history will have to be "the end of history." The dualism in the dialogue of historical understanding becomes a dialectic including a common third factor or shared middle term. This "future" belongs to historical phenomena and brings out their meaning. It must also accept responsibility for the present if it is to be historically present. This "future" mediates between past and present, making the dialogue of historical understanding necessary. For Bultmann, however, this line of thought soon breaks down. For him, knowledge of the end of world history is "presumptuous." The question of the sense of the whole course of history, therefore, is already meaningless. This resig-

---

[13] Cf. "Wissenschaft und Existenz," *Glauben und Verstehen*, Vol. III (Tübingen, 1960), pp. 113–115.

[14] *Ibid.*, p. 113.

nation, however, does not appear logical to the impartial reader. If a question cannot be answered because all of the previous answers show themselves to be inadequate, must the question therefore be meaningless? Does it not then become an open question? In this case, it has its basis in the openness of history. In the openness of history alone can the future be determined regarding the meaning and significance of the past and the present.

For the quest for sense and purpose of world history, Bultmann substitutes the search for the meaning of the history of existence, i.e., the search in the individual case for one's own being.[15] Only he who is moved to participation in history, he who accepts responsibility for the future, can understand the "language of history." This is evident; but his qualifying postscript is not: "Only he who is moved by the question of his own existence is able to hear the claim of history."[16]

Participation in history is still participation in the history of mankind, in political, social, scientific, and technical history. This participation, however, leads far beyond the search for the meaning of one's own being. There develops from it a responsibility for the future of the whole and for the future of that which is held in common. In this responsibility, one inquires after the goal, purpose, and significance of the course of history in its entirety. A universal historical understanding of the past does not develop out of this responsibility for the future itself. Now Bultmann replaces this universal historical quest for the future with the quest for existence, and thus replaces the theodicy question, which is the search for a just world, with the quest for the identity of one's own existence. This must not necessarily be taken as a "substitute." The summation of history in one's striving to be integral can also be understood as an anticipation of the future of world history. On this basis, what Bultmann would like to establish could then be meaningful, namely, the responsibil-

---

[15] Cf. R. Bultmann, *History and Eschatology* (New York, 1957), p. 155: "The *meaning in history lies always in the present*, and when the present is conceived as the eschatological present by the Christian faith, the meaning in history is realized."

[16] R. Bultmann, *Glauben und Verstehen*, Vol. III, p. 115.

ity of the present for the future of history. The meaning of an historical phenomenon for one's own existence in the present, then, would be a prolepsis of its meaning in its own future at the end of history.

Resurrection: Symbol of Protest

The existential interpretation, then, falls into the larger framework of an eschatological interpretation of world history. In a certain manner the "end of the world" is indeed present in the existence which has come into its freedom over against the world, that is, in the present, responsible decision. This is not hampered, however, by the fact that the "end of the world" is still to come; if it had already come, man would no longer have any responsibility for the social and political history of his present before that future. Theologically speaking, with the solving of the question of the identity of man through word and faith, the question of the whole suffering creation waiting for freedom is not yet solved. But in the freedom of the believer, the universal solution comes into view. The "end of the world" practiced in the freedom of belief is then the *end* of the *world* and the *goal* of history only when faith understands itself as the anticipation and the representation of the end of all things which is to come, when faith understands itself as the beginning of the liberation of the whole enslaved creation from the power of transitoriness. Faith, as an anticipation of the salvation of the whole, thus opens a future for the mortal body, for society, and for nature—in short, for everything which still lies in anguish.

In the horizon of the theodicy question, the resurrection of the crucified Jesus by God is understandable as the beginning of the new creation of God's righteousness which corresponds only *provisionally* to faith, but *conclusively* to a new world. In effect, this transforms faith from a deliverance from the world into an initiative that changes the world and makes those who believe into worldly, personal, social, and political witnesses to God's righteousness and freedom in the midst of a repressive society and an unredeemed world. In this, faith comes to historical self-consciousness and to the recognition of its eschatological task within history.

Revolutionary Historical Hermeneutics

On the way to a political hermeneutics, we cannot neglect Karl Marx. His purely political analysis of religion is intended as "irreligious critique" of religion. This is literally what Bonhoeffer set out to do in the inception of his "non-religious interpretation of biblical concepts." Still, for the young Marx, it is not so much a matter of an *interpretation* of the transmitted Christian tradition or a rationalistic *enlightenment* of the "essence of Christianity" (Ludwig Feuerbach). Rather, he is concerned with the historical (which means social and political) *realization* of religion: "What was an inner light becomes a consuming flame turned outward."[17] If, with Feuerbach, the beginning of the critique of religion lies in referring all religions back to mysticism, the reversal of mysticism into revolution[18] becomes the spear point of the Marxist criticism of religion. If we take this aspect into hermeneutics, the historical work in tradition and proclamation is changed. Rather than mere interpretation of past history, it becomes an effort to realize what is announced historically under present circumstances.

Religion for the young Marx is the illusory expression of the alienated man because this expression is held captive in a "perverted consciousness of the world." In it is set the "fantastic realization of the human essence, because human essence possesses no true reality."[19] Religion is thus a realization of the human essence, but only in fantasy. Its conceptions of the true nature of man are correct, but as mere conceptions they remain incongruent with the reality of the "vale of

[17] K. Marx, *Die Frühschriften*, S. Landshut, ed. (Stuttgart, 1953), p. 17.
[18] Cf. K. Mannheim, *Ideologie und Utopie*, Third Ed. (Frankfurt, 1952), pp. 184ff.
[19] K. Marx, *Die Frühschriften*, p. 208.

tears." While Bultmann criticizes the conceptions of religion as myths in order to interpret them existentially on the basis of man's self-understanding, Marx, on the other hand, criticizes the evil reality which forces man to represent the illusion of his fortune and his true nature in religious conceptions only. While with Bultmann the existentially interpreted myths still remain myths, Marx seeks a way of overcoming myths in a changed and new reality. Religious conceptions are determined by three factors: they are the *expression* of real affliction; they are *protestations* against real afflictions; and, as mere conceptions, they are the *opium* of suffering people.[20] Religion, therefore, originates in the concrete experience of the difference between existence and essence. It will be placed on its feet when its conceptions are no longer an escape from this painful difference into another world, when it no longer serves to promote resignation to these afflictions. But religion must be understood as direction for the overcoming of this difference in a revolutionary manner. The "protestation against real affliction" is the unmythological kernel of religion. In this way, the revolutionary realization of human fortune enters into the real inheritance of religion. Revolutionary criticism does not pull the flowers off man's chains so that he must come to terms with his chains but so that he breaks his chains and picks the living flower. To this extent this "irreligious critique" is an interpretation of religion through realization of what was only imagined by religion.

Christian Myth as Protest

If we admit this, then in no religion is the "character of protest" so vital as in the messianic faith of Christianity. One cannot grasp freedom in faith without hearing simultaneously the categorical imperative: One must serve through bodily, social, and political obedience the liberation of the suffering creation out of real affliction. If one grasps only the promise of freedom in faith and forgets the realistic demand for the

[20] *Ibid.*

liberation of this world, the gospel becomes the religious basis for the justification of society as it is and a mystification of the suffering reality. It results in the "soft-living flesh" of old and new "realists" when the critique of religion leads only to criticism of the heavens in demythologization and not simultaneously to the critique of the earth—to the criticism of politics and of the law. The radical consequence of the critique of myths is not existential interpretation, but revolutionary realization of freedom in present circumstances. As long as mythical conceptions are considered mere "expressions" of human understanding and not agonizing protests against real affliction, demythologizing interpretation remains in the dimension of the "fantastic" and does not approach the messianic kernel of the Christian proclamation.

The criterion for the criticism of Christian myths cannot simply be the changing of one's world view. It is the cross of Christ. When we understand the cross of Christ in this connection as an expression of *real* human affliction, then the resurrection of Christ achieves the significance of the true "protest" against human affliction. Consequently, the missionary proclamation of the cross of the Resurrected One is not an opium of the people which intoxicates and incapacitates, but the ferment of new freedom. It leads to the awakening of that revolt which, in the "power of the resurrection" (as Paul expresses it), follows the categorical imperative to overthrow all conditions in which man is a being who labors and is heavily laden. Paul has done this for his time (when religion and idols repressed mankind) with the gospel of free justification. Today the affliction of men is no longer determined by a coterie of idols to which one is subjected. How then must religion's character of protest appear to the present affliction of humanity? Religious Christianity has preserved the "inner light" down through the centuries. Again and again it has become the consuming flame directed outwards. How must the inner light force its way out today?

Within hermeneutical deliberations this continuation of the question of understanding into revolutionary change is possible as soon as the horizons of understanding are expanded. They must be broadened beyond the possibilities of human existence to include the "horizon of concern" (Wolfhart Pannenberg) for the possibilities of history. The biblical texts outline a horizon of concern between the Christ event on one side, and the future of Christ and the kingdom of freedom on the other. But if one is aware of this, then in the horizon of the present personal, social, and political lack of freedom, he must surely ask how the biblical horizon of freedom can be mediated to the oppressions of the present. From this vantage point, then, textual exegesis is no longer only a peculiar concern of self-understanding which will occasionally conform with comprehension. It is more a matter of a special understanding of the texts' concern which strives for practical congruence between the biblical tradition's horizon of concern and present circumstances. It also perceives the needs and the opportunities of present social reality. The desire for objective correspondence cannot get bogged down in endeavors at understanding. Then it would only be the mystification of the present. The energetic, revolutionary changing of the present state of affairs is rather the consequence of an intimate understanding of and familiarity with the biblical proclamation.

In this case, it will also be clear exactly *why* this Christian tradition and proclamation necessitates understanding and cannot, along with other traditions of the past, be appropriated arbitrarily or simply forgotten. Biblical texts present an horizon of concern which encroaches upon the whole affliction of the present and indicates for it the new possibilities of a future open to God. Out of an indeterminate historical view will come a passionate understanding, captivated by the future. Proclamation, through its announcement of new freedom, becomes the denunciation of the bondage and fettering of the present to the past. Just as the "inner light" in Marx's image forces its way outward as the "consuming flame," so the understanding of the biblical proclamation is turned from the inner agreement of faith to bodily obedience and to political work in the liberation of mankind from present affliction. This obedience is no longer the old heteronomy which had to bear the yoke of an authoritative tradition. It is understanding obedience which answers the concern of hope and freedom, as represented in the Christian tradition, in the circumstances of the present.

Political Hermeneutics

Hermeneutics falls into the danger of formalism when it only seeks in retrospect for an understanding of the past under the conditions of the present. A material hermeneutics must seek changes of the present conditions. There is, then, a parallel with the Marxist coordination of theory and practice which is kindled by the conviction that philosophy must be overcome in order to be realized.[21]

The unity of theory and practice designates the truth, which is produced by, and, at the same time, is the highest standard of reason; to the extent that within estrangement anything which advances efforts toward the establishment of truth can be called reasonable—reason is the entrance to future truth.[22]

Correspondingly, theological hermeneutics is abstract as long as it does not become the theory of practice, and sterile as long as it does not make "the entrance to future truth" possible. Theology serves future freedom in so far as it prepares the way for it in historical criticism, in ideological criticism, and, finally, in criticism of institutions. This criticism must always be directed first of all toward its own hindrance to freedom. If we find in the Bible the recorded promises of freedom and in proclamation the mission of this freedom, then it is the peculiar responsibility of an historical hermeneutic to outline the means and the methods of practical liberation. This hermeneutic can therefore be called a political hermeneutic because it apprehends politics, in the Aristotelian sense of the word, as the inclusive horizon of the life of mankind.

[21] *Ibid.*, p. 215.
[22] J. Hobermas, "Zur philosophischen Diskussion um Mark und den Marxismus," *Theorie und Praxis, Politica,* Vol. II, 1963, p. 316.

If we analyze the scriptural texts from this viewpoint, with the help of the form-critical method, we come upon the language of apostleship. We find this language among the missionized and missionary groups, in congregations of the tempted and persecuted. In their worship, their proclamation, and their disputations, they have not only interpreted the world and understood themselves, but they have also desired to bring something new into the world. Through his Gospel, Paul wanted "to bring about the obedience of faith" in all lands (Romans 1:5;16:26) and to extend the freedom of faith as the vanguard of the liberation of the world in the future of Jesus Christ. The content and forms of kerygmatic language are not understandable without consideration of this concrete, missionary initiative.

"The scriptures arose in the service of God, hence there is also appeal to and direction from them," Adolf Schlatter said.[23] The common ground and the common direction of the different proclamations and theologies in differing situations is therefore that social initiative which we most correctly describe as *mission*. They all stand in the movement of the apostleship of Christ in an unredeemed world. If we take notice of this direction, we can no longer read the Bible as "the charter of our religion" or tradition; it must rather be understood as the creative witness of our call and commission in the world. Only then does he who understands stand in the same alignment with these texts. If he stands in the same alignment however, it will be necessary to investigate the conceptions of the kerygma critically in every period of history. But this still remains on a superficial level. One must go deeper and consider the affliction from which the kerygma liberates man in his time. Then one will get to see both how the kerygma stands out of step with his time and how timely it really is. One sees that it does not correspond to his time, but that it brings the God of Christ to expression in a way that frees men and changes their circumstances. This contemporaneous non-contemporaneity is the thorn of the gospel

[23] A. Schlatter, *Der Dienst des Christen in der älteren Dogmatik* (1897), p. 69.

which is deeply embedded in history. In it there is expressed a future which has not yet been gleaned from any historical present.

Cosmological or Political Theology

When we find the Gospel in the garb of the cosmological metaphysics of another era, there is once again no sense in describing this as mythological and childish as seen from the plateaus of modern times. Behind this theistic representation of the world into which the kerygma enters, stands a real affliction of mankind: his suffering in chaos, in the absurdity of history, and the threat of transiency. The doctrine of the two natures was not ontological speculation. It was the Christian answer of freedom to the agony of transiency. Behind that cosmological representation of the world stands the question of theodicy, the question of suffering in expectation of God's just world. If that theistic representation of the world is outdated today, this interrogation of God about evil and pain is still not relegated to the past. The question has merely lost its old cosmological form. It has become more of a political and social question. Therefore this cosmological theology can develop into a political theology, because "politically" (in the broadest sense of the word) mankind suffers and struggles against, but also brings forth, evil. One can, of course, demythologize the answers of the fathers; but he cannot demythologize the foundation of the painful question which they wanted to answer. The old apocalyptical, world-historical eschatology has lost its cosmological language, but its lasting horizon is the theodicy question. Within the range of this question, one has to speak in a secular way of the righteousness of God. Here the proclamation of the resurrection of the Crucified One (i.e., of the righteousness of God which creates anew) attains its understandable as well as its practical meaning.

Since the beginning of modern times, the advance of the Gospel in the garb of an anthropological metaphysics has its real basis in the changed afflictions of mankind. If man has become the master of his world, then he no longer finds grandeur and misery in the powers of nature, but in himself. Behind the theological turn to anthropology in the "consciousness theology" of Schleiermacher, the "existence theology" of Kierkegaard, the "ethical theology" of Kant and his followers, man's identity question is hidden as the concrete experience of misery. It has become so agonizing for him that he connects it to the God question and often unifies them. The "Christology from below," the "doctrine of faith," and "existentialist interpretation" were and are accommodations to modern representation of the world, for which anthropology has become the central problem. They were and are, as well, the kerygma's concrete initiatives for liberating man from his modern afflictions. One must see the real agony behind man's search for himself. The Christian proclamation does not enter into this quest only to make itself understandable and to adjust its own tradition to the present. It enters into it for the sake of liberation. Today the limitations of existentialist interpretation become clearer because the real unredeemed state of mankind looks different. Therefore, one must arrive at an ideological critique of this existentialist interpretation.[24] But one must still keep in mind the concrete experiential content behind the outline of existence theology.

The question of man's identity becomes more and more pressing the more man becomes an historical being. But he becomes an historical being only in connection with the social changes of world history. Therefore, this agonizing and impelling identity question is the reverse side of the theodicy question which seeks the meaning of history. Practically, this means that persons and groups of men are to find their identity in history—not apart from history. But this identity is to be found only in concrete historical identification with projects involved in overcoming affliction and enslavement. Even Christians and Christian churches can lose their identity in social changes if their traditions are not critically related to the needs of the new situations of the present. But they

[24] T. W. Adorno, *Jargon der Eigentlichkeit* (Frankfurt, 1964)

can be regenerated from their origins, if these origins present themselves and can be presented as something necessary in the present distresses.

Hermeneutics: Living Documents of Freedom

Christian hermeneutics cannot concern itself exclusively with proclamation and language because they themselves stand in the larger political and social forum of public attention. Therefore, the political configuration of the Church and the ethical form of the Christian life belong in Christian hermeneutical considerations. If the totality of Christian expressions of life or charismata must be considered in the hermeneutics and significance of the Christ event, then it becomes clear why one can no longer derive hermeneutics from a principle. Hermeneutics is then not just the "act of understanding written expressions of life," but of understanding all the "living documents" or texts, institutions, and events in historical expressions of life within their political context. In *kerygma*, *koinonia*, and *diakonia*, the spirit of freedom and of the new future of God is brought into the whole present affliction. Thus, we arrive at a method which is not a principle, namely, the method of historical effectiveness in outline, experience, and criticism of this outline. Preaching needs to establish the text and scrutinize the conversation of the congregation. The Church needs to establish the Bible and scrutinize the public discussion. Obedience and love need to establish the discipleship of Jesus and need to scrutinize the working-out of present experience. This is an hermeneutical process which encompasses the whole history of Christianity. From it arises the method of realization of faith, community, and free life under the changing circumstances of affliction in the present.

In this process one must be aware of the following: 1. *The constant factor* in the changing situation of history is the relation of spirit and faith, of freedom and life to Jesus the Crucified One. Content and manner of proclaimed and lived freedom must be legitimized by reflections on their basis in the crucified Christ. The cross of Christ is the criterion for distinguishing between the spirits, i.e., for the separation of faith and superstition. The Church is only the Church of Christ as the brotherhood of the Crucified One. This is its criterion. The new life *in* freedom and *for* freedom is the discipleship of Jesus. This is its criterion. Where this fundamental connection is lost, proclamation, church, and life lose their Christian identity.

2. *The invariable factor* is the adjustment of proclamation, church, and life to the future of the Crucified One, i.e., to his parousia in bodily, political, and cosmic openness. No one can conserve our forefathers' conceptions and representations of hope. They arose out of the afflictions of their time, but always in the same direction and with the same intention. The conceptions, images and words are variable because they are determined by their time. Invariable, however, is their orientation toward the future of Christ and the coming freedom which he reveals to the afflictions of the present situation. Whoever abandons this orientation does not demythologize anymore—he breaks off the transmission of the gospel.

3. *Variable factors* are exegesis and application because new forms of alienation, sin, and affliction are continually produced. But there is a solidarity of afflicted men in history and time which, as Paul says, is found in their common lack of freedom and glory. Therefore, one can understand himself through the changing representations of the world and social order in the partnership of deprivation. And in this solidarity, the freedom of the "coming one" becomes the common future for all periods of history, until the kingdom of freedom overcomes the conditions of history. Figuratively expressed, the "wandering people of God," who go from affliction to affliction and from freedom to freedom through the course of history, can better represent the continuum in history than institutions which vacillate back and forth between orthodoxy and modernism, fundamentalism and accommodation. This is shown in a practical outline for the witness of the Christian in the modern world:

A. *The kingdom of God comes to those who labor and are heavily laden.* If Jesus, the Messiah of the kingdom, appeared to the poor, the afflicted, and the sick, he indicated thereby that through poverty, hunger, and sickness mankind is held in unworthiness and that the Kingdom of God will fill him with riches materially. The kingdom which Jesus preached and represented through his existence is not only the soul's bliss but *shalom* for the body as well: peace on earth and liberation of the creature from the past. "The body is meant . . . for the Lord and the Lord for the body" (I Corinthians 6:13). If, however, the body belongs to the Lord, the task of the Christian is to await and anticipate his dominion in the emaciated and exploited body. This is not just Christian *charitas*, but a practical proof of hope in the redemption of the body in this world. The social revolution against unjust circumstances is the immanent reverse side of the transcendent resurrection hope. Only because the Church limited itself to the soul's bliss in the heavenly beyond and became docetic did the active hope of bodily salvation wander out of the Church and enter into social-change utopias. In them, circumstances are represented in which those who labor and are heavily laden cease to be so, as Ernst Bloch correctly asserts (with an unmistakable biblical emphasis).[25] Therefore, the Church and Christians should recognize a spirit which is of the spirit of Christ in the movement of changing social relationships. It is, of course, not so much a matter of a "latent church" or an "anonymous Christianity" that appears here. It is much more the latent kingdom, for which the Church (in its own way) exists, that proves itself effective in these movements. Through a critical analysis of the cogency and possibilities of "one-dimensional" (H. Marcuse) humanity in modern society, hope for the kingdom can be joined to present possibilities and thus become practical.[26]

B. *The kingdom of God comes to the humiliated and abused.* Jesus, the Messiah of God's righteousness, came to those who

[25] Ernst Bloch, *Naturrecht und menschliche Würde* (Frankfurt, 1961), p. 13.

[26] Cf. W. Rauschenbusch, *Christianity and the Social Crisis*, R. D. Cross, ed. (New York, 1964), p. 91: "Ascetic Christianity called the world evil and left it. Humanity is waiting for a revolutionary Christianity which will call the world evil and change it."

had no rights, to sinners and tax collectors. With this he indicated that not only through poverty, but even more by deprivation of rights, is man retained in humiliation. With those who had no rights, he celebrated the eschatological banquet. His resurrection can be understood from the humiliation of the cross as the revelation of the new creation of God's righteousness. Christians are obligated to bring, with the Gospel and with their fellowship, the justice of God and freedom into the world of oppression. Men do not hunger for bread alone. In the most elementary way, they hunger for recognition and independence. Since the Church has limited itself to the forgiveness of moral and spiritual sins, the hope for justice wandered out of the Church and entered into revolutions for freedom. Many of the revolutions which today go through Africa, Asia, and the Americas are declarations of independence. They embody the right to be free and to determine one's own destiny so that one can live in a truly human way and find his own identity. One of the most difficult tasks today lies in the attempt at mediation between economic progress and democratic freedom. Foreign aid in terms of patronizing economic gifts is in continual danger of making men economically dependent. The "great leap forward" out of poverty and affliction is, on the other hand, too easily purchased with dictatorship, i.e., with renunciation of freedom. All kinds of protests and rebellions indicate that the compulsion for economic advancement encourages continual conflict between freedom and social accommodation in industrialized countries as well. Here, there is an open front for the commitment of Christians who should actualize the freedom of faith in an unfree world and justification in a repressive society.

C. *God himself comes to mankind.* Finally, it is not to be overlooked that Jesus forgives sins as only God can forgive. In him who was crucified and resurrected, the coming God himself is represented. The social and political commitment of Christians errs when it acts as if it did not contain behind and within itself the vivifying expectancy of God's own pres-

ence. It would be false if Christians expended all their energy
in political activity because of a bad social conscience. If
there were no hope against guilt and life's susceptibility to
emptiness, if there were no hope for the coming of God himself, everything else would be a renovation of the prison—
not a real break from the prison into the land of freedom.[27]
Luther called the scale of human affliction: sin, death, and
the devil. Leibniz translated this philosophically into the scale
of moral, physical and metaphysical evil. In the nineteenth
century, the distinction was made between the economic,
moral, and religious spheres of man's life. But if there were
no hope against the devil, against the metaphysical evil of
nothingness, and against the religious anguish over the pain
of mortality, whatever remains in human existence would
not be of much value. Hope for the coming of God himself
is described in Revelation 21 in the cosmological conceptions
of the new creation: in the city of God the succession of
day and night ceases because God himself and the Lamb are
"the sun." The first earth has passed away and the new earth
is no longer threatened by the waters. If we translate this
into ontological concepts, it would mean a new being which
is a participation in the pure being of God beyond the ambivalence of being and non-being in the first creation. The
ontological ambivalence determined through the *creatio ex
nihilo* is overcome in the *participatio in Deo*. Hope for the
coming of God himself is directed against the nothingness
at whose boundary everything that is exists. We do not find
this hope in social revolutions and wars for independence. We
find the sacrament of this hope in the Church anticipated in
Word and sacrament. The newness which the Church of Christ
advocates, and without which there is no advocate, means:

[27] The Social Gospel theology knew this quite well and in no
sense did it idealistically overlook it. Cf. W. Rauschenbusch,
op. cit., p. 47: "When the question of economic wants is solved
for the individual and all his outward adjustments are as comfortable as possible, he may still be haunted by the horrible
emptiness of his life and feel that existence is a meaningless
riddle and delusion. . . . Universal prosperity would not be incompatible with universal *ennui* and *Weltschmerz*."

"Behold, the dwelling of God is with man. He will dwell with them, and they shall be his people and God himself will be with them [Revelation 21:3]."

Here there are already hope and strength for mankind for a future in which conflicts other than social, political, and personal ones should cease. But on the other hand, these hopes can become the inexhaustible sources for social imagination and for legal and political visions in the name of freedom. Religion must not make this hope relative and irrelevant. It must intensify it and strengthen it against any defeat and disappointment.

When finally everything shall come to pass and God himself comes, when his presence changes the ontic condition of all things and relationships, then the interpretation of scriptural promises will take place, not just for the sake of the salvation and freedom of mankind, but for the coming glory of God himself. This is also a doxology, in the form of the calling out of the depths—a doxology that is the proclamation of God for God's own sake.

II: The Theory of Revolution:
Pro and Con

A Christian Looks at Revolution

George Celestin

George Celestin first assesses the significance of the martyred Colombian guerrilla-priest Camilo Torres, then catalogues the varieties of political and social revolution, and finally considers the phenomenon of revolution from a theological viewpoint. On the whole, his is a positive appraisal. He sees in revolution the possibility of its becoming "the cutting edge of humanization"; like the eminent Catholic theologian Karl Rahner, he regards the struggle for power as inevitable, and the pacifist's total renunciation of power as irresponsible. At the same time, he recognizes that for man moral ambiguity is also inevitable—that "not every revolution is necessarily good," and that "God is not always on the side of the revolutionaries." Celestin is an instructor in theology at St. Edward's University in Austin, Texas. His article is from the Spring 1968 issue of the Dominican publication *Listening: Current Studies in Dialog.**

WE ARE living in an age when to speak of "world-wide revolution" no longer sounds hyperbolic. Of the more than a hundred countries in the United Nations more than half have become sovereign states through some form of revolution. Faced with Mexico and Cuba we can no longer make Latin American revolutions into insignificant palace coups or "harem" revolts. Similar dissatisfaction of the under-privileged around the globe threatens sudden and violent social and political action, and Christians are finally waking up to the implications of the situations. The churches can no longer be content to alleviate the sufferings of victims of unjust social structures. Christians are becoming determined

* 2570 Asbury Ave., Dubuque, Iowa 52001.

to change unjust structures as quickly as possible. This will mean in some cases that the churches may have to preach violence.

Last year near the little town of El Carmen in Eastern Colombia, Camilo Torres, the priest turned guerilla, was ambushed and killed as he tried to man the machine gun of his ill-fated band. It was a painful and tortuous spiritual odyssey that finally brought Camilo to an unmarked grave. As his program for social reform tended more and more towards violence, Camilo was estranged from his aristocratic family and friends, became an enemy of the government and was finally rejected by his ecclesiastical superiors.

Protesting the fixed elections, seventy-five per cent of the Colombian electorate boycotted the 1964 election. With the corrupt government bureaucracy incapable of effective social reform, Camilo became convinced that only a violent revolution could change things. "The people," he wrote, "do not believe in elections. The people know that legal means are at an end. . . . The people know that only armed rebellion is left. The people are desperate and ready to stake their lives so that the next generation of Colombians may not be slaves."

With the news of Camilo's death, rioting broke out in Bogotá. Students recklessly roamed through the streets, demanding to see his body. Over television a priest blamed his church for having driven Camilo into the revolutionary camp. And in wretched villages throughout Colombia people shouted "Camilo lives! Camilo lives!" When Camilo died the Colombian people gained a new national hero and the Latin American revolutionary movement a new martyr.

Yet *social revolution* is the primary fact with which our generation will have to come to terms. Except in Latin America, the anticolonial struggle has now passed its peak; but the struggle of the poor and weak nations for a more equitable share of the wealth has just begun; and the revolution of the dispossessed within wealthier nations is in its infant stages. It is impossible for us to avoid or withdraw from the revolutionary struggle. Few thinkers today are as extreme as the quotable Fr. Torres shouting to his followers: "Every Catholic who is not a revolutionary, and is not on the side of the revolutionaries, lives in mortal sin." But in a recent surprising declaration from the hierachy, there came a positive statement on revolution. Under the title of *A Message from Some Bishops of the Third World*, the document states, "the Church cannot but accept those revolutions which serve justice." The bishops go on to encourage the oppressed to attend to their own liberation since, "they know by experience that they must count on themselves and their own energies more than on the aid of the rich." Although some rich nations or certain rich people within their own nation may help, it would be illusory for the poor to wait for the conversion of the majority of the rich, who "will not be convinced even if someone should rise from the dead."

Varieties of Revolution

To call our age one of revolution may seem like a misnomer since according to most authors the classical "Age of Revolution" would span the era from the beginning of the French or American revolutions to the nineteenth century. But our age also is preoccupied with revolution, as Adlai Stevenson pointed out in his Harvard lectures in 1954. "Great movements and forces, springing from deep wells, have converged at this mid-century point, and I suspect we have barely begun to comprehend what has happened and why. In the background are the opaque, moving forms and shadows of a world revolution, of which Communism is more the scavenger than the inspiration; a world in transition from an age with which we are familiar to an age shrouded in mist."

If revolution is indeed a central concern of our age, we must look more closely at revolution itself before investigation of the Christian's task in that concern. By now it must be obvious that we have been using the word revolution in a great variety of ways. We ought to explicate some of the various types of revolutions; "precise" more carefully what kinds we are talking about in this paper; and arrive at some insight into the nature and function of revolution.

Ever since the industrial revolution began in England in

the last century, it has been common to speak of the mush-rooming growth in technology as a revolution. In this paper however we wish to restrict ourselves to the political revolution and to omit as far as possible the revolution in science and technology. We say *as far as possible* because these two types of revolution are interrelated. Consider, for example, the vast discrepancy between the per-capita income of the rich and poor nations that is due to geometric progression of technological advances in the affluent nations. Much of the dissatisfaction among the earth's paupers is also due to technology. Communications have placed the once distant peoples next to one another. Consequently the have-nots can see better than ever before just what it is that they have not.

All political revolutions are obviously not cut from the same bolt of cloth. The French revolution, the Irish and the Cuban are all unique. Political scientists, however, have come up with typologies which allow us to group revolutions into categories for study. Perhaps one of the best for our purpose is that of Chalmers Johnson in his work *Revolution and the Social System.* We preface this analysis with the caution that the types are not ironclad and any one revolution may share characteristics of several of Johnson's categories.

Johnson recognizes six types of revolutions, specified according to the targets attacked and the means used:

The first type of revolution may be labeled *Jacquerie.* It is a spontaneous mass peasant uprising carried out in the name of traditional authorities, church or monarchy, for example— with the limited aims of purging the local or national elite. Such were the peasants' revolt of 1381, Ket's rebellion in 1549, and Russia's Pugachev rebellion in 1773–75.

Millenarian rebellion is the second type. An added feature distinguishes it from the first type: a utopian dream inspired by a living messiah. Examples are the 1494 Florentine revolution of Savonarola, the Anabaptist rebellion at Münster in 1533–35, the Sioux Ghost-dance rebellion inspired by the Paiute prophet Wavoka in 1890.

The third type is called *Anarchistic rebellion,* a romantic idealization of the old order and a nostalgic reaction to "progressive" change. In this category are the Pilgrimage of Grace against Henry VIII, 1536–37, and the reaction in the Vendée against the French revolution.

The *Jacobin* or *Communist revolution* is very rare. Entailing a sweeping fundamental change in political organization, social structure, and economic property control, it can only occur in a highly centralized state with good communications and a large capital city. The target of this revolution is the government, as well as society. The upshot of the revolution is the creation of a new national consciousness formed by a central military authority and a more efficient social order build on the ruins of privilege, nepotism, corruption. Examples: the French and Russian revolutions.

The fifth type is the *conspiratorial coup d'état*: the planned work of a tiny elite fired up by a sectarian ideology. It can qualify as a revolutionary type only if it actually anticipates a mass movement and inaugurates social change. Castro's revolution in Cuba and Nasser's in Egypt fall into this category.

Militarized mass insurrection, the last type of revolution, is a new phenomenon of the twentieth century. It is a deliberately planned mass revolutionary war guided by a dedicated elite. Since the rebels are completely dependent on broad popular support the outcome of the guerilla warfare is determined by political attitudes rather than military strategy or matériel. The ideology impelling these revolutions combines a preponderance of xenophobic nationalism with Marxism. This type of struggle has occurred in Yugoslavia, China and Vietnam.

One possible difficulty with this typology is that it does not specifically include the rebellion of the dispossessed and underprivileged within relatively prosperous and satisfied national populaces. The example close to home is the Negro "revolution" in America. In this case there is no question of overthrowing the existing government or constitution, but of forcing the government to uphold the constitution so that *de jure* rights may *de facto* be realized. The Negro is not seeking disassociation from American society like the Nat Turner uprising or the scheme of Elijah Mohammed for a separate Negro state. Rather the Negro wants to be completely integrated into the American mainstream.

The revolution of the dispossessed looms large today, as important perhaps as the peasant revolutions in the poor nations. Our definition of revolution, therefore, has to be wide enough to include both the revolution of governmental overthrow and that of integration or incorporation.

Revolution Defined

According to Carl Friedrich, it is the speed and violence with which a political revolution takes place that distinguishes it from others such as the industrial revolution, the scientific revolution or the revolution of rising expectations.[1]

For Chalmers Johnson, revolution is "a change effected by the use of violence, in government and/or society." This is perhaps a better definition for our purposes since it admits of a change in society without governmental overthrow. Notice that in both definitions violence is essential, as indeed it is in all the types of revolution which we studied briefly in the previous section.

Finally the definition of revolution given by the "bishops of the third world" seems best for our purposes, for it gives a final reason for revolution: the common good. Their definition reads: "Revolution . . . is a rupture with a system which does not guarantee the common good and the setting up of a new order more apt to procure it."

The introduction of this ethical notion of the *common good* brings us out of the realm of the sociology and history of revolution into the ethics, morality and theology of revolution.

Theological Aspects of Revolution

The history of Christian thought does not provide us with many theologians of revolution. Theology in our days is striv-

ing to once again catch up with the secular reality and interpret it in Christian terms. Among those who in the past *have*
broached the subject was Augustine. In his *City of God,* Augustine attributes the demise of the Roman Empire to God
himself working through human instruments. This idea occasions Augustine's speculation on the order in the city of
man. The peace of the earthly city depends on the order
motivated by human self-love. In other words, it is an order
which is always coming to be in the midst of conflict. Earthly
peace is unstable and temporary; men must often make war
to achieve peace. In this order, furthermore, God's judgment upon human pride often effects the collapse of certain
structures in society so that society as a whole may be reformed.

In the Middle Ages, John of Salisbury taught the legitimacy of tyrannicide. (This teaching, however, should be
taken within the whole context of his commonwealth theory.)
Lord Acton considered Thomas Aquinas the earliest expo-
nent of the Whig theory of revolution.[2]

In our own times, the Popes have addressed themselves to
the question of revolution. Pius XII proclaimed to a group of
Italian workers in 1943:

Salvation and justice are not to be found in revolution but in
evolution through concord. Violence has always achieved only
destruction, not construction; the kindling of passions, not
their pacification; the accumulation of hate and ruin, not the
reconciliation of the contending parties. And it has reduced
men and parties to the difficult task of rebuilding, after sad
experience, on the ruins of discord.

John XXIII, writing on the same subject in *Pacem in
terris,* says "It must be borne in mind that to proceed gradually is the law of life in all its expressions; therefore in
human institutions, too, it is not possible to renovate for the
better except by working from within them, gradually. . . ."
But in the same place he does recognize that those who cham-
pion revolution are often "particularly endowed with gen-
erosity" for bringing about justice.

In *Populorum progressio*, Paul VI also confronts the issue:

A revolutionary uprising—save where there is a manifest, long standing tyranny which would do great damage to fundamental personal rights and dangerous harm to the common good of the country—produces new injustices, throws more elements out of balance and brings on new disasters. A real evil should not be fought against at the cost of greater misery.

By and large, then, the Popes have been loath to recognize revolution as a legitimate recourse in resolving social injustices. Certainly we see nothing of the positive recommendation which the "bishops of the third world" have advocated.

For Christians who are horrified at the thought of revolution, perhaps the greatest fear is of the violence that history demonstrates is inevitably involved. Power and particularly its violent use generates traumas of conscience for many Christians. As they see it, the way of Christ is the way of peace and non-violence. Witness the interest of Père Régamey and of the late Martin Luther King, Jr., in the life and teachings of Mahatma Gandhi. Régamey maintains that:

War or revolution never lead to peace in itself, but to a state in which it may be possible to work for peace, and to achieve this only peaceful means are of any use. These are often likely to be compromised by the injustices of a so-called "peace," so that the settlement of a violent conflict is in fact nothing more than established violence.[3]

(It is interesting to note that in a recent statement on Camilo Torres, Régamey calls him a saintly exception to the Christian norm of nonviolence!)

Karl Rahner, in an excellent analysis of the Christian understanding and use of power, points out that the struggle for power is inevitable. It is a struggle, moreover, from which the Christian cannot absent himself. To do so would constitute a false spiritualism, an escape from the real material world. Rahner considers blanket renunciation of any kind of physical force not merely impracticable but also immoral, because it is in effect an abdication of responsibility under God. The very freedom of decision regarding the correct use of power is radically precluded by the extreme pacifist who denies the validity of this option. Thus Rahner asserts that "the intransigent pacifist is a greater threat to peace than those who reckon with the existence of force and its inevitable exercise, and therefore treat it as something real. . . ."[4]

Rahner's analysis is absolutely basic to any discussion of the theology of revolution. Violent use of power usually accompanies any revolution. Thus to write off any such use of power as evil, closes the case for revolution and ends all discussion. Appreciation of power as a basic good, which can be perverted but need not be, is fundamental. Man must use power as God intended.

God and Revolution

What role does God play in revolutions?

Some insightful answers have been arrived at recently by theologians working with the concept of the theology of messianism, a notion broad enough to cover God's activity in human institutions. In the Old Testament, God tore down in order to build up (Jer. 1:10), and in the New Testament divine power is praised for crushing the proud, the mighty and exalting the lowly (Lk. 1:50–3). God is concerned with the progress of humanity. Thus the theology of messianism focuses on what God is doing *right now* in the world to make man's life more human. In this context revolution can become the cutting edge of humanization.

In the same vein, theologians such as Van Leeuwen see Christianity bearing within itself the seeds of humanity's progress. The entire Western mentality formed by Christianity is revolutionary. It was not accidental, therefore, that the industrial revolution and the great political revolutions first took place in the Christian West.

As the first groping attempts at theorizing on God's role in revolution, these speculations perhaps must be somewhat simplistic. In this there is no real harm, so long as we realize that the reality under consideration is more complex than our theoretical concepts. The ambiguity of the Christian life becomes clear when one tries to come up with the religious significance of revolution.

Hopefully theologizing about revolution will bring understanding to those Christians who face the real possibility of revolution. But the final moral decisions must be made by those on the firing line. This is the time when the ideas of theologians must be tested in the crucible of life, where there is neither black nor white, only shades of gray. This is the time when the earnest revolutionary is haunted by the realization that not every revolution is necessarily good; it may be oppression in a different form. God is not always on the side of the revolutionaries.

NOTES

[1] Carl Friedrich, "An Introductory Note on Revolution," in *Revolution Nomos VIII, Yearbook of the American Society for Political and Legal Philosophy* (New York: Atherton Press, 1966), p. 5.

[2] Lord Acton, *Essays on Freedom and Power*, ed. Gertrude Himmelfarb (Cleveland: World-Meridian, 1948), p. 88.

[3] P. Régamey, *Non-violence and the Christian Conscience* (New York: Herder and Herder, 1966), p. 56.

[4] Karl Rahner, "The Theology of Power," in *Theological Investigations*, Vol. 4 (Baltimore: Helicon, 1966), p. 401.

Ecumenical Theology of Revolution

J. M. Lochman

Despite the fact that divergent views in regard to a theology of revolution were much in evidence at the Conference on Church and Society, held in Geneva, Switzerland, in the summer of 1966 under the auspices of the World Council of Churches, in the opinion of J. M. Lochman the beginnings of an ecumenical consensus on this controversial subject did emerge at the conference. In outlining the points of convergence, Lochman notes that the conference participants generally agreed that the possibility of developing a theology of revolution should no longer be anathema among churchmen, and that a correct reading of the dynamic biblical perspective—and biblical eschatology in particular—makes it incumbent upon the Christian to work for the transformation of society, and to do so in untraditional ways. Especially instructive is Lochman's discussion of how the conference dealt with the crucial question of whether the church may sanction the use of force to achieve social transformation. Professor Lochman, a member of the Comenius Theological Faculty in Prague, Czechoslovakia, recently traveled to the United States for a term as visiting professor at Union Theological Seminary in New York City. His essay appeared in the June 1968 *Scottish Journal of Theology.**

Revolution in Geneva

ONE of the most stirring moments of the World Conference on Church and Society held in Geneva in 1966 was during the third plenary session on 14th July. For that evening the subject was "The Challenge and Relevance of

* Don House, 46 Don Street, Aberdeen, Scotland.

Theology to the Social Revolutions of our Time." It had been chosen with some hesitation by the preparatory Committee; for although the relevance of the subjects on the first and second evenings—the technological and social revolutions of our time—was clear to all the delegates, the importance of a "theological revolution" seemed simply incommensurable in comparison with the others. However, this evening proved to be a real challenge to the Conference (and also in its repercussions on the social-theological thinking in the ecumenical movement) and its influence on the discussions afterwards was lasting and varied. The "theology of revolution" presented itself as an extremely burning issue for ecumenism.

There were three main speakers on the theme: a Protestant theologian from Western Germany, a Presbyterian from the U.S.A. (who spoke primarily about the experiences and views of the Churches in Latin America), and an Orthodox Archpriest from the U.S.S.R. Thus widely differing forms of Church and society belonging to the ecumenical movement were well represented. What theological perceptions were expressed, and what points were stressed?

"It is the great revolutions of modern history, first in England, then in France, Russia and China, which have created the world in which we live."[1] These were the opening words of the well-constructed address by Professor *Heinz-Dietrich Wendland*. He stressed the fact that it is not we (the Church and the theologians) who have chosen the theme of revolution; the theme presents a challenge to us owing to the fundamental facts of our world today. Especially the "total revolution" (as Wendland calls it to distinguish it from the political and social revolution of the past as the most important type of revolution today), namely the tremendous upheavals in every sphere of modern life resulting from science

---

[1] I quote from the mimeographed versions of the addresses given at the Conference on Church and Society, to which the page-numbers refer. The three addresses were as follows:

H.-D. Wendland: "The Church and Revolution"

Richard Shaull: "The Revolutionary Challenge to Church and Theology"

Archpriest Borovoy: "The Challenge and Relevance of Theology to the social revolutions of our time."

and technology, is becoming the global factor which confronts everyone living in the world today.

However, in the midst of this revolution the Church is not by any means being driven into a strange sphere by the blind destiny of historical progress. Reflection on the message of the Bible shows that the Gospel itself contains a "revolutionary element" which has helped to make the modern world what it is. "The question then arises: what is the connexion between the revolutionary element in the Christian message and revolution in history?" (p. 12). It is answered dialectically by referring to the thinking of Paul Tillich and Arthur Rich, who maintain that there is an affinity with the biblical thinking about revolution, but that the Bible also places limits on revolution. The affinity (say Tillich and Rich) lies mainly in the eschatology of the Bible, in the message of the coming Kingdom of God, whose dynamic force confronts Christians (also in society) with the basic principle *societas semper reformanda*. It is stressed by the anthropology of the Bible (which is the source of man's infinite power over the world) and by the Christian "ethic of action." "Man is the administrator who organises and reforms the state, the economy, society" (p. 15). Moreover it is never a "Christian revolution." Christians "do not set up any 'Christian' orders, systems, states and societies; for their task is to *humanise* the secular orders and the slightest real progress that can be attained there is more important than the most perfect Christian Utopia, because it guarantees real help to definite people or social groups" (pp. 16–17).

What is said above already indicates the distinction between the "revolutionary element" in the Bible and secular-revolutionary absolutism or fanatical Utopianism. No historical revolution "opens the door to the reign of freedom, which at the same time offers the inexhaustible satisfaction of all human needs" (p. 6). The Kingdom of God will never be directly established within this aeon.

In Wendland's view the effect of the revolutionary element in the Bible is to be understood differently: "The rule of God *indirectly* has social and political repercussions, not by stirring up rebellion, not by the use of political and military force, but solely through the 'quiet,' unarmed, loving action and service of Christian groups scattered all over the world, and yet united in Christ" (p. 13). "Thus the Church itself becomes the source of constant revolutionary changes in state and society" (p. 18).

The carefully weighed statements of Professor Wendland were immediately followed by a real thunderbolt—the revolutionary theology of *Richard Shaull's* address. It was awaited with tense expectation. Professor Schaull (who is a professor at Princeton Theological Seminary) had written the first chapter for the first preparatory volume for the present Conference.[2] This chapter, entitled "Revolutionary Change in Theological Perspective," was a passionate plea for a "revolutionary theology" and for its concrete application to the burning social issues of our time, of which Professor Shaull has had personal experience through his very active participation in the questions of church and society in Latin America. In the present world situation, which is characterised by an unprecedented gulf between the different societies (especially between the "rich" and the "poor" nations), the social revolution is the first question which must be honestly faced by our generation. The crucial questions of the humanisation or de-humanisation of human life in the contemporary world are decided "on the frontiers of revolution."[3] "As a political form of change, revolution represents the cutting edge of humanisation."[4]

In his address to the Conference Shaull expressed the same view of the world situation and drew the same consequences for Christian ethics and Christian action. He mentioned Wendland, but then went resolutely further, stressing that in certain situations it might be incumbent upon Christians to take part in revolutionary action which involved the use of force. His arguments were directed especially against those

[2] *Christian Social Ethics in a Changing World*, edited by John C. Bennett, Association Press, New York, 1966. It really is a pity that the German preparatory book (*Die Kirche als Faktor einer kommenden Weltgemeinschaft*, Stuttgart, 1966) does not include Shaull's contribution.

[3] *Christian Social Ethics in a Changing World*, p. 25.

[4] *Op. cit.*, p. 32.

who, in regard to the highly developed technical structure of the industrial countries, exclude the possibility of a revolutionary change there.[5] In face of this, Shaull did not proclaim the "end of revolution" but "a new strategy of revolution." This consists in "developing those bases from which a system unwilling to initiate major changes when they are most urgently needed, can be constantly bombarded by strong pressures for small changes at many different points" (p. 3). In this connexion Shaull refers to the strategy of "guerilla warfare."

What then is the relevance of theology for such revolutionary thought and action? Not mainly to issue warnings against turning revolutionary ideologies into absolutes (although that is also one of theology's tasks), and certainly not to draft "abstract principles or ideas" (like that of the responsible society). It is much more important for Christians to bear witness to the revolutionary of those perspectives "which free him to break the bonds of the secular, empirical ethos, dream new dreams about the future of man, and cultivate the creative imagination so as to be capable of thinking about new problems in new ways, and defining new goals and models for a new society" (p. 5). What is required of the theologian is "not a new language, but a new involvement, in those places in the world where God is most dynamically at work"; an effort "to keep going the difficult but not impossible running conversation between the full biblical and theological tradition and the contemporary human situation" (p. 7).

As a sort of counterpoint to the above addresses, the third speaker was Archpriest *Vitalij Borovoy* of the Russian Orthodox Church—a Church "which has lived for almost half a century in the conditions of the social revolution which lies at the root of almost all the social revolutions of our time" (p. 1). He spoke about these actual experiences—without concealing the difficulties of the theme nor the reality of the revolution. Particularly for Orthodox Christians it was difficult to find an open-minded attitude towards revolution,

[5] For instance André Philip in the second preparatory volume *Responsible Government in a Revolutionary Age*, p. 120.

owing to their tradition: "Of all Christian cultures, Byzantium is the one which contributed most of all to the mere sanctification of social evil" (p. 3). "Our Church, in the persons of part of its hierarchy and part of its clergy, went through all the stages of rejection, opposition and even direct action against the revolution and the changes it brought to the life of the Church. . . . As a result, the Church lost millions of believers" (p. 5).

However, a conflict between the Church and revolution (and especially between Christian and revolutionary thinking) is not inevitable. On the contrary, biblical thinking in its original form is "social and revolutionary." If revolution means "change of relationships," "regeneration," "new life," these are clearly "basic Christian concepts." The biblical concepts of "rebirth" and "repentance," and the "conversions" of the great saints and ascetes, are "evidence of a spiritual revolution" (p. 3). "Christian life begins in crisis; it also continues in crisis" (p. 3). This insight is true not only of the individual soul but also of man's social existence. One may therefore sum up by saying: "Christianity is by its very nature revolutionary; and the new life required by Christian social ethics is more radical, more profoundly revolutionary, more novel than any other social system or doctrine which has grown up outside Christianity" (p. 4).

Here lies the promise for the relevance of biblical Christian theology and the Church also in the age of social revolutions: "New in its form, but biblical in its content, the theology of development and revolution will have a positive influence on the course of history, and on the thinking of the new revolutionary and socialist societies" (p. 5).

Ecumenical Divergences

If one tries to compare the addresses given at Geneva, in order to discover signs of an ecumenical consensus on the question of revolution (bearing in mind also the discussions evoked by these addresses), one soon encounters difficulties. It is not easy to reduce the three "revolutionary speakers" to one common denominator. They do not speak in unison, but with three somewhat discordant voices.

To begin with, each of them has a different concept of revolution. Borovoy appeals for Christian understanding for the social revolution, by drawing an analogy between the concept of revolution and the starting-point of the spiritual life—"conversion," "change of heart" and "new life." Wendland's concept of "total revolution" goes far in another direction (and corresponds to some extent to the central theme of the Conference, which speaks not only of the social revolution but also of the technological revolution).[6] To Wendland "total revolution" means the all-embracing revolutionary process of our technological-scientific civilisation with its upheavals not only in the social sphere, but also in the realms of culture and religion. Shaull does not ignore the general background of this "total revolution," but he deliberately concentrates on the most crucial aspects of the revolution of our time, namely the social aspects; his main concern is to bring about a radical change (which is long overdue) in the unjust national and international "order."

These differences in concept did not facilitate the discussions in Geneva. The word "revolution" soon developed into one of the slogans of the Conference which kept cropping up in widely differing contexts, but every time one was obliged to ask oneself what was really meant by "revolution" in that particular case. The question was raised not only by those who were opposed to any kind of "theology of revolution" both at the Conference and after it; it was raised also by those who did not dispute the need for change. As one can easily understand, there was a demand for a theological clari-

---

[6] "Christians in the Technical and Social Revolutions of our Time." At first it had been planned to convene the Conference under a more neutral title, "God, Man and Contemporary Society." But during the preparations the explosive character of contemporary society became more and more apparent (on this point the Christians in the developing countries were most insistent) and the concept of revolution was increasingly clearly adopted as the main theme—understood in a very broad sense (bearing in mind the differences between the "revolutionary changes" in the different areas of the world).

fication of the concept. (This dynamic Conference already had to face too many urgent problems, and was sometimes unable to cope with the task.)

Already in the plenary session directly after the addresses, the speakers were asked to answer some important questions. Roger Shinn, an American theologian, asked whether, in concentrating so much on the problem of revolution, they were not only seeking a "theology of revolution" but at the same time an "ideology of revolution." Is not "revolution" almost being turned into a general law to which the Church is firmly bound (e.g., in the minds of many young American theologians who want to be "where the action is taking place")? Denys Munby, an economist from Oxford, formulated the classical theological question: what is meant by talking of God's revolutionary action in history ("places in the world where God is most dynamically at work")? Is not this concept far too vague and general? Does it not vaguely regard God as identical with the process of history and its crises? These questions must be considered seriously; it is true that many points have still to be clarified (both linguistically and theologically), especially perhaps in Shaull's address.[7] For this reason alone it is difficult to arrive at an ecumenical consensus on the concept of "revolution."

[7] If some people thought they could trace signs of a new (perhaps "red") variation of the "German Christian" heresy in the ideas of Shaull and his friends, in my own view this was unfair. In the whole of his revolutionary thinking, which is thoroughly comprehensible, Shaull shows that he is no vague enthusiast nor romantic in his concept of revolution. He is deeply aware of the ambiguity of all revolutionary commitment, and gives clear expression to it: "The struggle for a new order takes place in the midst of opposition, repeated failure and the constant appearance of new threats of dehumanisation" (*Christian Social Ethics in a Changing World*, p. 38f). His whole emphasis is the following, however: the Christian choice cannot be to moralise while "keeping one's own hands clean," taking anxious care not to become involved in any dangerous situations. Admittedly, the Christian does not simply swim with the current of revolution; but on the other hand he is not a spectator watching from the bank either. Shaull expresses this as follows: "The Christian

The sharpest difference, however, is in relation to the concrete ethical problem: the problem of force. In the theological reflections about revolution this question has always played an important role. It was also the crucial point (explicitly or implicitly) of the discussions at the Conference. Already in the addresses this question gave rise to open dispute. Despite all the insistence on the possibility and the need for a Christian-revolutionary commitment, in Wendland's view the use of force (especially of military force) is excluded as a legitimate instrument which Christians could use for "transforming the world" (p. 16). On the other hand, Shaull takes the view that "there may be some situations in which only the threat or use of violence can set the process of change in motion" (p. 4). In the discussions some supported one of these views, some the other—with different nuances.

Sometimes the division cut right across the geographical and confessional fronts. But sometimes a certain "rule" was apparent. Most of the delegates from the developing countries (especially from Africa and Latin America) approved the use of revolutionary force in order to effect changes in the unjust social structures; they did not take this view lightly, but they were quite definite about it. This position was summed up very impressively by Dr. Castillo-Cardenas of Colombia in his address to the Conference. He said that if Christians are coming more and more to realise that the present order is "an affront to God because it is an affront to man" (p. 5); and when they realise how many forms of force are employed in order to protect this unjust order against the under-privileged and oppressed, the poor and the weak, then (if they really love their neighbour) they cannot content themselves with "certain isolated reforms equivalent to social anesthesia." What is required is "to take power away from the privileged minorities and give it to the poor majorities."

---

looks for stability on the other side of change; he is therefore free to be fully involved in the revolution. At the same time, his understanding of what is going on there obliges him to work constantly for reconciliation" (*op. cit.*, p. 32).

"Therefore, revolution is not only permitted, but is obligatory for those Christians who see it as the only effective way of fulfilling love to one's neighbour"[8] (p. 5).

On the other hand, the delegates from the highly industrialised countries on the whole showed a more reserved attitude to the problem of force; not only the pacifists (who were of course represented at the Conference) but also "realistic politicians." This view was summed up in the second preparatory volume by Professor André Philip, one of the Chairmen of the Conference: "violence seems to be impossible, even apart from any ethical considerations." For "the technical structure is too elaborate and the different elements overlap too much for any sudden break to be made without upsetting the whole system of production and consequently impoverishing the masses." Consequently, in these countries it is only "through limited action, which does not jeopardise the structure as a whole, that improvements can be introduced, by methods that are bound to be democratic, attempting creatively to mobilise public opinion as a whole."[9]

If one compares these two concepts and places them in the context of the social situations involved, the question arises: is not the problem of force in the ecumenical movement today "ideological" rather than "theological"? Do not the different answers simply reflect the different social positions in the "world-wide struggle" of our time between the rich and the poor nations? The "poor" nations want revolution, even if it involves the use of force. The "rich" nations regard the use of force as a problem—apparently a theological one, but in reality an ideological one. This aspect of our ecumenical discussions should not be swept aside in a self-righteous manner. The "ideological" aspects and the non-theological factors certainly do play a role and we ought to take sober account of them (especially in our own minds). And yet the

[8] Gonzalo Castillo-Cardenas: "Christians and the Struggle for a new Social Order in Latin America" (mimeographed conference-document, p. 5).

[9] André Philip: "The Revolutionary Change in the Structure of European Political Life" (pp. 120-1), article in the Second Preparatory Volume for the Conference entitled *Responsible Government in a Revolutionary Age.*

problem of revolutionary force cannot be solved ideologically. It is certainly not only those who defend a privileged "status quo" who express serious misgivings about the use of force; sometimes it is quite the contrary. Many of them support the need for a radical change in the social structures. The problem has a still deeper level—namely the theological one.

After the Conference, but clearly in relation to it, *Helmut Gollwitzer* (in an important statement on the work of the Prague Peace Conference) drew attention to the strange paradox in the ecumenical discussions today concerning the use of force. Owing to the nihilistic consequences of the brutal use of violence during the last world wars, in the theological work of the great European Churches the traditional sanctioning of the use of force in the Christian ethic is at last being questioned. Understanding is growing for Christian pacifism and for "non-violence as the most appropriate form of Christian witness." And now "just at this moment, when we . . . are inclined to regard as mistaken the traditional approval of Christian participation in the use of military force and to hoist the flag of pacifism . . . we hear from our brethren in the under-developed countries (where the situation is a revolutionary one) that they consider it incumbent upon them to participate in national and social revolutionary struggles which involve the use of force."[10]

The paradox of this situation is tremendous. It cannot be solved by theological statements and considerations. Nevertheless it is worth while making a first attempt at an ecumenical reflection. The Conference on Church and Society also tried to do so—and not entirely without success. Especially in the report of the Second Section dealing with "The Nature and Function of the State in a Revolutionary Age" there are several paragraphs on this question (paragraphs 83, 84 and 85). These paragraphs definitely approve the renunciation of force and the way of peace, and urge Christians not to resort to force. The Christian should familiarise himself ecumenically with the strategy of non-violence (where it has proved effective in practice) and should try to discover those forms of

[10] Helmut Gollwitzer, published in *Junge Kirche*, 1966, p. 637 (free translation).

non-violence that are appropriate for his own situation. Even in the most unfavourable situations, in his struggle against the evils in society the Christian should always take the path of non-violence.

Nevertheless force is a reality in our world—either open or concealed. Thus in certain situations a genuine question can emerge: "whether the violence which sheds blood in planned revolutions may not be a lesser evil than the violence which, though bloodless, condemns whole populations to perennial despair" (paragraph 84). If Christians accept this view, however, they must regard violence as a last resort which is justified only in extreme situations. "The use of violence requires a rigorous definition of the ends for which it is used and a clear recognition of the evils which are inherent in it" (paragraph 85).

These statements clearly do not offer any solution to our paradox; they are merely the first hesitant steps towards seeking it ecumenically. Further steps are urgently required.[11] But

---

[11] For instance, a step of this kind is represented by a statement presented in October 1966 to the Consultative Committee of this movement by the theological study-group of the Christian Peace Conference. Referring to the problems raised at the Conference of Church and Society, this study-group tried to answer the question of the possibility of participating in revolution involving the use of violence. The study-group answered the question in the affirmative, making the reservation however that military force can be resorted to only as an *ultima ratio*. *Ultima ratio* means:

(a) if violent measures have already been used by the oppressors . . .;

(b) if all possible methods of legal criticism and legal actions have been courageously and patiently tried, without success;

(c) if a situation has arisen which (owing to the action or failure to act of the oppressors) is more harmful to human beings than a violent revolution would probably be.

The document concludes with an important theological explanation: "If Christians support revolution, they derive the right to do so not from the idea of revolution but from the Christian Gospel. In so doing the goals of humanisation and justice (which are the goals of revolution) are not made relative. On the contrary, we should understand these goals more deeply, more objectively, more concretely. This means that our participation in revolu-

these first steps point in the right direction. The "tension in the field of ecumenical ethics" revealed by them may prove fruitful, if the two "positions" are understood not as being "complementary" (as two static, co-existent variations on a common theme) but as a "lively dialectic." "Lively" in the most literal sense, because they both spring from that movement into which Christians in the Church (and in society) are drawn by "the Lordship of Christ." In this movement there will be no doubt about the "trend" of our social discipleship: the maintenance of non-violent love is clearly the "first essential" in our political Diakonia. It is the essential framework within which all theories (and all practical forms) of Christian force must be placed. At the same time, however, the "pacifist" is warned: the testimony of non-violent love is not true if it is understood quietistically or ideologically (as a luxury-attitude in which the *beati possidentes* can indulge); it is true only if it is expressed in serious Christian testimony, i.e., in a revolutionary way, attacking the inhuman, godless structures of the world in the light of God's Kingdom. It is only through ecumenical solidarity with the hungry, oppressed people in the developing countries, and by supporting their justified revolutionary demands, that the privileged Christians of Europe today can make a testimony of non-violent love which will carry any conviction. It is only through this solidarity with them that our theological struggle with the problem of violence and non-violence can maintain that ecumenical tension, and perhaps solve it step by step.

In this connexion a Czech theologian is bound to recall with gratitude the tremendous struggle of the *Reformation in Bohemia*. The amazing actuality and relevance of this Reformation for our own time was brought home to us afresh by the Conference on Church and Society. That applies already to the problem of revolution. It is not an unfamiliar

---

tionary action must not be motivated by hatred, nor by confidence in force, but solely by sympathy and solidarity with those who suffer . . . and by the hope of a new, just order, by readiness to forgive" (*Junge Kirche*, 1966, p. 658f).

theme for the tradition of the Bohemian Reformation. In Hussite Bohemia and Moravia the Word of God really was understood and explained in a revolutionary sense, in the attempt to change not only the Church but also society (in accordance with the Gospel). The "social dimension" of Christian obedience was very clearly recognised from the time of Hus onwards, and it was also expressed in practice. It was no blind "enthusiasm": even in the Hussite "Sturm und Drang" theological reflection was not thrown overboard. Recent research shows that even the important question of a "theology of revolution" was tackled—at least an important beginning was made. For years the Hussite theologians grappled with the problem of a *bellum iustum*, which was really a constant attempt to solve the problem of a *revolutio iusta*.[12]

The Bohemian Reformation also provides very valuable ideas even for the ecumenical paradox on the question of non-violence and violence. This was the crucial question raised by the tremendous tension between the theologians who supported revolutionary force and those who insisted that the struggle was a spiritual one and must be waged in a Christian spirit without resort to violence. (This latter view was held by Peter Chelcicky and later by the Czech Brethren.) This tension did not take the form of a paralysing paradox between two extremes; it expressed itself in a "lively dialectic" in which both views endeavoured together to seek the way of God's Kingdom. This theme of Christian discipleship linked the whole Reformation together—even when opinions diverged as to what form that discipleship should take. Among the Hussites it expressed itself in the attempt to change the whole life of society (involving the burning issue of a responsible use of force). In the case of Chelcicky and the Czech Brethren it took the form of an attempt to give the binding authority of Jesus Christ full expression in the Christian minority-church, without the use of violence. Both these attitudes (the common theme and the different ways of in-

12 See A. Molnar, "Mezi revoluci a valkou" ("Between Revolution and War"), theological annex to the *Krestanska Revue*, 1967, No. 1. See also F. Seibt, *Hussitica* (Zur Struktur einer Revolution), Cologne, 1965, on our subject, especially chapter 2.

terpreting it) inherited from the Bohemian Reformation may be relevant to our ecumenical work even today.[13]

Dynamic Convergence

The tensions and divergences in the ecumenical theology of revolution are strong. In spite of this, can one speak of a certain convergence, or even of a consensus? I should like to answer in the affirmative. In support of doing so, three points may be made.

1. Revolution in ecumenical social ethics

I understand this ambiguous slogan simply as a definition of an incomparably greater role which the phenomenon of revolution should play in Christian thinking on social ethics today. For centuries revolution was the "step-child" of Christian social ethics. Usually it came up only on the periphery of ethical considerations, and was overshadowed by other problems (e.g., that of "the orders"). "Hitherto theological ethics have paid inadequate attention to the problem of revolution."[14] To put it more bluntly: "There is no authoritative theological literature in this field at all."[15] The way in which

---

[13] It is not by chance that the Czech theologian J. L. Hromadka was one of the pioneers of an "ecumenical theology of revolution." See my paper "Zur Frage der 'Geschichtsphilosophie' J. L. Hromadkas" ("On Hromadka's philosophy of history") published in *Evangelische Theologie*, 1965, pp. 413–28.

[14] See E. Fahlbusch, *Evangelisches Kirchenlexikon*, III, Sp. 646. Fahlbusch's article is one of the best things written on the subject by a Protestant.

[15] See Wendland's paper at the Conference on Church and Society, footnote 6 (p. 6). If one studies the standard works on Christian Ethics, one finds hardly any mention in them of the question of revolution, or merely a superficial one. This applies to N. H. Søe (*Christliche Ethik*) who is Lutheran, to Emil Brunner (*Das Gebot und die Ordnungen*) who is Reformed, and to B. Häring (*Das Gesetz Christi*) who is a Catholic. W. Trillhaas (*Ethik*) and H. Thielicke (*Theologische Ethik*, II/2) also devote only short sections to the question.

the theme is handled is also "step-motherly," as if it were an unwanted illegitimate child who presents a menace to the legitimate children (the traditional Christian orders of the West). Thus the traditional social ethic was inspired with an anti-revolutionary spirit. For the conservative mentality, revolution means "downfall, destruction, decadence, the decline of morality and religion, the end of all true culture and a contempt for history."[16] The conservative view of the theme has therefore "helped to 'daemonise' the phenomenon of 'revolution' rather than to cast light on the concept and on the challenge."[17]

In this connexion the Conference on Church and Society, and the years of work on social ethics which preceded it, reveal a very definite change. Not only did this Conference

[16] Wendland's address at the Conference on Church and Society, p. 5. This conservative rejection of revolution is apparent especially in German Lutheranism even at the time of the Reformation (i.e., in Luther himself, especially in his decision to oppose the peasant's rebellion). The anti-revolutionary spirit reached its climax probably after the French Revolution. In his lecture entitled "Von Ordnung und Revolution" (*Posthumous Works*, 2, Munich, 1966, pp. 153–92) Hans-Joachim Iwand traces its different forms very perspicaciously. To Julius Stahl revolution was simply "the rule of sin" and "the opposite pole" to Christianity. And in the view of A. Fr. Vilmar the Church is the last stronghold of legality and of divinely appointed authority, it is therefore anti-revolution incarnate and will "victoriously outlive democracy and despotism, with which it has nothing to do" (quoted by Iwand, p. 157).

This mistrust of revolution is still apparent in German Lutheranism today, not only in Otto Dibelius (who almost consistently maintains the view of the nineteenth century, see p. 122, n. 4) but also in W. Trillhaas (who writes that revolution means "the release of egoism, the falsification of truth, the breakdown of all respect; the lowest come up on top and the upper classes (the nobility) are forced down" (*Ethik*, vol. 2, Berlin, 1965, p. 424). It is even apparent in Bonhoeffer, who says, "According to Holy Scripture, there is no such thing as a right to revolution" (*Ethik*, vol. 2, Munich, 1953, p. 273). However, Bonhoeffer, through his personal action, broke through these hard-and-fast concepts and has thus perhaps helped to change the traditional anti-revolutionary attitude of Protestant ethics. See also Iwand's essays on the Christian right to resistance, *op. cit.*, p. 193–242.

[17] E. Fahlbusch, *op. cit.*, p. 641.

bring the problem of revolution from the periphery into the very centre of ecumenical social ethics; it also transformed the whole approach to the problem. Admittedly some cautious warnings were issued at the Conference concerning the "theology of revolution"; but the problem was not "daemonised" and anathematised as in the past (nor was it at the Second Vatican Council). So in this connexion, despite the serious divergences, a certain convergence seems to be taking place. The "theology of revolution" is a legitimate and important theme for Christian theory and practice.

2. From the ethic of the "established Orders" to the ethic of "Change"

The phrase about "revolution in ecumenical social ethics" cannot, of course, be understood only as an indication of the increasing importance of the theme of "revolution" in the ecumenical movement. It also denotes the change which is taking place in the social ethic itself. Ecumenical thinking on social ethics is moving on from an "ethic of the established Orders" to an "ethic of change." In his article (already mentioned) "On Order and Revolution" H. J. Iwand shows how the principle of order became the guiding principle for all Christian ethics for the typical conservative thinkers of the nineteenth century—in opposition to the "anti-Christian" principle of revolution.[18] They were not pioneers; they took their stand on the Christian *ethica perennis* and strengthened it. Since the Middle Ages the ethics of the Church had increasingly developed into an ethic of the established Orders; the first and last concern of Christian ethics was to arrange natural and supernatural life in accordance

---

[18] Vilmar formulates this as follows: "Law and property, marriage, family, education, authority and obedience, rulers and subjects—all these are the general bases (or general concepts) on which society (even in the pagan world) rested and still rests." And now: "it is these orders (which are the 'indispensable preconditions for the vocatio gentium') that the Ministry must advocate unreservedly and to the utmost of its ability, using all their human energy and also the full power of the Holy Spirit" (quoted by Iwand, *op. cit.*, p. 159).

with a *lex naturae* or *lex divinum*. In society this ethic aims
at protecting the Christian (i.e., the traditional) order. This
explains the conservative trend of traditional Christian ethics
—not only in the Roman Catholic Church.

This form of traditional ethic is being challenged in the
ecumenical movement today. Admittedly the "established
Order" and the "established Orders" in Church and society
may have a significance which is ethically genuine and true.
But they are out of place if we regard them as fixed stars
whereby we can make our ethical decisions.[19] For in the world
of very ambiguous orders the first concern of Christian obedience cannot be to sanctify this ambiguous world by giving
it religious approval (as the Church usually did in relation
to the given society). The concern of Christian obedience is
rather to change this world, to "humanise" it—not theoreti-
cally but in actual fact, in the light of Christian humanity.
This perception, that the Christian ethic today should be primarily concerned with the transformation (and not the "con-
firmation") of society reached at the Conference was another
important aspect of an ecumenical consensus.[20]

3. *Dynamism of the biblical perspective*

The trends of thought in the ecumenical theology of revolution did not spring solely from outside influences, i.e., from
shattering experience of the revolutionary upheavals of our
time. Of course, it would be senseless, and also theologically
wrong, to deny that external events have influenced that

[19] With regard to the "Order-theologians" of the nineteenth
century Iwand rightly asks: "Does not the ethic of the New
Testament spring from the distinction between the two aeons,
and is not the Christian life related to the 'powers of the future
world?' Why then do the Lutheran theologians keep looking
backwards at that past epoch thus acting according to the old
Thomist principle: gratia non destruit, sed reparat naturam" (*op.
cit.*, p. 160).

[20] On the theme "How can the Church contribute to the transformation of Society?" see my own address at the Conference
on Church and Society (printed in *Communio Viatorum*, 1966,
pp. 217-20).

thinking. The Church, which lives by the incarnate Word, never thinks in an autocratic immanence of a "pure doctrine." It lives under the pressure of its world, and comes to grips with it, and carries on its theology through that encounter. Nevertheless its thinking remains "theological" only if it is based on the truth entrusted to it. This also applies to all "theologies of revolution"—if they wish to be theologies and not merely ideologies.

Among the voices which determine the ecumenical theology of revolution that we have so far described, the intention and the claim to represent a programme based on theology cannot be ignored. The theological basis varies, of course: from the Orthodox theology of the resurrection and of rebirth (Borovoy), via the concept of the Kingdom of God and social action (Wendland), to the radically secularising and humanising motives of Shaull.[21]

However, a surprising convergence is taking place amid all these divergences; this theology is impelled by the dynamism of the biblical approach. Especially it is biblical eschatology which plays the guiding role here. Our world is not a self-constituted quiescent world. We are living "between the aeons" and are therefore caught up in the eschatological movement of God's Kingdom. "The Kingdom of God presents a challenge to the present constitution and form of this world, in so far as it is not in accordance with the holy, life-giving will of God."[22] The future is therefore opening up to the

[21] Shaull is very critical of traditional theology: "the old images and concepts have lost their power" (p. 6). He has understanding for the most radical "death-of-God" theologians. Nevertheless his theology is not simply a "secularised" and "humanised" version of the biblical message. He has an amazing sense (like his friend Paul Lehmann) for the central pronouncements of the Christian tradition (e.g. for the Messianism of the Bible) and also for the dogma of the Trinity. The "transcendental" themes of the Kergyma are very important to him—and he interprets them in a revolutionary way (Cf. *Christian Social Ethics*, pp. 27f, 31f).

[22] Wendland, p. 12: "The Kingdom of God presents a challenge to the present constitution and form of this world, in so far as it is not in accordance with the holy, life-giving will of God." The moving dialectic of God's Kingdom is expressed in a similar way by Shaull: "The Kingdom of God always stands over against

transforming action of the Christian. Consequently we are no longer bound to the existing orders of a "status quo." The theory of a "realistic scepticism" ("the world does not change and people do not change"[23]) is not true. "The eschatology of the Christian faith (releases) a 'revolutionary humanity.' "[24] "God's revolution against 'all the godless wickedness of men' " (Rom. 1:18)—as Karl Barth called it[25]—inspires our social-ethical Diakonia.

If the ecumenical theology of revolution takes this "revolution of God's" as its guide, then it cannot be considered "a clearance-sale of the spiritual substance of the Church."[26] If, amid all the divergences (to which the ecumenical movement must devote a great deal of further thought) the theology of revolution can maintain that promising "convergence," it may open up new roads of Christian social ethics for Church and society in our revolutionary world.

---

every social and political order, thus exposing its dehumanising elements and judging it. At the same time, the Kingdom is a dynamic reality; it is 'coming' through the work of him who is restoring the nations" (*op. cit.*, p. 36).

[23] W. Trillhaas, *op. cit.*, p. 425.

[24] A. Rich, *Glaube in politischer Entscheidung*, Zürich, 1962, p. 96.

[25] *Kirchliche Dogmatic*, III/4, p. 626.

[26] Otto Dibelius's view is the following: "May God preserve us from a 'theology of revolution' as advocated in Geneva. During the twentieth century the clearance-sale of the Church's spiritual life has gone so far that this final suggestion is really not necessary" (quoted in *Junge Kirche*, 1966, p. 640).

Christian Faith as Scandal in a Technocratic World

Richard Shaull

Author of *Encounter with Revolution* and coauthor (with New Leftist Carl Oglesby) of *Containment and Change*, Richard Shaull lived many years in Colombia and Brazil, where he was intimately involved in the elaboration of a theological analysis of the Christian community's role in societies rapidly undergoing social, economic, technical, and political change. Herein he calls upon the Christian community to sound a clear *No* to the bourgeois-bureaucratic-technocratic perspective, which contends that all change must be orderly and rational and within the present system. For what that system really offers is not the liberation of man but "a new form of enslavement." Shaull sees "a small sign of hope for the world" among those who are relating their Christian experience to a revolutionary perspective and commitment. Shaull's essay appeared, in tandem with one by Josef Smolik, in the booklet *Consumers, or Revolutionaries?* published by the Foyer John Knox Association of Geneva, Switzerland;* the two pieces were originally lectures delivered at the Foyer. Dr. Shaull is Professor of Ecumenics at Princeton Theological Seminary.

WHEN society is at peace with itself and the church at ease in Zion, Christian faith often reveals an unusual capacity for disruption, as it challenges the accepted presuppositions of a culture and violates the norms of thought and action until then taken for granted. The outstanding example of this in our century is provided by Karl Barth, who

* 27 Chemin des Crêts-de-Pregny, 1218 Grand-Saconnex, Geneva, Switzerland.

negated what appeared to be the inevitable thrust of modernity and challenged its then uncontested assumptions in the name of Revelation, communicated through that "strange new world" of the Bible.

I would wager that the time has come for a new Christian scandal, not in the realm of dogmatics proper so much as in what Professor Johann Metz calls "political theology." In our contemporary understanding of society in the West, we function in terms of a perspective which it seems absurd even to question. Its basic ingredient in our liberal-bourgeois trust in natural harmony, with its assumption that our society is moving progressively toward greater justice and fuller human life within the framework of institutional continuity. This outlook has been tremendously strengthened by the structures and *ethos* of modern technology. As a result of this marriage, we assume that technology represents the great *revolution* of our time, and that its amazing success in the mastery of the physical world will now be duplicated in the social order for the greater good of all. We take for granted that it offers a rational way of defining and solving social problems, creates a new mentality capable of serving it enthusiastically, and brings about a gradual movement of man toward economic well-being, as well as more freedom and wider choices.

Those who function within this framework do not deny the seriousness of the problems we face, but they are convinced that these problems can be met and solved within the given institutional structures, according to the rules of the game as already laid down. André Philip declares:

"It is through limited action, which does not jeopardize the structure as a whole, that improvements can be introduced, by methods that are bound to be democratic."[1] At the Church and Society Conference here in July 1966, Max Kohnstamm was the incarnation of this, as he pleaded for the sanity which devotes itself to patiently planting seeds in the

[1] "The Revolutionary Change in the Structure of European Political Life," in Matthews, Z. K., ed., *Responsible Government in a Revolutionary Age*, pp. 120–121.

little cracks in the system, wherever they appear. In the words of Philip:

We no longer dream about a future revolution, because we are already living in one, in a continual process of destroying existing structures and rebuilding them; and man's role is to influence events in such a way as to turn them in the direction he considers favorable.[2]

As this statement clearly shows, these men are much concerned about change and innovation—but of a very specific type. It must be ordered and rational change, which can occur within the present system. Its hidden assumption is that life moves upward in spirals, that the lot of the dispossessed world can be improved without fundamentally upsetting our position in it, and that the values and patterns of life which we have labored long to develop will sooner or later be accepted and appreciated by the rest of the world.

How could it occur to anyone to challenge such a rational outlook, so firmly grounded in the ethos and achievements of our western world—especially when we have no critical tools by which to do so? The collapse of a metaphysical world view and the gradual process of secularization have led us to think in functional and operational terms, without any ultimate point of reference. In the social sciences, we tend to deal with radical departures from the accepted social norms under the rubric of deviant or pathological social behaviour. And if psychoanalytic theory originally postulated the most basic kind of conflict between the individual and his culture, today it does not quite know what to make of the new patient, who "is likely to come now for help in building an identity acceptable to the demands of society rather than in maintaining his own character productively in the situation which these demands create."[3] Those who dare to challenge this overwhelming rationality obviously must have something wrong with them. If they come from the Third World, they

[2] *Ibid.*, p. 120.
[3] Edgar Z., *The Dignity of Youth and Other Atavisms*, p. 61.

are reacting to conditions there which of course are not ours; and they can be dismissed as naive for they fail to understand the complexity of our society. And those few from the West who should know better are hopeless "romantics of revolution" enamored, in the opinion of one German theologian, with "the poetry of guerrilla action."

Now I hope that I have no special psychological compulsions to be different, if I affirm that the time has come when there must arise, from within the Christian community, a clear *No* to this general perspective. Granted, we cannot refute its logic as long as we accept the paradigm within which it operates; the trouble is that this paradigm is no longer adequate as an instrument for opening contemporary reality to us.[4] And over against the assumptions that this order is working for the liberation of man, we must contend that what it really offers is a new form of enslavement, plus the prospect of death under the suffocating weight of conformity and containment.

This affirmation does not mean that I am intent on developing a "theology of revolution," some sort of systematic re-interpretation of Christian faith which would justify a revolutionary approach to life today, and make the claim that only those who are revolutionary are faithful to the Gospel. But I would make a more humble proposal: that a revolutionary perspective and commitment is taking shape as some men and women today relate their experience in the Christian community and the symbols of Christian faith to the struggle in which they are engaged; that the insights and perspectives here emerging are authentic products of the Gospel, and that this development may constitute a small sign of hope for the world in which we now live. Here I can only point, very rapidly, to what I mean by this.

---

[4] Here I am indebted to insights provided by Thomas Kuhn, in his recent book, *The Structure of Scientific Revolutions*. He shows, in his analysis of the development of paradigms in the realm of the physical sciences, how closely logic is related to the dominant paradigm. When an old paradigm is no longer adequate, and a scientist proposes a new one, the truths of the new cannot be judged on the basis of the logic of the old.

Intensified Conflict on the Road to Ultimate Freedom

All of us, if we hope to understand or act, must attempt to make some sense out of what is going on around us. For the Christian this involves a certain compulsion to discern the direction in which western history may be moving. This compulsion flows in part from the biblical emphasis upon the purposiveness of God's action in history; it also stems from the belief that the impact of Jesus Christ and his teachings has progressively affected our on-going history. As Dietrich Von Oppen puts it, the person of Christ represents a "transforming entry into the world," which has given an unchangeable and irrevocable direction to world history. For Von Oppen this means a movement toward ultimate freedom as the power of sacral institutions is shattered, and structures emerge which are open, flexible, limited in their area of influence and subject to critical examination. Van Leeuwen discerns a similar process, which he describes as the gradual collapse of all ontocratic structures of existence and the increasing freedom which this brings—to man and society—to create the future. In his chapter on "The Revolutionary West" (in *Christianity in World History*) he traces the progressive penetration of this virus into diverse realms of our social existence.

Another Dutch theologian, Prof. H. Berkhof, reminds us however (in his *Christ the Meaning of History*) that this movement toward human liberation does not go unchallenged. In fact, as the biblical imagery of the anti-Christ suggests, the growing influence of Christ leads to the union of those adversaries called to live by his action; i.e., to those forces which stand in the way of human liberation but which have already been defeated by Christ through the destruction of the very foundation of their system. For Berkhof, this means that the greatest adversaries of the Gospel are those movements which give man the illusion of being delivered from pagan ontocracy, "without in the least giving him the freedom which comes with the appearance of Christ" (p. 108).

Berkhof believes that Islam is today the incarnation of this. I would like to come nearer home and apply it to what is happening in our western society of advanced technology. For what some of us discern today is a climactic moment in this struggle. What we have in the rising nationalism of the developing nations, the Negro revolution in the USA or the growing unrest among youth and students in many parts of the world, is a new human self-consciousness grasping for the new dimensions of freedom to which they are destined in the face of the collapse of all traditional authority structures. But this new longing is not being satisfied; it is rather being met by the overwhelming power of a system which increasingly blocks its realization. The traditional paternalism of the powerful may be completely undermined, but it continues to express itself in a variety of subtle ways, when we assume that we can help the poor nations or solve the problems of the dispossessed in our own society. The emergence of a new self-identity of many national and ethnic groups, as well as that of a new generation, is met with extraordinarily well organized and effective pressures for conformity which make real independence and opposition almost impossible. And the longing of the powerless for power to determine their destiny is met by an expanding system of domination no longer held in check by effective countervailing power. In this situation—and herein lies both its tragedy and its hope—those in power are so bound to their past and to their irrelevant ideologies, that they are no longer able to respond creatively to the challenges of a new day; while those who find themselves enveloped in the shroud of the old order have the choice of slow death or rebellion. We may indeed be witnessing the end of an era, from which we can emerge only as we attempt a new beginning.

The Revolutionary Character of the Struggle for Liberation

As we participate in this world, our thought, illumined by the Christian symbols, may lead us to a further conclusion: today we are being pushed to the threshold of a new order; and we have arrived at a moment in which the nature of the struggle for liberation, as well as instruments for its attainment, should be defined in a new way. If there is any truth in this reading of our western history, it will be only in and through this struggle that contemporary man can move to a fuller and richer life.

I would describe the struggle as an attempt to realize two goals which may be somewhat in tension with each other: (1) the more rational use of technology on a worldwide scale; and (2) the creation, within a technological society, of conditions permitting free men to decide for and create their own future. One of the paradoxical results of the development of technological rationality is the fact that it is so irrational. Nowhere is this more evident than in the economic sphere. Modern technology has made it possible for us to be no longer obsessed with the production and distribution of goods. We can now cut the economic realm down to size, put this particular form of human activity in its allotted place, explode the myths surrounding it and free ourselves from obsession with it and its rewards. To the degree that we establish proper political controls over the economic order, i.e., to the degree that society at large decides to take it in hand, we can gradually learn how to establish the goals we want in this area and work out the most rational ways to achieve them. Something similar, in terms of the rational ordering of society, can and must be done in other spheres as well.

But this struggle, long and arduous as it may turn out to be, must be accompanied by another one: to create a society in which all sorts of diverse communities—national, racial, social, professional, and a wide variety of primary, face-to-face associations—can overcome the pressure to conformity and containment, carve out new spheres of freedom and make it possible for modern bureaucracy to function more creatively. These developments, disturbing as they may be for the stabilities and consensus of the established order, could open the way to a new enrichment and dynamization of life as we strive for reconciliation in the midst of diversity and tension.

If this is the nature of the revolution in which we are involved, it will not be an easy one to achieve. Modern technological society is so all-embracing that those who want to change it cannot stand completely outside it. But those who stand within it are easily neutralized. In fact, the pressures and rewards of the present system tend to blind us to the issues and incapacitate us for the struggle. Once again, revolution will depend upon a vanguard that is free to see what is happening, discern the shape of the future, and accept a new vocation over against the system. That vanguard is not today the industrial proletariat, but rather those who are victimized by the present order: i.e., those who have been excluded from the benefits of the system—or have rejected them—and are at the same time discovering a new self-identity, which they may as yet not be able to articulate clearly. I refer to the Negro in America, a new generation in the developing nations, youth and students around the world. At the present moment, the decisive question about the future may well be whether these groups will be able to transform their dissatisfaction with their marginal position into an authentic revolutionary vocation.

Here, the Christian imagination and a dynamic Christian community could play a significant role, as they orient us toward the future, break the dominance of the past, and provide us with signs of hope that a new order can and will come. At this point, recent developments in theology, centering around a theology of hope, seem to me to be especially important. As Professor Moltmann (*Theology of Hope*) has worked this out, the Christian symbols point to a God who goes ahead of us and who is bringing a new future into being. His word is essentially a word of promise, that awakens in us the hope for a new future. It is a word that upsets old stabilities, arouses dissatisfaction with the old order, and frees us to expect and serve the things that are to come.

Professor Moltmann has done such a masterful job that I need say nothing more about this. What I would like to do, however, is add a very important element not clearly developed in Moltmann: *The biblical symbols and images stress discontinuity, judgment, the end of the world and the emergence of the radically new.* Time and again, in the Old Testament, the movement toward the fulfillment of the messianic hope was blocked by human egotism and power, and the prophets proclaimed that God would have to tear down in order to build up. In the New Testament, the eschatological and the apocalyptic are closely intermingled. As Rosenstock-Huessy has pointed out, the Christian understanding of history focuses on death and resurrection; we await the end of the world which comes again and again in the midst of historical existence. History often moves ahead by leaps; the social order does not stand open to the future; again and again it has to be broken open. When institutions become sclerotic, they often have to be reproduced, i.e., remade from the bottom up.

What this means, I believe, is that Christian faith can provide resources for being authentically revolutionary. It can produce the type of person whose own inward experience of death and resurrection equips him to let the old die when its time has come, and frees him to give form to the new possibilities open before him. This is what we most desperately need today: men liberated for creativity, participating in a community in which they are forced to die daily in order to create new ideas, new perspectives, new experiments, new institutions, new political possibilities. In other words, our western world needs cadres of men and women who are as seriously concerned as the Marxists in China or earlier in Eastern Europe, to bury the dead, violate the old and create the new. When such a moment arrives, the distinctiveness of the Christian witness does not lie in its emphasis upon the values to be preserved from the past, but rather in the freedom it offers to bury the dead without remorse, to create the new in response to the future rather than in reaction against the past, and to preserve an iconoclastic attitude throughout the revolution.

Priorities for the Christian Community

Given our limitation of time, I can only mention several points which, if my thesis has any validity to it, deserve further examination. In the revolution of our time, the church should not expect to be a *power structure* working for radical change nor attempt to create Christian revolutionary movements. But it is just possible that among those Christians engaged in revolution, certain things may happen which can have a parabolic significance in the present struggle.

1. The Christian community can offer a structure and the dynamics for human liberation. To do this, we will not only have to overcome the "privatization" of Christian existence so dominant today in many circles, but also discover how to contribute effectively to the formation of personal and group self-identity over against the system, the development of increasing critical awareness, and the creation of a style of life that breaks the power of the old order over us, challenges its values, and makes it possible for us to play a new game by a new set of rules. If that is to happen, then it is our task to be especially sensitive to those individuals and groups who are open to and prepared for such an adventure. Perhaps only those who have no future within the system —because they have been excluded from it or have repudiated it—can be the creators of a new future.

2. The time has come when we must rediscover—in church and society—the meaning of our sectarian heritage. Those who are *in* but not *of* the established order will be the agents of revolution in our advanced technological society. This means the development of the *sect*, the encouragement of the *dissenter* and the re-affirmation of *heresy*, for only thus will it be possible to call into question the accepted presuppositions and drive a wedge into the established order that will provide a fulcrum for change. Here our western liberal society needs badly the resources provided by the Christian sectarian tradition. But these can be made available through the church only to the degree that we are free to encourage the formation of new sectarian communities in the Church itself. Professor Smolik has indicated what it means, in his country, to draw upon this heritage. For us in America, it may mean, among other things, the rediscovery of the work of the early Niebuhr and his development of the Fellowship of Socialist Christians.

3. Speaking in Geneva, I cannot resist making one remark about the relevance of all this to the future of the Ecumenical Movement. Given the present tension between the drive toward the universal organization of technological rationality and the significance of the new independent self-identity of groups, races and peoples around the world, the Ecumenical Movement has an extraordinary opportunity for parabolic action. In many ways its history prepares it for incorporating this tension into its life, and working on the problems emerging from it. For that to happen, however, it will be necessary for it to give full expression, within its life and structure, to new discordant voices of our time, such as those of the new nationalism, new cultural selfhood and pluralism, black power, and the protest of a new generation.

But more important than this, the Ecumenical Movement will have to find a place, within its life, for a new international sectarianism. If the church is to be present in the revolution, rather than coming along fifty years later to enter into dialogue with it, it will have to encourage contact and mutual support, across national boundaries, for those who have taken this leap into the midst of the revolutionary struggle. Just as the lines of missionary advance in the past were set in the context of the colonial structure, so today, the new dialogue about the faith and the search for a new style of life will have to move back and forth between the internal and external proletariat of the western world, to use Toynbee's phrase: between those in the West who are convinced that they can work for the future of man only if they enter into a total struggle with the system, and those in Asia, Africa and Latin America, who struggle against the same system on the periphery of it. In a planetary world, in which the powers of the old era function across all boundaries, radical communities of Christians cannot fulfill their tasks without such relationships. I have no hopes that the established Ecumenical Movement will undertake such a daring adventure, but it is just possible that the same spirit which gave birth to the Ecumenical Movement some decades ago could be *reproduced* among the younger generation, and take this form.

4. Given the powerlessness of those working for change

over against the overwhelming power of the established technological system, we thus far have no satisfactory answer to the question of strategy. The Christian community will have no special insight on this point, but we may find that we are free to engage with others in study and experimentation along two lines: first, the development of new bases for power and a new politics. This involves the encouragement of critical political awareness and a new sense of participation among a variety of groups in our society open to this possibility at present; constant exposure of the way the system functions and of its failures to deal with the crucial questions; the formation of pressure groups, and the organization of various movements of eventual political significance. Secondly, it requires what Orlando Fals Borda, a distinguished Colombian sociologist, calls the systematic *subversion* of institutions as those within them discover how to use these institutions for their own transformation in spite of themselves. In other words, if modern bureaucracy tends to solve all minor problems but to overlook more basic ones, and to stifle initiative and creativity, it is essential now to develop, within institutions, small groups of people committed to constantly upsetting their stability, taking new initiatives and launching new experiments—and willing to pay the price of such subversive acts which will not always be appreciated.

For most of us, contented bourgeois protestants, such a vocation may be as difficult as passing through the eye of a needle. But then, we still worship a Christ who was considered so subversive that the political and religious leaders of his time put him to death. We are called to live in the world as a pilgrim people and to possess what we have as though we had it not. If a small minority of the Western middle class is to become a vanguard in the transformation of technological society, is it too much to hope that some of its numbers might come from a community in which such symbols are at work?

A Theology of Rebellion

Rolland F. Smith

Revolution, contends Rolland F. Smith, S.J., ends by denying the human value and liberty that it begins by affirming;
"it absolutizes its present or future forms and so becomes
demonic and nihilistic." Rebellion, on the other hand, is a
continual revolution; "the new system is ever in process of
being established and the victory or victories are always still
ahead." Moreover, rebellious thought has connection with
Judeo-Christian thought, particularly the eschatologically oriented theology of hope, which sees God as "the power of our
future." "Rebellion affirms past, future, *and* present, memory, expectation, and activity, faith, hope, *and* love to overcome the faithless tyranny and hopeless servitude of a
loveless world." The substance of Father Smith's essay was
delivered as one of three lectures at the annual Bellarmine
Disputations, December 1967, at the Bellarmine School of
Theology, Loyola University, North Aurora, Illinois, where he
is a member of the faculty; the essay subsequently was published in the April 1968 issue of *Theology Today*.* Father
Smith says of himself: "I have been engaged in Alinsky-style
organizations in both Detroit and Chicago, and I am very
sympathetic to the movement even with its dangers of anti-
intellectualism, utopianism, and its own arrogance of power."

WE LIVE in an age of crisis, we are often told—
especially in an election year. Crisis means possibility for good
and for evil. Hence we are confronted daily with two apocalyptic pictures: (a) a great society of international justice, peace,
and plenty, and (b) a devastated, radioactive world due to a
wargame without rules or referee. Crisis means possibility of

* P.O. Box 29, Princeton, N.J. 08540.

a new order of freedom or of repression. If emerging Asia and Africa or even Latin America are too far away from us, Watts, Detroit, Harlem, Lawndale are not. Here men have quit reading Gandhi and are turning to the wisdom of Mao; they are collecting bombs and bullets for a new day of Yahweh. They are not waiting for an evolutionary change; they seek the forceful overthrow of the present social-political-economic structures.

At this moment two major ideologies compete for the minds of man: Judeo-Christianity and Marxism. Christianity accuses Marxism of being atheistic, of losing continuity with the past, and of being another means of self-elevation that is doomed to failure. Marxism accuses Christianity of being un-revolutionary, of championing the structures of the past against the possibilities of the future for the poor, deprived, enslaved. But Marxism and Christianity are forced to become allies against a third force found within both ranks, that of secularist man who cares for neither past nor future. He is neither Christian nor Marxist; he is man without hope. He will drug himself into vegetable existence or he will absurdly lash out to destroy all along with himself.

When we look at the churches, whether in Johannesburg or Chicago, we find evidence for the Marxist accusations. Social anthropology has demonstrated the conservative role of religion in culture, and the Christian religion is no exception. The churches embody a code of mores for proper, private, and passive behavior. The poor are preached patience, and the rich are asked to offer paternal charity. Saul Alinsky's use of power is labeled "sub-Christian." Stokely Carmichael is "anti-Christian." Father Groppi and Pastor King are deviants tolerated by the churches, but less and less as they become more and more revolutionary. The churches have little to do officially with the Vietnam protest, with Students for a Democratic Society, with Black Power. The more a university is influenced by a church, the more it seems to avoid student or faculty rebellions against government or administration policies.

Harvey Cox has spoken to American Christians: "We are living in an age of revolution without a theology of revolution. The development of such a theology should be the first item on the theological agenda today."[1] It is the objective of this essay to indicate the ambiguity, also the need, of rebellion and to show that Christianity must be its occasion and the theologian one of its prophets. This theology of rebellion is a theology of hope which opposes the ideology of revolution which preaches presumption, as well as the ideology of annihilation which spreads despair.

I

A classic study by Mircea Eliade contrasts two basic views of history, that of archaic man and that of biblical man.[2] Archaic man organizes reality according to ideal models or the primordial cosmogonic act. All present happenings are seen as manifestations of the archetypes or repetitions of the eternal act. Men, through their religious rites and daily activities, repeat the primordial act of the god. This they do in the establishment of centers in which a sacred space is organized as well as by rejuvenating the seasons in returning to the beginning of sacred time. Thus archaic man is anti-historical: concrete, unique, new events cannot be. Nothing is new under the sun since everything is but a repetition of the primordial act. The *past* is the real, the happening *in illo tempore*, which is present as an eternal now. The *future* is sameness and repetition. This anti-historicity serves the valuable function of keeping archaic man in contact with the real, with order and meaning, amidst the sufferings and catastrophes of historical existence. Catastrophe can be understood and so tolerated because it is a repetition of the primordial struggle to bring order from chaos. Time is characterized by "revolution"—an astral term which signifies the eternal return of the heavens, of the seasons, and of men.

The Hebrews discovered a God who was neither within na-

---

[1] Harvey Cox, *The Secular City* (New York, Macmillan, 1965), p. 107.
[2] Mircea Eliade, *Cosmos and History* (New York, Harper, 1959).

ture, eternally revolving, nor above nature as an archetype or ideal manifestation. Yahweh, for this nomadic people, was *in front* calling a man and then a people to leave completely the former places and plunge out into the new. Resignation to an eternal repetition is replaced by faith, which is an acceptance of the uniqueness and novelties of history as manifestations of God who calls the people into the new by means of his promise. The *past* for biblical man is promise; it has a once-for-all character and so is truly over and past; and yet it is present in so far as it is an anticipation of the present and future. Hence memory in writings and cult is important, but not as a looking back with nostalgia upon a golden age.[3] The Deuteronomist was interested in the today of Israel and appealed to Israel's memory to urge her future actions. The Psalms ask Yahweh to remember the days of old, and they recall to Israel all that Yahweh has done in order that Yahweh will be encouraged to act again and that Israel will continue her pilgrimage. The *future* for biblical man is a truly new event in history which does not exist now but is anticipated or promised in the acts of the past and present. Hence, instead of abolishing history and idealizing worldly events, biblical man finds the revelation of Yahweh in the unique and novel events of history itself. With the prophets especially, we find the two concepts of history warring against each other.[4] By finding the act of Yahweh in the acts of the Assyrians and Chaldeans, by condemning the securities of temple and ritual, by attacking the worship of the fertility god Baal, by rebelling against the present order, the prophets were proclaiming the God of pilgrimage who acts in the new events of history and who calls men to continually transcend the securities and forms of the past. They were rejecting the god of the eternal now who constantly repeats the primordial activity within nature and whom man influences by his own repetitions of the cosmogonic act.

[3] Brevard Childs, *Memory and Tradition in Israel* (London, SCM Press, 1962).

[4] Cf. Gerhard von Rad, *Old Testament Theology*, Vol. II, translated by D. M. G. Stalker (Edinburgh, Oliver and Boyd, 1965), pp. 99–125.

But where is "Christian" man in relation to archaic man and biblical man? If we take Rudolf Bultmann as an expression of Christian man, we must say that he is biblical man regressed to an archaic mentality. Bultmann's *Theology of the New Testament* uses Heidegger's concept of history as a concern for authentic possibilities. Thus the historical statements of the New Testament are understood, not as the record of past objective occurrences, but as significant for present existence. The cross is the culminating act of the life of Jesus of Nazareth. To believe in the cross of Christ is not to believe that an objective event once happened, but it is to accept Christ's cross as one's own. The cross is made present to me. It is an "eschatological event"—a term Bultmann uses to translate Heidegger's notion of "authentic repeatable possibility."[5] The cross expresses a radical self-surrender and an achievement of authenticity, or freedom from the tyranny of the public, from the world of things, and from death. This authentic repeatable possibility was first given to man on Calvary and is still offered to him in the proclaiming of the word. "Resurrection" is a symbol expressing the cross as eschatological, that is, as significant for me. Rather than implying that a miracle once happened, it expresses the belief that a miracle of new life can happen for me now through my free decision of faith which has been made possible by the preaching of the word.

In this way Bultmann demythologizes both the world-view of Gnosticism and Jewish Apocalypticism. But the paradox is that, in his efforts to demythologize, he not only dismisses the Gnostic three-story universe, but he also abolishes history

[5] Cf. Rudolf Bultmann, "The New Testament and Mythology," in *Kerygma and Myth*, edited by Hans Werner Bartsch (New York, Harper, 1961), p. 36. Also John Macquarrie, *An Existentialist Theology*, pp. 159–192. I am perhaps unfairly using Bultmann as a "whipping boy." He could counter that authentic repeatable possibilities offer new perspectives for the future. But I am emphasizing an emphasis which leads, I believe, to a distortion. Also space does not allow us to consider other Christian positions here, such as those of Barth and Tillich. We are using Bultmann merely to state the problem for Christian man: Does the "finality of Christ" mean a loss of the reality of history?

for a very mythological, antihistorical world-view of the eternal return. Revelation becomes self-realization or the achievement of personal authenticity through a repeatable act. By my decision of faith, I repeat the primordial act that took place *in illo tempore* and is expressed in the mythic language of incarnation-cross-resurrection. The Hebrew notion of the continual possibility of new revelation in world history is abolished. The Christ-event is isolated and detached from history to become an eternal now, an eschatological event, an authentic *repeatable* possibility. Both its past and its future are neglected. For it is not seen in continuity with all other events in history within the Hebrew and world communities. Moreover it has no future, that is, no possibilities of transcending the present by future revelations in the events of history. In this way Bultmann exemplifies the problem of Christian man: Must every Christian, because he insists on the finality of the Christ-event, say that the eschaton has arrived and is realized, that the last word has been spoken, that the time of revelation is over, that the book of revelation is closed with the death of the last apostle, and so not look forward to new revelation in culture and history and to the very transcendence of Christianity in its present forms? Must he simply continue the same Christ-event by his preaching, whereby he repeats the word of salvation to the hearers and so occasions a decision for authentic existence just as the original disciples were confronted with the same decision?

II

"Revolution," from *revolvere* meaning "roll back or again," originates in astronomy. It refers to the eternal return of a celestial body or to the completion of a cycle (of years). Later it came to mean the overthrow of one system (political, scientific, moral, etc.) and the substitution of another. "Rebellion," from *rebellare* meaning "to make war again," is the acceptance of and participation in rapid social change. To contrast revolution and rebellion, we can define them in terms of each other: a *revolution* is a successful rebellion; the victory has been won and the new system has been established. A *rebellion* is a continual revolution; the new system is ever in process of being established and the victory or victories are always still ahead.

Eric Hoffer[6] analyzes three stages of a revolution: (1) the stage of the men of words which is a stage of preparation through ideology; (2) the stage of the fanatics which is the stage of overthrow and terrorism; (3) the stage of the practical men of action which consolidates and stabilizes the mass movement. The first stage of words, ideas, and ideology should not be underestimated (a constant temptation of the fanatics). One of de Tocqueville's major contributions to revolutionary theory was his study of the function of ideas in the French Revolution.[7] Max Weber has argued that ideas influence the choice and direction of political courses of action: "Ideas define situations so that an alternative may be perceived or blocked by a person's or group's view of the world, or by the categories in which he or it thinks."[8] C. B. Macpherson has demonstrated the importance of ideology in the revolutions of this late twentieth century: "The leaders of the new revolutions, themselves, generally intellectuals, politicized by training abroad, have had to bring a pre-political people to a sense of nationality and national self-esteem, to create a political and national consciousness, and to infuse a hope and a faith that great things can be done by the new nation. This is a task for ideology."[9] Hence the men sitting in library or classroom should not feel that they are unconnected with what is going on out in the streets; and this is another expression for the need of a *theology* of rebellion.

Crane Brinton points out that the second stage of a revolu-

---

[6] Eric Hoffer, *The True Believer* (New York, Harper, 1951).

[7] Melvin Richter, "Tocqueville's Contribution to the Theory of Revolution" in *Revolution*, edited by Carl J. Friedrich (New York, Atherton, 1967), pp. 91–102.

[8] *Ibid.*, p. 99.

[9] C. B. Macpherson, "Revolution and Ideology in the Late 20th Century," in *Revolution, op. cit.*, p. 142.

tion is the most acute.[10] This is the stage of a Robespierre, a Sam Adams, a Lenin and Stalin, where the roles are reversed, the rebels become masters using force, terror, and injustice. In this "despotism of liberty against tyranny" or "dictatorship of the proletariat," one absolute is substituted for another, the revolutionary ideal becomes demonic, the rebellion becomes a revolution.

Albert Camus shall be our guide here.[11] First he describes the rebel, then he contrasts rebellion with revolution. The rebel is one who says "no" to his master. But at the same time, he is saying "yes" to a limit which is based on a value that he discovers in himself and in all men in the very act of saying "no." Rebellion risks and accepts death which indicates that the "affirmation implicit in every act of rebellion is extended to something that transcends the individual in so far as it withdraws him from his supposed solitude and provides him with a reason to act."[12] The act of rebellion is an act of fellowship, for it is an affirmation of a *human* value; it gives man a feeling of identification and founds his solidarity. In sum, rebellion is one of the essential dimensions of man; it is his historical reality; it is his very existence. And so Camus can replace Descartes' old *cogito* with a new *cogito*: man is not merely a thinking being, but a rebelling being whose very act founds his solidarity with all men. "I rebel, therefore, *we* exist."[13] But *revolution* exceeds the limits that rebellion sets for itself and so turns against its rebel origins. What it began affirming, it ends by denying; namely, human value and liberty. Revolution becomes an absolute negation of the past; it absolutizes its present or future forms and so becomes demonic and nihilistic. Thus "every revolutionary ends by becoming an oppressor or a heretic."[14] For to escape its absurd destiny of either tyranny or servitude, revolution must rediscover (in the third stage) the creative source of

[10] Crane Brinton, *The Anatomy of a Revolution* (New York, Vintage, 1965).

[11] Albert Camus, *The Rebel* (New York, Vintage, 1956).

[12] *Ibid.*, p. 16.

[13] *Ibid.*, p. 22.

[14] *Ibid.*, p. 249.

rebellion. As Camus writes: "In order to exist, man must rebel, but rebellion must respect the limit it discovers in itself—a limit where minds meet and, in meeting, begin to exist. Rebellious thought, therefore, cannot dispense with memory: it is a perpetual state of tension."[15]

III

There is an historical connection between rebellious thought and Judeo-Christian thought. Camus asserts that the problem of rebellion has no meaning except within our western society where a theoretical equality conceals factual inequalities and where the world is not metaphysically or sacrally fixed. "If in a world where things are held sacred the problem of rebellion does not arise, it is because no real problems are to be found in such a world, all the answers having been given simultaneously."[16] Harvey Cox connects rapid social change to the process of secularization which has its roots in the Bible and the disenchantment of nature, the desacralization of politics, and the deconsecration of values. "When we look at history as a process of secularization, it becomes for us at the same time meaningful *and* open-ended. It suggests that history has a significance for man, but it does not impose a meaning on him. In fact, it topples inherited metaphysical and religious meaning and turns man loose to compose new ones."[17] Ernst Benz traces Christian eschatological thinking from the early Fathers to Teilhard de Chardin; he shows the connection of such thinking whether in the early church, or in Joachim de Fiori and Thomas Müntzer, with social revolutionary action. He quotes Wilhelm Mühlmann saying: "The tendency for revolt was created by the Jewish-Christian doctrine of apocalypse. The principle of rebellion has existed since then."[18]

[15] *Ibid.*, p. 22.
[16] *Ibid.*, p. 20.
[17] Cox, p. 109.
[18] Ernst Benz, *Evolution and Christian Hope*, translated by Heinz G. Frank (New York, Doubleday, 1966), p. 62. It is true

Christian theology *is* eschatology, according to Jürgen Moltmann and Johannes Metz.[19] Eschatology is not merely the doctrine of the last things, a distant utopia with little relation to the present world. It is the straining after and anticipating the future of Christ which is the future of the world; it is a revolutionizing and transforming of the present. The Christian God is the God of the exodus and of the resurrection; he is not eternal presence, but the God of promise, the God in front, the God with future as his essential nature, whom we "await" and "follow" with active hope. Christian eschatology is not an ideology of the future or a blueprint of what is to come. But it sets out from a definite reality in history and announces the future of that reality. That definite reality is Jesus Christ.

The crucified Jesus is the Christ and has a future because of his resurrection. This historical reality is announced in terms of promise; that is, the promise of the future of the Christ which is the future of the world. In the promise, the hidden future already announces itself and exerts its influence on the present through the hope that it awakens. Statements of promise stand in contradiction to the present, to "this-world," because they are the conditions of possibility for a new experience, a new present. Thus hope and the statements of promise are not based on history; rather history is based on hope. Present and future, experience and hope are in contradiction; hope is directed to the not-yet experienced. But it is not utopian or a striving after things that have "no-place," but is a striving for things that have "no place as

---

that certain elements in the apocalyptic expectation tend to retard actions, such as deterministic and escapist attitudes. But Benz points out that these waiting attitudes are still "virtually for action" and can suddenly switch to revolutionary action. It should be further added that late Jewish apocalyptic was adapted by Paul who did not take over the determinism and excessive use of the future of apocalyptic literature.

[19] Jürgen Moltmann, *The Theology of Hope*, translated by James W. Leitch (London, SCM Press, 1967). Johannes B. Metz, "The Church and the World," in *The Word and History* (New York, Sheed and Ward, 1966), pp. 69–85. Johannes B. Metz, "Creative Hope," *Cross Currents*, Spring, 1967, pp. 171–179.

yet" but can acquire one. Only with hope is Christian love possible, which is a love directed toward the nonexistent, the worthless, the lost, the god-forsaken, and the dead; for it springs from a hope in a *creatio ex nihilo;* it is a love for man and for the world as *possible*, and it strains after their future actualization.

We may summarize some of the major theses of this theology of hope:

(1) Christian theology is eschatology based on the biblical scheme of history in terms of promise and fulfillment.

(2) God is revealed as the power of our future. He is a future that does not come out of our present possibilities, but which allows them to be. "For only a future which is more than a correlative and a projection of our own possibilities can free us for something truly 'new,' for new possibilities for that which has never been."[20]

(3) The cross-and-resurrection of Christ reveals the power of God who fulfills his promise beyond all expectations, who contradicts the present by initiating the new. This event becomes the central promise and basis of hope for this world. It is a historical event because by promise, hope, and contradiction it makes the reality of man historic. The Christ-event "sets the stage for history, on which there emerges the possibility of the engulfing of all things in nothingness and of the new creation."[21] It does not fulfill all promises but itself becomes promise. Hence the Christian mission is not a repetition of the event, but an expectation of new "fulfillment of the promised righteousness of God in all things, the fulfillment of the resurrection of the dead that is promised in the resurrection, the fulfillment of the lordship of the crucified one over all things that is promised in his exaltation."[22]

(4) "The Christian consciousness of history is a consciousness of mission."[23] The future of Christ is a mission for the future of the world. Hence it is a continual criticism and trans-

---

[20] Metz, "Creative Hope," p. 174.
[21] Moltmann, p. 227.
[22] *Ibid.*, p. 229.
[23] *Ibid.*, p. 225.

formation of the present because it is open towards the universal future of the kingdom. The church, then, is an exodus church which is both creative and militant. It is that body of Christians who, relying on the promise expressed in the cross and resurrection of Christ, and hoping for its fulfillment, engage themselves in the world to attack and to call the world into its history, its transformation in Christ. It is easy to see from this latter point why both Moltmann and Metz consider the theology of hope a theology of revolt.

The preceding sketch of the contemporary expression of the theology of hope does not pretend to include all of even its major points. However, it perhaps indicates the direction and emphasis of this theology enough for us to make three observations.

(1) This theology introduces a welcome new trend in a Germany dominated by the dialectic dualism of Barth and Bultmann. However, it is not clear that it is so new to America which, in a tradition of Rauschenbusch, the Niebuhrs, and Cox, has been socially and secularly oriented.[24]

(2) With the stress on the future and on the contradiction of the present, there is danger of distortion. Paul Tillich, the master of polarities, has said that the doctrine of eschatology should not be divorced from the doctrine of creation.[25] God is not only Future-Telos; he is also Ground-Archē. Secular culture now is the arena of God's activities and has contributed and will contribute to the realization of his reign.

(3) On the other hand, one wonders if the new theologians of the future have gone far enough in their critique of the theologians of the eternal-return. For though they speak of the *future* of Christ, they seem to make the Christ-event a new event that will not be transcended until the end of time. But the Christ-event must be seen in continuity with the events of its past which it has transcended and with the transcending events of its future. Only with such a view does

[24] Cf. Langdon Gilkey, "Social and Intellectual Sources of Contemporary Protestant Thought in America," *Daedalus*, Winter, 1967, pp. 69–98.

[25] Paul Tillich, *Systematic Theology*, Vol. III (Chicago, Univ. of Chicago Press, 1963), pp. 298–299.

the believer enter into biblical history and become open to the new action of God in every historical event in the world. The danger here is that the theology of rebellion will turn into an ideology of revolution which so absolutizes a past *or future* idea or event so as to deny the continual possibility of newness and the continual creative activity of God in the movements of culture and history.

"The Kingdom of God," the New Testament symbol for the content of Christian hope, is a double-barrelled notion. It is used to denote both future reality and present reality. It is the future coming of God among his people (so retaining the apocalyptic orientation). But it is also in our midst—at times identified with Jesus himself, at other times signifying the concrete community of believers. Christian hope must retain this tension, neither demythologizing Jewish apocalyptic to such an extent that new events in salvation history are impossible, nor stressing eschatology to such an extent that the present movements in culture, whether in science, art, or politics, are totally rejected. Christian hope which is an expectation for the future involves faith which is entry into communal history through the sharing of *past* memories; and it involves love—the acceptance of and response to men and women as they are *now* without sacrificing them for some abstract ideal.

IV

We can compare present day America with the ancient kingdoms of Israel and Judah. We are a nomadic, pilgrim people who have arrived and have been established. The days of the pilgrims and the days of immigration are over. In holy war and manifest destiny the land has been secured. We have even avoided the tragedy of a divided kingdom of the north and south. The American rebellion has been successful, and the last frontier has been settled. But now, like the Hebrew kingdoms, we are in danger of losing the frontier spirit that leads us continually out of the old into the new. We are in danger of changing our rebellion into a revolution which absolutizes and repeats our past rebellion. We are in danger of forming an ideal of our rebellion that takes it out of the ambiguities of history to become an archetype that admits neither criticism of the "American Way" nor historical transcendence of "Democracy." We are in danger of exchanging Yahweh for Baal, the exodus God who leads to new positions in history for the static agrarian god who guarantees the cycles of nature and frees man from history, change, and from freedom itself.

By absolutizing our forms, our ideals, and our history, we fall into the sin of self-elevation and self-revelation. We lose the faith that opens us to new revelations in history which do not come from our own power. We become superpatriots "with God on our side." We achieve what Senator Fulbright calls "the arrogance of power." In our righteousness, we do not see that in violently repressing rebellion in our cities and in other countries, we may be opposing the God of the future. Gamaliel the Pharisee spoke to us guardians of the status quo: "So in the present case, I tell you keep away from these men and let them alone; for if this plan or this undertaking is of men, it will fail; but if it be of God, you will not be able to overthrow them. You might even be found opposing God" (Acts 5: 38–39). And in this time of self-glorification and reliance on our own nuclear strength and own "good old American know-how," the prophets have arisen. Like the earlier prophets they have proclaimed that God is also with the "enemy"; they have preached the message of social justice and have championed the oppressed; they have spoken of a new frontier which leaves behind the old securities of past forms and police power. Also like the earlier prophets, they have been mistrusted and hated, jailed and killed. For the worshippers of Baal cannot take criticism because they cannot take history. Criticism means questioning the forms of the past; but the archetypes are the *raison d'être* of Baalism. Dissent is a rebellious act and it is an act of faith; it is a stepping out into an unknown future by contradicting the arrogances of the present.

Rebellion and its theology oppose the ideology of revolution which expresses the desire for an absolute form. Revolution is the desire to arrive at a state where one has become god, or it is the claim that one has already arrived. It is anti-historical in so far as it desires a terminus to history whether in Stoic conflagration or Buddhist nirvana. It is idolatrous because it makes a humanly constituted form, whether present or to come, a god, before which all other values are sacrificed. And here revolution becomes nihilism. But the theology of rebellion fights idolatry by its continual war on forms; even the forms which rebellion helped to establish in the past. But it also rejects iconoclasm because it maintains its memory or continuity with the past as it helps bring in new forms in fulfillment of preceding ones. Rebellion is *faith* because it situates the rebel in a community whose memory and past he shares and of which he does not lose sight. Rebellion is *hope* in the future as future; it affirms the infinity and transcendence of a God who will never be exhausted by a particular form; it is continual openness to the new. Rebellion is *love*; for it founds human solidarity of the present and so experiences the continuing divine activity in the movements of present society. Rebellion affirms past, future, *and* present, memory, expectation, *and* activity, faith, hope, *and* love to overcome the faithless tyranny and hopeless servitude of a loveless world.

It is fitting to end with a quotation from a man of hope, a man who remained a rebel to the end, allowing himself to constantly change and challenge even his own former positions, a man who best exemplifies the rebel that Camus describes, who chooses heresy over oppression, and faces death to affirm a value in himself and in all men. From *The Autobiography of Malcolm X*: "I believe that it would be almost impossible to find anywhere in America a black man who has lived further down in the mud of human society than I have. But it is only after the deepest darkness that the greatest joy can come; it is only after slavery and prison that the sweetest appreciation of freedom can come. For the freedom of my 22 million black brothers and sisters here in America, I do believe that I have fought the best that I knew how, and the best that I could, with the shortcomings that I have had. I know that societies often have killed the people who have helped to change those societies. And if I can die having brought any light, having exposed any meaningful truth that will help to destroy the racist cancer that is malignant in the body of America—then, all the credit is due to Allah. Only the mistakes have been mine."[26]

[26] *The Autobiography of Malcolm X* (New York, Grove, 1966), p. 379; pp. 381–382.

Marx and Religion:
An Impossible Marriage

Louis Dupré

Notwithstanding the setback it suffered as a consequence of the Soviet Union's assault on Czechoslovakia, the Christian-Marxist dialogue proceeds apace in many quarters. But Louis Dupré—whose article was originally published before that lamentable invasion, in the April 26, 1968, *Commonweal**—raises some perceptive questions about the burgeoning dialogue. Though he affirms that Marxists and believers can cooperate in constructing a more human world, he doubts that doctrinal reconciliation is possible—at least not so long as communism adheres to Marx's closed economism. Economic determinism "strikes the death blow" to religion, contends Dupré, for it excludes the existence of any reality independent of the economic production process. What hope there is for reconciliation lies in the possibility that communism will "incorporate into its theory the changes which are taking place in its own living praxis." Dr. Dupré, a native of Belgium, is Professor of Philosophy and Theology at Georgetown University, Washington, D.C. Among his writings are *Kierkegaard as Theologian, Contraception and Catholics,* and —most pertinent in this context—*The Philosophical Foundations of Marxism.*

CAN a true Marxist be a religious believer? During an international conference of Marxist scholars two years ago, I asked that question of three Eastern European philosophers. All three agreed that Marxists and believers can peacefully coexist and cooperate. Two also thought that religious beliefs would be no obstacle to the adoption of Marxist

* 232 Madison Ave., New York, N.Y. 10016.

doctrine. The third one, a highly intelligent liberal, had serious doubts whether religion and Marxism could be combined. His negative answer, however, was not based upon the materialism and scientism that are part of the official doctrine of most Communist states. All agreed that these apocryphal theories are quite foreign to the spirit of Marx's philosophy. The real reason why religion cannot be combined with Marxism lies, according to the one dissenter, in Marx's theory of action. Who is right?

It is obvious that the tension between most Communist regimes and the Christian Churches has softened. The expediency of atheistic propaganda is openly questioned in Communist countries. Political pragmatism has replaced dogmatic rigidity. Positive cooperation between Communism and the Churches now seems to have become a distinct possibility. The dialogue already exists. Does it also justify hopes for a full doctrinal reconciliation? Could the two greatest moral forces in the world ever join in the creation of a new humanism? Of course, such a spiritual merger would require that the Christian abandon some of his other-worldly detachment toward social problems and that the Communist become somewhat less simplistic in the economic interpretation of history. But neither one of these conditions implies the reversal of an essential position, and both parties could only gain by such a compromise. On one point, however, no compromise is possible: atheism must be dropped. Can this be done without jeopardizing the essential doctrine of Marx? According to some participants in the dialogue (mostly Christians), atheism was never an essential part of authentic Marxism. The latter rejects only idols: the refusal of true religion is, however genuine, incongruous with Marx's philosophy. All it would take, then, to reconcile religion with Marxism is to relinquish the spurious elements of both doctrines.

While fully supporting cooperation in constructing a more human world, I am less optimistic about a doctrinal reconciliation. Atheism understood as a denial of *any* God belongs to the essence of Marx's philosophy. A Czech Communist, Julius Tomin, put the matter quite correctly in an article, "Beginnings of Dialogue," in the *Prague Literary Weekly*:

"Marxism cannot be content with a struggle which only touches religion but is unable to refute it or which refutes only the utterly reactionary and backward forms of religion. It is important to refute religion even in its most developed forms." This position by no means renders the dialogue with Communism useless. On the contrary, a more serious study of Marx's attitude toward religion could lead to the abolition of the speculative, belligerent sort of atheism which is still prevalent in most Communist regimes. For theory or practice directly aimed at the abolition of religious beliefs conflicts with Marx's philosophy. What ought to be attacked is the *basis* of these beliefs, namely, the social frustration which religion merely expresses and mythologizes. To attack religion itself rather than the conditions which produce it, is both ineffective and wrong according to Marx. Marx's own negative attitude toward religion was never based upon speculative arguments for the non-existence of God. He rejected religion because it was incompatible with his theory of action. That is why the sort of "scientist," speculative atheism advocated in the Soviet Union, which stems from Engels, Lenin and Stalin, basically conflicts with Marx's philosophy, even though Marx is indirectly responsible for it.

Inheritance from Feuerbach

It is true that Marx was an atheist long before he developed his theory of action. He inherited a speculative atheism from Feuerbach. But as his own theories grew, this atheism underwent such basic changes that the two can no longer be considered to be of the same kind. Feuerbach's atheism is rooted in a speculative theory of man. According to Feuerbach, religion expresses man's relation to his own nature, but to his own nature not recognized as such. Since all the predicates which man ascribes to God are purely human, Feuerbach argues, there is no reason why the subject of these predicates should not be human also. Man is his own God. The God of religion is an extrapolation of man's own powers of striving, thinking and feeling. Such an extrapolation is inevitable in the earliest stages of the development of consciousness. As long as man is unable to conceive of human nature as a reality that far transcends its individual realizations, he projects his own infinite powers onto a superhuman being. Unfortunately, at a later stage when man ought to know that the potential of the human race far surpasses the powers of single individuals, he nevertheless maintains this projective attitude. Feuerbach attributes man's strange refusal to reappropriate what is his own to an immature desire for sharing the humiliating restrictions of one's private existence with the entire human species.

In *The Essence of Christianity*, we read: "Man identifies himself immediately with the species—a mistake which is immediately connected with the individual's love of ease, sloth, vanity and egoism. For a limitation which I know to be merely mine humiliates, shames and perturbs me. Hence to free myself from the feeling of shame, from this state of dissatisfaction, I convert the limits of my individuality into the limits of human nature in general." The notion of alienation in Hegel's philosophy describes the dialectical opposition between the thesis and the antithesis of the dialectical movement. Feuerbach now applies it to the operation by which man estranges part of his own powers and projects them into an external, infinite being. For Feuerbach God is *the* alienation of man: the self-estrangement preceding the reappropriation of the divine into the human.

The young Marx accepted Feuerbach's view of religion as an alienation of man and never changed his position on that issue. In the *Economic and Philosophical Manuscripts* of 1844 which inaugurate his own philosophy, Marx writes: "If I *know* religion as *alienated* human self-consciousness, what I know in it as religion is not my self-consciousness but my alienated self-consciousness confirmed in it. Thus my own self, and the self-consciousness which is its essence, is not confirmed in *religion* but in the *abolition* and *supersession* of religion." At the same time he felt that Feuerbach did not explain satisfactorily the origin of this alienation. There must be more serious grounds for maintaining man's self-estrangement than sloth and vanity. In an early commentary on

Hegel's *Philosophy of the State* written under the direct influence of Feuerbach, Marx points to the social and economic conditions of modern life as the source of man's alienation. In fact, these conditions *are* man's true alienation. Religion is only an expression of it: man takes refuge in the phantasy world of the beyond because he is profoundly frustrated in his earthly existence. Nor is religion the main culprit in maintaining these frustrating conditions. For it is the political structure which legalizes and protects the social *status quo*. Feuerbach's theory of alienation, therefore, applies to the State more than to religion. "The *political constitution* was, until today, the *religious sphere*, the *cult* of people's life, the heaven of its universality, as opposed to the earthly existence of its reality." Yet, neither State nor religion reveals the roots of alienation, for these lie in the economic conditions of a society determined by private property.

How much religion is subordinated to man's social-economic conditions Marx illustrates in an early article on the Jewish question. His former friend, Bruno Bauer, had proposed the thesis that the Jewish problem could be solved instantly if the Jew would cease to claim religious privileges from the State. By doing so, he maintains the religious State in existence and prevents his own as well as other people's emancipation. The emancipation of man requires a secular State that recognizes neither Christianity nor Jews. Marx agreed that the existence of religion always indicates an incomplete emancipation, but he denied that religion is the cause of the problem and, for that matter, that political rights are the solution. Bauer simply identified religion with alienation and political equality with emancipation. But political emancipation is by no means human emancipation. In fact, political emancipation may very well coexist with a thriving religious life. "To be *politically* emancipated from religion is not to be finally and completely emancipated from religion, because political emancipation is not the final and absolute form of *human* emancipation" (*Early Writings*). The situation of the United States offers an interesting illustration of this point. The American State is entirely separated from the Church and Americans should, therefore, be fully emancipated, according to Bauer's theory. Yet, Marx points out, the U.S.A. is considered to be the religious country *par excellence*. Far from implying the suppression of religion, political emancipation grants man the right to worship according to the religion of his choice. Even if the State would suppress religion, its own existence would remain a profane expression of an alienation which in time would irresistibly produce its religious form. So, instead of being a remedy against religious alienation, the secular State is the purest symptom of its presence. More than religion, the State keeps alive the inhuman conditions that separate man from his fellow man and thereby prevent mankind from realizing its full potential. If religion means deception, the State is more religious than the Church. "The members of the political State are religious because of the dualism between individual life and species-life, between the life of civil society and political life. They are religious in the sense that man treats political life, which is remote from his own individual existence, as if it were his true life; and in the sense that religion is here the spirit of civil society, and expresses the separation and withdrawal of man from man" (*Early Writings*).

However, religion is not merely an *expression* of alienation—it also is a *protest* against it. In his "Introduction to a Critique of Hegel's *Philosophy of Right*," written around the same time, Marx uses the famous expression that religion is the opium of the people. Yet, he adds immediately: "The abolition of religion as the illusory happiness of men, is a demand for their real happiness. The call to abandon their illusions about their condition is *the call to abandon a condition which requires illusions*." The French Marxist Roger Garaudy concludes from this text that only the reflection aspect (the ideological content) of religion is illusionary, while the element of protest expresses a profound truth about the human condition. It would be mistaken, according to him, to describe Marx's view of religion only in terms of alienation. As an expression of human misery and protest against it, religion rightly questions the structure of society. Religion is false only in its answers, but it is most true in the questions which it raises.

Garaudy's interpretation is entirely correct, but it does not provide a legitimate basis for the continuance of religion in the Marxist society. Nor does it justify its present existence. For the religious way of questioning man's situation already implies a wrong answer. The right answer cannot be given as long as the protest remains religious. So, even as a form of social protest, religion can only slow down the advent of the Communist society. The first step toward a solution, therefore, would be to abandon a way of posing the problem which makes a solution impossible. Yet the abandonment of religion is merely a pre-condition and not, as Marx's atheist friends believed, the solution itself. Communism is much more than atheism, even though atheism is a preliminary requirement for it. "Communism begins where atheism begins, but atheism is at the outset still far from being Communism; indeed it is still for the most part an abstraction" (*Early Writings*).

It is small comfort to religion that Marx considers it an authentic cry of distress as long as he does not take seriously the content of this cry. For Marx religion is a symptom of social disease, not an articulate symbol. To expect the symptom to provide a cure would be most unreasonable. Rather will the symptom disappear with the disease. Marx's distaste for Feuerbach's atheism does not originate in a more open attitude toward religion but rather in his conviction that atheism alone is insufficient to cure the ills of the human situation. Atheism attempts to cure the symptoms without eradicating the disease itself, namely, man's social-economic condition in capitalist society. Theism will never be compatible with a free society, yet neither is atheism sufficient to produce such a society. That religion must be unmasked as a deception is self-evident to Marx, but more important is the question: What causes man to deceive himself? Neither Feuerbach nor any other atheist philosopher ever seriously attempted to answer that question. If they had, "the critique of heaven would have been transformed into a critique of earth, the critique of law, the critique of theology into a critique of politics" (*Early Writings*).

The Atheism-Communism Link

In the important *Manuscripts* of 1844, Marx attempts to determine the precise connection between atheism and Communism. Again he states that a full reappropriation of what man has alienated from himself cannot be achieved by a mere annulment of God, but only by an annulment of the social structure of private property which produces the need for God. Private property and religion are complementary aspects of the same alienation, while Communism and atheism are the two facets of the same reappropriation. "Atheism as the annulment of God is the emergence of theoretical humanism, and Communism as the annulment of private property is the vindication of real human life as man's property. The latter is also the emergence of practical humanism, for atheism is humanism mediated to itself by the annulment of religion, while Communism is humanism mediated to itself by the annulment of private property. . . . Atheism and Communism are not a flight or abstraction from, or loss of, the objective world which men have created by the objectification of their faculties. They are not an impoverished return to unnatural, primitive simplicity. They are rather the first real emergence, the genuine actualization of man's nature as something real." Although the reappropriation process has a theoretical aspect, it ultimately consists in reestablishing the true relationship between man and nature, and this relationship is an active one, a *praxis*. For Marx as for the existentialists, to be human is not *to be* something but *to do* something. Not leisure and contemplation but work and material production constitute man's fulfillment.

It is most incorrect to brand this productive view of man as materialism. In a few remarks jotted down in 1845 and later published by Engels as *Theses on Feuerbach*, Marx clearly rejects materialism as a simplistic reduction of consciousness to nature. "The chief defect of all materialism up to now (including Feuerbach's) is that the object, reality, that we apprehend through our senses, is understood only in the form of the *object of contemplation*; but not as sensuous human *activity*, as *practice*; not subjectively. Hence in opposition to materialism the *active* side was developed abstractly by idealism—which of course does not know real conscious activity as such." Only the *praxis* holds both poles of the human reality, nature and consciousness, as well as their relationship, simultaneously present. All interpretations of man or of nature which explain either consciousness or nature independently of the active relation to the other term, are *a priori* false. Marx rejects such purely theoretical constructions as "ideologies." All idealist systems in which consciousness is the only active element are obviously ideological. But materialism is just as ideological, for any theory that considers nature independently of consciousness, in which alone nature reveals itself, is an abstract, mental construction. The only true philosophy is the philosophy of action, for the truth of man is in what he *does*, not in what he knows or claims to know independently of his active relation to nature. This is the meaning of Marx's famous dictum in *Thesis XI on Feuerbach*: "The philosophers have only *interpreted* the world differently; the point is to change it." Atheism as a *speculative philosophy* is not based upon the *praxis* and is therefore pure ideology. It misses the *practical* origin of all ideas, its own as well as the idea of God. Its entire approach to truth is therefore wrong even though it accidentally results in correct conclusions. Its mistake lies in the assumption that ideas are independent of the social conditions of action and, consequently, that they can be changed without changing these conditions.

The recent emphasis on Marx's anti-materialist attitude and of his final rejection of speculative atheism, has aroused new hope of reconciling religion with Marxist pragmatism. To me this hope seems unjustified. For to open Marxism to religion it is not sufficient to prove that Marx was neither a materialist nor a speculative atheist. The very same argument which disposes of speculative systems as atheism and materialism, also disposes of religion. Any theory that does not have its roots in man's active relation to nature and the social conditions necessitated by this relation lacks the only possible basis of sound theory. Now this is obviously the case for religion, for in religion man claims precisely to transcend his relation to nature.

Is Religion Positively Excluded?

However, one might ask, does the absence of a foundation in the *praxis* positively exclude religion? Could one not argue that a consistent Marxist pragmatism ought to adopt a neutral rather than a hostile attitude toward any private beliefs that do not positively counteract the progress of socialist humanism? Such is already the attitude of most socialist parties in Western Europe. Why could it not be adopted by Communist regimes as well? Individual Communists have argued, like Roger Garaudy in *From Anathema to Dialogue*, that religion may have some practical justification in the fact that religion, as all ideologies, is a "project" and that all action requires some "projecting" in order to transcend the given and to anticipate a new reality.

Interesting as this acceptance of a transcendent dimension is, it cannot change the Marxist position on religion, for the Marxist transcendence must always remain *within* the immanence of human possibilities. Action compels us to project beyond the present, but does not allow us to project beyond the human. Garaudy himself seems to be aware of this, for he writes about the transcendence projected by Communism: "This new frontier of hominization, making of every man a man, questioning and creative, will mark a new detachment from the earth. The detachment, this time, will be from all the alienations which have been crystallized for thousands of years and have become so thoroughly customary as to seem to us like a *given* nature, like earth itself. It will free the spiritual energies of each man and of all men with such force that it is absolutely impossible . . . to imagine their nature and their use. This future, open to the infinite, is the only transcendence which is known to us as atheists." This frank and unambiguous statement shows how much the Communist has in common with the believer. It also shows why they can never agree on the basic issue, even after the believer has disposed of all his idols and the Communist of all his preju-

dices. The Communist transcendent cannot be God, for, as Garaudy writes, "it is impossible to conceive of a God who is always in process of making himself, in process of being born." The Communist transcendent is transcendent with respect to the present, not to the future of man. Any absolute transcendence is out of the question. That is the reason why, from a Marxist point of view, religious belief must always conflict with a truly humanist attitude. Creationist dependence and full human autonomy are incompatible. As Marx writes in the *Manuscripts*: "A being does not regard himself as independent unless he is his own master, and he is only his own master when he owes his existence to himself. A man who lives by the favor of another considers himself a dependent being. But I live completely by another person's favor when I owe to him not only the continuance of my life but also its creation, when he is its source." Even the question of creation cannot come up for Marx, because it conflicts with the *praxis*.

Does not such a positive exclusion of an absolute transcendent constitute a return to speculative atheism, and hence to pure ideology? Not really, for the independence of man which Marx asserts is primarily an independence of *acting*. Atheism as denial of supernatural *reality* is merely a conclusion concerning the independence of man's *being* which is implied in his independence of *acting*. That is the only reason why Marx supports his practical humanism by some atheistic considerations. If it were not for the ontological implication of an autonomous *praxis*, Marx would not even bother to call himself an atheist. For atheism is speculative and negative, while the entire attitude of the Communist is practical and positive. "Creation conflicts with the choice of autonomy: that is the core of Marx's argument. He does not undertake a metaphysical analysis of the structures of the real or a phenomenological description of dependent behavior. His considerations are not true proofs, they rather provide apologetic weapons to support a thesis accepted on a different ground: creation is not possible because it conflicts with the choice of autonomy; that is a postulate." So George Cottier notes in *L'athéisme du jeune Marx*.

For Marx the *praxis* is an absolute which admits no further questioning. The speculative question: "How did man and nature originate?" is ultimately meaningless because it views as non-existent the very act from which all questions of existence must originate. Marx mentions spontaneous generation, but that is merely an expression to shrug off the problem. No questions of being can be asked *beyond* the *praxis*.

Two conclusions follow from the preceding. 1. Religious beliefs are totally incompatible with the philosophy of Marx. 2. Atheism, which was the original starting-point of Marx's philosophy, gradually lost its primary importance until it was reduced to a mere implication of the *praxis*. Primary now is an absolute autonomy of the *praxis* which excludes any transcendent principle of acting. This closed autonomy is what gives Marx's philosophy its forceful simplicity. But Marx pays a high price for this simplicity. For aside from excluding an entire dimension of human experience in which man knows himself as a contingent being, Marx's philosophy unduly restricts the *praxis* to a material production process. Space does not permit me to do full justice here to a thesis which I have developed at length in a work on *The Philosophical Foundations of Marxism*. But even a superficial look shows that Marx's theory of superstructures has unjustifiably narrowed his interpretation of action. Marxist man is autonomous only in his material life process. All cultural values intrinsically and indissolubly depend upon this original process. It is the economic character of the *praxis* which has led Communist theoreticians in the past to interpret Marx in a materialist way. The interpretation is wrong, but texts as the following (*The German Ideology*) on the origin of ideas show how much responsibility Marx himself bears for the misinterpretation: "We set out from real, active men, and on the basis of their real life-process we demonstrate the development of the ideological reflexes and echoes of this life-process. The phantoms formed in the human brain are also, necessarily, sublimates of their material life-process, which is empirically verifiable and bound to material premises. Morality, religion, metaphysics, all the rest of ideology and their corresponding forms of consciousness, thus no longer retain the

semblance of independence. They have no history, no development; but men developing the material production and their material intercourse alter, along with this their real existence, their thinking and the products of their thinking." All claims of independence are "ideological" mystifications and embellishments of social conditions that need idealization. Consciousness is determined by social-economic relations, and these relations are determined by forces of production.

Yet Marx never denies the originality of consciousness. He says explicitly that man could no more establish social-economic relations without consciousness than he could be conscious without social-economic relations. The same mutual causality applies to the relation between nature and consciousness. Marx never reduces consciousness to a physiological or chemical process *of* nature. The production process which determines man's thinking presupposes an *active* relationship with nature in which consciousness has as much impact upon nature as nature upon consciousness. Consciousness as such is not a product of nature. The moment it becomes consciousness it opposes itself to nature.

Engels, who is usually held responsible for Marxism's later development toward materialism, goes even further and admits at one point a *mutual* causality between the production process and the other processes of consciousness. "Political, juridical, philosophical, religious, literary, artistic, etc., development is based on economic development. But all these react upon one another and also upon the economic basis. It is not that the economic condition is the *cause* and *alone active*, while everything else only is a passive effect." If this line of thinking had been pursued, the situation of Marxism with respect to religion would have looked entirely different. For in that case Marxism would merely have asserted the interdependence of the various levels of consciousness as well as their dependence upon the economic production process. The thesis that all states of consciousness are *conditioned* by the attainment of a certain level of economic production is perfectly compatible with the acceptance of religious values. But that is not what Marx and Engels say. They claim that all states of consciousness are *intrinsically determined* (which is quite different from *conditioned*) by the economic production process. Even Engels' just quoted text, which is probably the most reconciliatory in the entire Marxist literature, concludes with the following sentence: "There is, rather, interaction on the basis of economic necessity, which *ultimately* always asserts itself." This implies that the ultimate explanation of all ideal values is to be found in economic processes. Such an economic determinism leads to unsatisfactory results in all fields of culture. To religion it strikes the death blow, for it excludes the existence of any reality independent of the material production.

The economism of the concept of *praxis*, then, as well as its absolute autonomy are the ultimate reasons why Marxism is incompatible with religious belief. Are they also the final word on Communism's attitude toward religion? The question amounts to asking whether Communism must necessarily retain all the principles of Marx's philosophy. Several have been abandoned already. Marx's prediction about the demise of capitalism and the proletarization of the masses, is one important example. Lenin's "adaptation" of Marxism to the Russian situation is another. In some parts of Eastern Europe it is considered poor taste to quote Marx on economic matters. So then, why could Marx's theory of the *praxis* not be widened from a closed economism into an open humanism? True enough, autonomy and economic determinism belong to the core of Marxism, which cannot be changed without deviating from Marx's basic intuition. Yet even Marx's authority should remain subordinate to the cause of socialist humanism which he brought to the world. As long as the authority of its prophet remains an obstacle to the further development of its content, Marxism cannot claim to have fully overcome the anti-humanist dogma of Stalinism. Communism in the past has constantly decried *revisionism* as a halfhearted return to bourgeois theory. But has the time not come to incorporate into its theory the changes which are taking place in its own living *praxis*? Such an attitude would ultimately be more consistent with Marx's philosophy than the rigid preservation of a theory which is rapidly proving too narrow to interpret the fullness of human action.

III: The Practice of Revolution: Theological Reflection

A. RACE

B. PEACE AND CONSCIENCE

C. THE CHURCH

The Afro-American Past

Vincent Harding

If American society is ever to undergo the kind of radical transformation that is essential to its survival, it must first give close attention to the tragic story of the Afro-American past. "We cannot move towards a new beginning until we have faced all the horror and agony of the past with absolute honesty." So argues Vincent Harding, and he argues compellingly. Black historian Harding knows his people's story in all its stark dimensions, and he is too realistic to hazard any assurance that there will be time "before the last night." Yet precisely because his people have endured their ordeal, he eschews cynicism and despair. "The Afro-American past leaves a man with no illusions, but even in the heart of chaos it does not strip him of his hope." A Mennonite lay preacher as well as a historian, Dr. Harding is chairman of the History Department at Spelman College, Atlanta, Georgia, and director of the Martin Luther King, Jr., Library Project, which is part of the Memorial Center being established in Atlanta in honor of Dr. King. One of many journal contributions to his credit, Dr. Harding's article is from the April 1968 issue of *motive*.*

NEGRO history suffers the same fate in the overall American story as the individual Negro's integration into American society. That is, small but prominent doses of "Negro History" can be dropped into the national saga, but these black drops should never be numerous or indelible. For if they are too many and too black, these encroachments might necessitate unpleasant rereadings, reassessments and rewritings of the entire story.

* P.O. Box 871, Nashville, Tenn. 37202.

An American history which cannot contain the full story of the black pilgrimage is no more worthy than an American society that cannot bear the full and troublesome black presence in its midst.

Just as America can know no survival worth considering unless it finds a way of facing its black counter-image, so too our history is a tale told by fools if it does not incorporate the Afro-American experience with unflinching integrity. And if such open encounter between black and white history should produce the same insecurity as we now experience in the human encounter, so much the better.

The analogy doesn't end there. The urgency some of us feel for creating such a new American history is no less critical than the pressure impelling us to seek for the lineaments of a new American society. Obviously, the tasks are not unrelated, for there will be no new beginnings for a nation that refuses to acknowledge its real past.

Any American history that ignores the central role of black people as actors and foils on this maddening stage is a falsified and misleading history. Such a history ignores the ironic symbol of that summer in Jamestown more than three centuries ago when representative government and African bondsmen had a mutual beginning of sorts, a beginning that seemed to lock the rhetoric of democracy and the reality of black inequality into the American heart. It is a history that tries to explore the making of the Constitution without understanding the major price in its integrity that was exacted by the system of slavery and its proponents, both north and south. It is a history that attempts to speak of the Peculiar Institution as if there were no human beings involved who produced no authentic historical materials. (Thus a major publisher could attempt recently to produce a collection of documents on slavery without one document from a slave.) It is a history that speaks of Jacksonian Democracy as if the expanded white franchise were not purchased at the cost of the black northern vote in many states.

Such a vacuous history treats Reconstruction as if it were an unfortunate mistake, rather than one of the nation's greatest lost chances to be honest and free. This kind of history deals with the turn of the nineteenth century without suggesting the way in which the brutality against blacks and Indians at home may have permanently poisoned the nation's attempts at expansion among non-white peoples elsewhere. It is a history that tries to understand the urban crisis of the 1960's without tracing the long and bloody lines of Negro migration since Reconstruction. It is a history that attempts to interpret current American culture without any appreciation for the major role black people have played in creating the popular culture of the nation, especially since the 1920's.

A history without the Afro-American story may indicate why this nation can now be so numb to the brutalization of a Vietnam thousands of miles away. In denying the physical and spiritual destruction of black persons which has become a part of the American Way of Life, a callus has grown on whatever heart the nation has.

This history has contributed immensely to the miseducation of the American people and has not prepared them to face a world that is neither white, Christian, capitalist, nor affluent. Such history may yet prove poisonous, and if there is any possible antidote on the American scene, it could be the hard and bitter medicine of the Afro-American past. Is it too late for a society that still insists that its drops be few and painless?

Even when one acknowledges the grotesquely slow pace at which black people are moving onto the American stage, the knowledge of their history is still absolutely indispensable as they cast off the roles of the past and seek for new ones. If they come to the integrated scene with integrity, they must come with a knowledge of themselves and of the many-splendored gifts they bring.

Black students in formerly white schools must not enter as suppliants who are going to be transformed from "disadvantaged" to "advantaged" by such a move. They must be so aware of their black fathers and the wealth of their spiritual and intellectual heritage that they will illuminate sharply the disadvantages inherent in an isolated, beleaguered middle-class white world. If they are to become more than black Anglo-Saxons, then they cannot accept the old doctrines of slavery which encouraged them to believe that God somehow blessed darkest Africa with the light of Christian guns and ships and chains. Neither the ancient Kingdom of Songhai nor the modern Kingdom of Harlem was benighted without whites, and black young people need to know the measurements of the light—in both places.

Any society that would encourage black children to live in a state of permanent amnesia or shame—or both—concerning their fathers and their fathers' ways of life is a society not worth knowing. Any men who would enter such a society on its amnesic terms would only add to its corruption, whether they entered through the door of the ninth grade or by the carpeted way of a General Electric executive suite. But it must also be acknowledged that such knowledge is exceedingly dangerous, for if it were faithfully presented, a reading of the Afro-American past might cause black exiles to refuse many an open door. Indeed some doors might be torn from their hinges. This is not teaching hatred of whites. Rather it is the necessary and healthy explanation for the existence of the hatred and fear that most black men have known from childhood on. Any society lacking the courage to take such risks with light lacks the courage to live.

Those white persons who first encounter the token blacks in their new roles also are in desperate need of the Afro-American past. For without it they will be tempted to feel that they are doing a favor for the students or the junior executives by letting them in. Properly read, the pages of the Negro past will reveal that it is black people who have done the favor by doing so much to build the nation under such horrible circumstances, and by letting such ambiguous doors stay on their hinges for so long a time. Compassionately understood, the black past will teach all benefactors that *they* are receiving a favor in being allowed what may be the one last chance to do justice, that they are being graced by the presence of a people whose pilgrimage is perhaps the only true epic poem that America has ever known. Such a reading of the Afro-American past might even shatter the general illusion that token acceptance of token Negroes will ever bring any basic hope for the survival of any of us.

Perhaps the issue of survival suggests another level of our need for the story of this dark journey in America. Not long ago, the most highly esteemed newspaper in America asked an author to write his reflections on the reasons "for the current breaking of America into two parts, based on race." When it rips apart all the easy generalizations of our textbooks (written largely by, for and about white America), the new coming of black history would cast such a question into limbo. For any perceptive apprehension of the Negro-white encounter cannot fail to reveal that there have always been two major communities in this nation—based on race.

The breaking began in West Africa and continued in every colony and state that came into being. If we read with both speed and comprehension, it may not be too late to ask the right questions, questions based not on Newark or Detroit in 1967, but on Jamestown and Philadelphia and Springfield and St. Louis over the centuries. For it is only as America faces a Denmark Vesey, a Nat Turner, a W. E. B. DuBois, a Paul Robeson and a Malcolm X, that the nation will begin to be ready to understand a Stokely Carmichael, a Rap Brown and the host of black radicals yet to come. Such a reading would identify each one as "Made in America, Product of its Broken Community." How shall this land create new and whole men if it refuses to examine its past production record, a record strewn with the crushed bodies and spirits of black radicals hurling defiant curses and urgent pleas for renewal from the same dying lips?

These angry young men's lives demonstrate the fact that the Afro-American past and the black present are no longer matters of limited national concern—if they ever were. Indeed they suggest to us what may be one of the most profound and universally significant uses of this history: that is, its service as an entrance to the non-white, non-Western world. One of the most gifted and least celebrated American political analysts, A. J. Muste, used to say that the basic division in the world now and for some time to come was not based on communism versus capitalism. Rather, Muste said, the world was divided now between those people who had rarely if ever known defeat and humiliation as a national experience and those who had lived with this for centuries.

In a sense, Muste was simply echoing the profound insights expressed by W. E. B. DuBois half a century earlier. However formulated, the concepts of these men remind us that the world experience of the last 500 years has meant that the vast majority of the earth's humiliated people has been non-white, and their humiliation has come at the hands of the white, Western world. Moreover, it appears that this nation now stands as the self-proclaimed leader of that unhumiliated world, and finds itself at once the most powerful and one of the least comprehending national states.

One of America's most critical blind areas is in the realm of understanding the oppressed, the wretched of the earth. Our vaunted experience of virtually unbroken success, our alabaster cities undimmed by human tears (except for the unseen tears of the poor and the black?) and our movement into the strange joys of advanced corporate capitalism—all these have cut this people off from the rest of the world in significant ways.

A nation that combines the American predilection towards violence, the American stockpile of weapons and the American lack of empathy for the earth's humiliated peoples is a dangerous nation. Perhaps it can begin another life by introducing itself to the invisible men in its midst, by seeking to know the quality of suffering and hurt and the rebellion they spawn. Such an introduction must include—if not begin with—the past.

Nor are black Americans excused from such a task, for we are constantly exposed to a terrible temptation to forget the black and bloody ground out of which we sprang, as the price for American acceptance. As DuBois put it more than a decade ago, ". . . most American Negroes, even those of intelligence and courage, do not fully realize that they are being bribed to trade equal status in the United States for the slavery of the majority of men." So the Afro-American past must remind black people that we are children of the humiliated and the oppressed, that our fathers were colonized and exploited subjects, and that the ghettos we have recently left are still too often filled with the stench of poverty and despair.

Such history must remind Afro-Americans that all of our greatest leaders have begged us to stand in solidarity with the black and anguished people of the earth. We are their spokesmen in the midst of the world's foremost antirevolutionary power. If we forsake them, we forsake our past, our fathers, and our own best selves. If we forsake them, there may be no future for our children or theirs. If we forget our own father's burnings in village squares and don American uniforms to set fires against the world's desperate revolutions, we will deserve nothing but the scorn of men and the judgment of the gods.

Some years ago, D. W. Brogan, an English expert on American affairs, referred to what he called The Myth of American Omnipotence. This phrase referred to his conviction that the reading of the American past was distorted by a conception of this nation as an entity incapable of failure, powerful and pure enough to succeed at anything it chose. The corollary of this myth, said Brogan (in the days of McCarthy's reign), was that any American failure at home or overseas had to be explained by subversion or conspiracies, or—at worst—a mistake in well-intentioned American judgment.

Related to Brogan's myth is what might be called The Myth of American Romanticism. Ever since the nation's beginning it has been plagued by this equally crippling misconception of itself. Succinctly put, it involves a belief that American history is the story of a society moving on a straight upward line from perfection to perfection, from goodness to betterness, from being better than other nations to being the best and most complete nation God has ever stood over (I take it that is the implication of being "under God"). This mythology was intensified to the point of indoctrination after World War II when history became a tool of Cold War, and it became necessary to prove consistently the superiority of America over every conceivable communist, socialist or neutralist model in the world.

This self-image is on a level with fairy tales and happiness-for-ever-after. It is the self-understanding of those whose adult development has been aborted by the fear of the risks of growth. Most importantly, it is a refusal to recognize the bloody, tragic line that whips its way through all of life. Failure to face the tragic is failure to mature in national as well as personal spheres, so in the midst of this pabulum view of history a serious implanting of the Afro-American past could be the difference between death and growth—at least spiritually.

Were American historians and American citizens at large to face this story, many—if not all—of their liberal, superficial myths about, and hopes for, American society might be transformed. They would need to face again the fact that two of their greatest heroes, Jefferson and Lincoln, were convinced that black and white people could never live on a basis of true equality in America. They would be pressed to realize that The Great Emancipator cared far more deeply for a cheaply won white reconciliation than for the very costly black liberation, thereby helping to lead the nation down bloody paths of malice for all.

A close reading of the black past might reveal how fully this broken people has tested every line of American democratic rhetoric and how fully each word has shrunk before the ultimate test in every generation. (They would also see the pathetic and perennial sight of esteemed national leaders offering solutions a generation old to wounds long past such ancient salves.) A reading of the black preachers, poets and editors, a sensitive listening to the singers of our songs, would face the nation with the ceaseless rage that has been the lot of men in every strange land who have been called upon to sing, to dance, to laugh, and to be grateful. And in those pages any searching eye would easily spy the century-old predictions of black alienation, sedition, rebellion, and guerrilla warfare. Tragic disaster has always lurked at the American door, created largely by blindness to the nation's fatal flaw.

Not only would the tragic nature of American life perhaps become more clear, but the Afro-American story would remind the nation that it was conceived as an experiment, an experiment that could yet fail, miserably, utterly, explosively. Almost a century ago Henry Adams described the America of 1800 as very healthy "except for the cancer of slavery." The irony and the tragedy of a "very healthy" cancerous body is still the American condition, and though no cure has yet been found for the cancer, it may not be too late to open the blind eyes to see its sources in the past. And what if we open our eyes only to discover that Jefferson and Lincoln (and many black men) were right, that present white prejudice and black bitterness, and unbroken lines of injustice from the past now make it impossible for us to continue together in integrity? Is it better to go on in blind, self-righteous rage towards internecine struggle or to see, finally see, with sad and mature clarity the pathway down from all our past romantic dreams—including the dream of integration?

The black experience in America allows for no illusions, not even that last, ancient hope of the chosen American people whom God will somehow rescue by a special act of his grace. America began with such hopes, but they were tied to the idea of a Covenant, that men would have to do God's will for them to remain as his chosen ones. Somehow, just as America forced black men to do so much of its other dirty but productive work, the nation evidently came to believe the whites could be chosen while blacks did that suffering which has always been identified with the chosen ones. Now that is over. The black past has begun to explode and to reveal to a hiding chosen people that to be the anointed one is to be crushed and humiliated by the forces of the world. After almost 400 years of exile, the black branch of the chosen people has grown louder than ever before in its refusal to take the sufferings apart from the privileges of the chosen status.

So, for all who would see it, the Afro-American past illuminates the meaning of being chosen. Perhaps this is what white Americans must see: that they will either join the ranks of suffering and humiliation (beginning perhaps with "losing face" in Vietnam?) or there will be no chosen people on these shores. Either they will submit their children to some of the same educational terrors they have allowed black children to endure or there is no future for any. Either they will give up their affluence to provide necessities for others or there will be neither affluence nor necessities for anyone. Perhaps we were chosen together, and we cannot move towards a new beginning until we have faced all the horror and agony of the past with absolute honesty. Perhaps integration is indeed irrelevant until the assessment of a long, unpaid debt has been made and significant payments begun. Perhaps atonement, not integration, is the issue at hand.

Of course, one last, shattering possibility may remain. It could be that the message of the Afro-American past is this: only one branch of the chosen people has really paid the dues of suffering—with the scars to show for it. Therefore it may be that only the black branch will be allowed to shape the future of the nation and determine its calling for the world. Perhaps only black people are open, sensitive, and scarred enough as a group to lead this nation into true community with the non-white humiliated world. Perhaps that world of suffering will trust no American leaders save those who bear the marks of oppression in their souls. Perhaps it will listen only to those who know the tragic sense of life and are not blind and calloused bearers of death.

Perhaps it is already time for the last to be first in our nation. How shall that overturning come? That knowledge may be too great for even the Afro-American past to bear. Perhaps our black history can only bear witness to the truth, and living men must shape that truth into new action and new history.

To those who would close their ears to such interpretations of the black past, to those who would tune out because such strange musings seem unrelated to the historian's vocation, I cite the word of a white radical who read black history with some care. Before an audience of well-meaning whites, in a time of similar crisis, he spoke on the Afro-American past, focusing on the greatness of a black leader named Toussaint, holding L'Ouverture above the great white heroes of the age. Then Wendell Phillips set out these words: "You think me a fanatik tonight, for you read history not with your eyes but with your prejudices."

So spoke a man who believed that there was no healing for America either in small black drops of history or in small black drops of Negro freedom. Had the nation heard his word and followed his uses of the past, we might well have been spared most of the bloody days between and the terror-filled nights yet to come.

Will there be time before the last night? We who have lived in night and waited long in darkness may have a special word of light for a stumbling power-bound people. We do not panic easily. Shall the word be heard? Only those with ears can say. It is our calling, our vocation, to speak it. And if the last darkness should fall, it is preferable that we be found standing faithful to all the agonizing sorrow-joy of our Afro-American past than lost and sullen black defenders of a world that sucked out our memory and bleached our minds.

Such a land deserves no defense. Better that it pass and make way for whatever is yet to come—even if it be the long-delayed last silence. Or will it be the drums of morning? I do not know. The Afro-American past leaves a man with no illusions, but even in the heart of chaos it does not strip him of his hope. We have come too far, through too much chaos, to cop out here.

Martin Luther King—Unsung Theologian

Herbert Warren Richardson

The year 1969 marks the one-hundredth anniversary of the birth of India's Mahatma Gandhi, the martyred spiritual leader who spearheaded his country's nonviolent struggle for independence. The year also marks the first anniversary of the martyrdom of another spiritual leader, a black man who considered Gandhi his mentor and who led his oppressed people in a comparable struggle for freedom and equality. Like Gandhi before him, Martin Luther King, Jr., was convinced that "to meet hate with retaliatory hate would do nothing but intensify the existence of evil in the universe." As Herbert Warren Richardson points out, King was well aware of the pervasiveness and ideological character of evil in our time; it was *because* he was thus aware that he believed the way of reconciliation and nonviolence to be the only practical method of dealing with evil and effecting social change. In eloquent tribute to King, Richardson, Assistant Professor of Theology at St. Michael's College, University of Toronto, tells why King "is the theologian for our time," and why "he deserves our head as well as our heart." Best known for his book *Toward an American Theology*, Dr. Richardson wrote his article not long after Martin Luther King's assassination; it appeared in the May 3, 1968, *Commonweal.**

MARTIN Luther King was the most important theologian of our time, not because of the plentitude of his literary production, but because of his creative proposals for dealing with the structure of evil generated by modern relativism, viz., ideological conflict. Over against this understand-

* 232 Madison Ave., New York, N.Y. 10016.

ing of social evil, King created not only a new theology, but also new types of piety, new styles of Christian living.

Relativism is like gnosticism in that it affirms knowledge to be acquired only in a privileged way; but relativism is like scientific naturalism in that it claims the object of knowledge to be natural. The peculiar demonic tendency of relativism arises from the combination of these two factors. With respect to the fact that it affirms access to knowledge to be privileged and not public, relativism posits the same irrevocable and irreconcilable separation of the *cognoscenti* from outsiders that is found in gnosticism. But whereas the gnostic object of knowledge is supernatural, the relativistic object of knowledge is natural. Whereas gnosticism asserts an opposition between the natural and supernatural orders of reality, relativism asserts an opposition within a single natural order between those who truly understand the meaning of life and those who do not. In this way, modern relativism generates a unique institution: ritual ideological conflict. This conflict is undertaken both because of and in order to confirm ideological commitments. It is not, in fact, conflict over particular problems; hence it is unresolvable in principle.

Modern relativism brings the dualism that is characteristic of religious gnosticism down into the natural order of time and space. In this situation there is inevitably conflict, for there is no basis for peaceful coexistence among parties that are ideologically opposed. Faced with the inevitability of ideological conflict, the relativists have replied that conflict, even war, is not only a necessary but also a valuable part of life. They say that it creates values rather than destroying them. Conflict not only encourages pluralism and diversity; it even creates or strengthens such values as justice, brotherhood and equality.

Relativism so pervades the world today that conflict, even violent conflict, is glorified not only by the extreme right and the extreme left; it has been increasingly structured into the whole fabric of modern culture. Faced with this demonic tendency, the Church must oppose relativism with a faith which will open it to a transcending redemptive reality.

Now, if we seek a conception of faith which is appropriately correlated with relativism, we shall understand faith as the power of reconciliation which works to unite the many relative perspectives and to thwart ideological conflict. In this context, faith is the commitment of man to oppose the separation of man from man. It is a commitment to struggle against attacks on the common good, against racism and segregation, and against the fragmentation of man's intellectual and spiritual life.

The most important proponent of a theology of reconciliation was Martin Luther King, who developed this theological principle into a new method for effecting social change. In his theology, therefore, faith affirms reconciliation in opposition to the relativism that denies its possibility. In intellectual discussion, faith hopes for agreement and not only dialogue. In war, faith expects and works for peace. In economic struggle, it calls for the common good. In the working together of churches, it anticipates ecumenical reunion. In all these acts, faith affirms something relativism cannot see, i.e., the power of divine unity working in all things to reconcile the ideological conflict generated by relativism itself. Quite concretely, too, faith as the affirmation of such a power of reconciliation also affirms that all those institutions and movements of our time which are working to overcome ideological conflicts are special instruments of redemptive power. One thinks immediately of King's support of the United Nations, of his development of the Southern Christian Leadership Conference, and of his concern for peace and ecumenism. These are the institutions where God is working in the world today. But only the eyes of faith can see it.

The struggle against ideological conflict anywhere in the world is the struggle for the unity of men living together in the world. Conversely, because the struggle against racism is really a struggle against ideological conflict, Martin Luther King recognized that he had to oppose this kind of conflict wherever it appears. He was, so to say, under this obligation *in principle*. Hence, King was the first of those who linked the civil rights struggle to opposition to the Vietnam war.

Civil Rights and Vietnam

It is instructive now to recall that many active supporters of King's civil rights program opposed his opposition to the Vietnam war. King, they said, was mixing up the civil rights movement with the problem of the war and this would weaken the struggle for integration. But these critics supposed that these were, in fact, two different problems rather than two manifestations of the same structure of evil: ideological conflict. By the very fact that King refused to separate these two issues, he showed the profundity of his theological insight into the nature of evil today. And who, today, would deny that what he first affirmed as a lone prophetic voice has now come to pass and been acknowledged by all among us as a basic social fact? Racial discrimination is but one form of the peculiar form of evil which characterizes our time— the presence of ideological hate within the world denies the possibility in principle of the unity of man with man.

King's perception of the human problem today as rooted in a certain structure of social evil led him to emphasize again and again that his struggle was directed against the forces, or structure, of evil itself rather than against the person or group who is doing the evil. Christian faith sees neither particular men nor particular groups as evil, but sees them trapped within a structure of ideological separation which makes ritual conflict inevitable. In order to overcome this kind of evil, faith does not attack the men who do evil, but the structure of evil which makes men act violently. Hence, there must be an *asymmetry* between the form in which evil manifests itself and the form of our opposition to evil. We should meet violence with non-violence. The philosophy of "black power" assumes that there must be a symmetry between the form in which evil manifests itself and the form of our opposition to it. But King saw that such a symmetrical response only perpetuates the structure of evil itself. In describing his work in the Montgomery bus boycott, King said:

"In my weekly remarks as president, I stressed that the use of violence in our struggle would be both impractical and immoral. To meet hate with retaliatory hate would do nothing but intensify the existence of evil in the universe. Hate begets hate; violence begets violence; toughness begets a greater toughness. We must meet the forces of hate with the power of love; we must meet physical force with soul force. Our aim must never be to defeat or humiliate the white man, but to win his friendship and understanding."

In this statement, the asymmetrical character of the struggle against evil is clearly noted and, as we have seen, the affirmation of the possibility of this asymmetry grows out of the vision that grounded King's theology. Face to face with the white man, bound, so to say, to the realm of relativism, to the order of visible differences and diverse histories, one can find no grounds for agreement, unity, or friendship. In such a realm, there are, as one theologian even today affirms, "only individuals and fights." But the vision of faith is that there is an invisible unity that makes the white and black man one in love, in holy communion, in common goal and good. But this realm of unity is seen only by faith, and the one who responds to evil asymmetrically, returning good for evil, is the man who lives by faith.

It should be noted that King did not argue for nonviolence on a fideistic or confessional ground—as if hereby we are making an eschatological witness to the Lordship of Christ, a witness that must, in our time, always be defeated. King argues that non-violence is the sole *practical* way to struggle against evil because it alone is based on a right understanding of reality itself. To struggle against evil within the system of ideological conflict never solves anything, but simply perpetuates the problem by confirming the structure of evil itself. This is why so much concerned social action is counter-effective—because one ideology lives off its opposition to another and thereby strengthens that which it opposes in the very act of opposing it. King's profound understanding of the way in which structures of evil in the world drive men to act evilly, i.e., oppress men until they are sick and filled with hatred and fear for all "outsiders," is what gave his theology a critical focus that is duplicated nowhere else on the contemporary scene.

Not only was King's understanding of the character of evil in the modern world precise and relevant, but so too was his vision of the goal of the struggle against evil and his understanding of the relation of the two. King identified the goal of the struggle against evil as the total interrelatedness of man with man, an ability to live together with those who are different, even opposed. We should not seek "to defeat or humiliate our opponent, but to win his friendship and understanding." Note King's stress on friendship as the ultimate value of human life. Protestant theology has so neglected the development of an adequate value theory or the idea of a chief good of life that we can scarcely understand why King holds that friendship is this good, why it is the purpose of all that we do. Protestants have, moreover, twisted the concept of Christian love to the requirements of the doctrine of justification by faith, i.e., to the demands of Reformation dogma, affirming that Christian love is self-sacrificing agape—not personal communion. To describe Christian love as self-sacrificing agape is to put the cart before the horse. According to King, self-sacrificing love grows naturally out of the love of friendship, out of the sense of being in communion with the one to whom good is returned for evil. Self-sacrifice cannot *establish* personal friendship, it can only manifest it. If it does not manifest it, then this love is only a more insidious form of evil, "the heaping of coals."

Emphasis on Christian love as friendship involves an important reversal of a pervasive Reformation error. Such a reversal could come, I surmise, only from a perspective that was itself not wholly at ease with the magisterial reformation, i.e., only from the "third wing," the spiritualists, the Baptists. One can understand today why Harvey Cox should say that the life and work of King make him proud to be a Baptist. And we should not forget this: that King's spiritualistic concern for the sanctification of the world and his vision of Christian love as friendship give his theological ethics a specificity that contrasts markedly with the other contemporary options.

We can understand the significance of King's insistence upon the unity of persons in friendship (brotherhood) as the goal of all life by contrasting it with an ethics that regards self-sacrificing agape (or the "faith" that receives it) as the chief good of human life. Such an ethics must regard evil as a necessary (even good) condition of human life. For in order for self-sacrifice to be possible, there must be an evil to be suffered. Self-sacrifice is good, therefore, not in itself, but because it deters or limits evil. In this framework, the fundamental fact of life is seen to be the ineradicability of evil—and by elevating self-sacrificial agape into the principal ethic, we know not the "essential good" but only the "deterrent good." In our own time, Reinhold Niebuhr reintroduced this Reformation, though semi-Manichean, understanding of evil back into American theology—and King's writings show a constant wrestling against him and the problem he raises. King's reply, his decisive repudiation of the Niebuhrian scheme, comes in his different, but more profound, understanding of evil as the structure that engenders ideological conflict, a structure that is to be opposed not by settling for proximate justice in the political order, and acknowledging the legitimacy of violent force to restrain evil, but by striving for a holy community of love in this world by the nonviolent striving to overcome evil with good.

King was regarded as a civil rights leader and as a man of extraordinary personal valor, but he has not been understood as a brilliant and mature theologian: the first two would, however, have been impossible without the third. It would be a tragedy, I believe, if we were to remember him only as hero and not as thinker—by still giving our minds over to the authors of ponderous tomes and the orators on prestigious lecture platforms while giving over only our hearts to him. He deserves our head as well as our heart. He is the theologian for our time.

The Foundation and Meaning of Christian Pacifism

Hans-Werner Bartsch

Unlike many of the contributors to this volume, Hans-Werner Bartsch disallows altogether any Christian sanction of the use of violence, whether for revolutionary or other purposes. Though he would disentangle pacifism from the onus of legalism and casuistry, he nonetheless sees the pacifist stance as basic to faith—basic because one cannot proclaim the gospel and bear witness to the love of God in Christ and at the same time engage in killing. No doubt many readers will balk at Bartsch's making pacifism *the* presupposition of Christian witness; but it cannot be denied that his argument manifests logic, conviction, and considerable scriptural undergirding. A New Testament scholar, Dr. Bartsch is Professor of Theology in Johann Wolfgang Goethe University in Frankfurt, Germany. His article was given as an address while he was teaching at Bethany Theological Seminary (Church of the Brethren) in Oak Brook, Illinois, in 1966–67; it later appeared in the Winter 1968 issue of *Brethren Life and Thought*.* Though none of his books has yet been translated into English, he is the editor of the distinguished two-volume work *Kerygma and Myth*.

PACIFISM is contracted from two Latin words, *pax* and *facere* (meaning "peace" and "to make"). Thus it is the abstraction of the Greek word *eirenopoioi*, which means "peacemakers" (Matthew 5:9). Any Christian understanding of pacifism should therefore start with an active interpretation of the word. Since Christians who adopt this word as a designation of their own commitment obviously try to im-

* P.O. Box 121, Oak Brook, Ill. 60521.

plement the demand of Matthew 5:9, pacifism has a genuine
Christian rootage and has to be understood apart from other
movements which proclaim nonviolence. The difference between the two words, *pacifism* and *nonviolence*, must not be
overlooked because the former designates an active movement and the latter a passive attitude. Nevertheless, this does
not exclude nonviolence as an attitude of pacifists, for it
really is the main feature and best-known behavior of them.
However, pacifism is not restricted to such a passive attitude;
it has necessarily the active counterpart of making peace,
promoting endeavors toward peace, and eliminating any discernible causes of war and hatred. Without this active and
positive endeavor, pacifism is not really what the name claims
to imply, and one should not speak about pacifism as identical with nonviolence.

This distinction is most important in the theological evaluation of pacifism. Generally, theological criticism is directed
against the merely passive attitude of nonviolence, and thus
the reproach of legalism is made. The passive attitude of nonviolence is understood as an attempt to avoid transgression
of the commandment, "Thou shalt not kill." Moreover, this is
not even a Christian endeavor, but it is due to a legalism
which is in principle independent of the commandment
and the teaching of Jesus in the Sermon on the Mount. It
could just as well have been derived from reverence for life, a
philosophical and not a theological doctrine. The commandment understood as a principle is already ossified and as such
taken as a tool of self-justification. The accusation of legalism
leads then to the reproach of casuistry since pacifism is looked
upon as a way by which the Christian may stay righteous by
rejection of participation in warfare. Because pacifism asks,
"What is commanded?" it is understood as casuistic.

This is the strongest argument of Karl Barth against an
adoption of pacifism which seems to be the logical inference
of his theology. As John Yoder has shown, Karl Barth has
turned away from the traditional stance in Protestant theology in regard to the problem of war. His position, which
Yoder calls a "relative pacifism," is far closer to pacifism
than to any kind of justification of participation in war. His

objection against a Christian pacifism is the alleged "legalism" and "casuistry" which he sees as a necessary feature of it.

Since this is the most frequent reason for the rejection of pacifism, we may deal with this question more generally. Actually, the accusation of legalism is imposed on pacifism by its opponents but is not a feature of pacifism itself. Since everybody acknowledges the commandment, "Thou shalt not kill," the possibility of a justified participation in war is given only if certain exceptions are assumed. Thus Luther exempts God and the state from the validity of the commandment, so that any person who acts officially in the name of God or of the state may kill without being guilty. Since pacifism asserts that there is no exception possible, it has to deal with the assumed exception, and this appears to be casuistic. But the reason lies in the nonpacifist assumption—an exception which is already casuistic. The pacifist who is arguing with a nonpacifist does this casuistically because he has to speak with his opponents on their own terms.

This is most evident with the assumption of an "extreme case" in which the transgression of the commandment is supposed to be no transgression. The nonpacifists have to use the concept of extreme case, which in itself gives evidence that their way of arguing is casuistic. On the other hand, "extreme obedience" is the least casuistic and legalistic, since any argument about cases is excluded. To argue about cases would mean to doubt the validity of the commandment. Thus extreme obedience is the only way to avoid casuistry while holding to the aim of obedience. But extreme obedience actually leads a step beyond mere obedience insofar as obedience is understood as a human endeavor or achievement. This may be understood from a practical case. Helmut Gollwitzer gave the following consideration when he was asked to deliver his pistol, at the end of the Second World War.

Up till now I had got through this horrible war without using a weapon against anyone, and had I got to make up for it now? Against the partisans? In self-defence? What about self-defence? Does that justify what is otherwise forbidden? Somebody tries to kill me: I get in first and kill him. It is he or I—just like that. Providing, that is, that death is something that must be avoided at all costs. That also justifies what he is trying to do to me, so no sensible man would react otherwise. But the Sermon on the Mount says something quite different, so there is, after all, another way. Perhaps that way might be more sensible, for it promises more in heaven and on earth. Perhaps, I thought, the Russians or the partisans, who are trying to catch you, need someone to sacrifice himself for once, rather than to fight, to suffer injury rather than to injure. Self-defence is solely in one's own interest. . . . It is clearly a false, un-Christlike reaction, the reaction of one who is already defeated, who is subject to the situation, not master of it, and who is still afraid.[1]

This consideration at the decisive moment shows clearly that obedience is not only a formal subjection to a commandment, but, in the extreme case, liberation and victory. A further consideration about what is going on in such a decision may prove this. If I am confronted with somebody so that the question is "he or I," I evaluate his life against mine. But how am I entitled to say that my life is more valuable than his? I may kill the other one only if I assume that my life is more valuable than his, and this assumption is possible only if I evaluate life according to human achievements, if I understand life as at my disposal. This is a non-Christian understanding, and hence self-defense is definitely a non-Christian or pre-Christian device. Understanding life as a gift of God brings about a complete change. If our lives are given to us, it is impossible to evaluate them. Recognizing this does not mean to submit to a commandment but to understand the gospel, which tells us that God has given us everything. But by understanding this, it is possible to comprehend the meaning of the commandment so that obedience becomes more than a legalistic action. It becomes the conscious consent to that which the commandment means. Since these considerations are still in terms of the general idea that obedience is the main aim of Christianity, legalism is not completely avoided. But we get a hint as to how to overcome legalism by extreme obedience.

However, obedience is not understood that way in most

[1] In his book entitled *Unwilling Journey*.

theological ethics. The interpretation of the fifth (sixth) commandment in theological ethics gives evidence that obedience is always understood as a limited obedience. The ethical problem is the question how far and by what obedience may be limited. Therefore, it is useful for our considerations to look at the structure of obedience in the New Testament.

The main commandment in the New Testament, that which is specifically given to the Christians, the disciples of the Lord Jesus, is obviously that at the end of the Gospel According to Matthew: "Go therefore and make disciples of all nations . . ." (Matthew 28:19). This commandment is founded upon the Lordship of Jesus, to whom all authority is given. The same commandment is reported by Luke in a slightly different way. In Acts 1:8, Jesus says to his disciples: "You shall be my witnesses[2] in Jerusalem and in all Judea and Samaria and to the end of the earth."

The ambiguity of the translation is significant. Actually the commandment can be understood as a prediction that is a promise. The commandment is only a form by which the disciples and the early church understood what was actually a necessary consequence of their being disciples. It is therefore awkward to call the early Christian mission an act of obedience because it is more; it is an act of their life as Christians but not an act which is an end in itself, an achievement of a true Christian life. The connotation of achievement which obedience necessarily has is avoided if we understand the early Christians' mission as an act of their life through faith and therefore the commandment of Jesus as a prediction, a promise of that which necessarily will happen.

This is consistent with the understanding of Paul as to his mission. He understands his mission as being entrusted with "the ministry of reconciliation. So we are ambassadors for Christ, God making his appeal through us" (2 Corinthians 5:19, 20). And he emphasizes this: "For necessity is laid upon me. Woe to me if I do not preach the gospel!" (1 Corinthians 9:16). If we would interpret this in terms of obedience, we have to say that the first commandment for Paul

---

[2] RSV. "You will bear witness for me"—NEB.

is to proclaim the gospel, and that he tries to carry out this commandment by extreme obedience. But it seems to be more appropriate not to understand Paul's mission as an act of obedience inasmuch as it is not a second act, after his conversion, separated from his accepting the gospel and answering God's gift by faith. His mission is the act of accepting the gospel itself. In the letter to the Galatians he is very careful to point out that without delay he went into Arabia after the appearance of the Lord. Therefore the main topic of Christian ethics should be witness instead of obedience. It is the first and main task of any Christian to bear witness to the deed of God through Christ. Woe to us if we do not do this, for it would mean that we would stop being Christians.

This presupposition, granted the question of pacifism and war, appears completely different. It is not a question of obedience to a specific commandment anymore, but it is the question of consistency with the Christian witness. Instead of asking whether it is possible under certain circumstances for a Christian to participate in warfare, we have to ask whether participating in warfare is a possible way of proclaiming the gospel. Thus it is not the question of whether warfare leaves enough space to be a Christian, as Luther put the question . . . "whether the Christian faith, by which we are accounted righteous before God, *can tolerate, alongside it,* that I be a soldier, go to war and slay and stab, rob and burn, as one does to enemies, by military law, in times of war."[3] If my whole life is to be a witness to the love of God, and if this means faith, then we cannot look for a space "alongside the faith" and ask whether faith can tolerate that I be a soldier. The question is whether my being a soldier may be a possible way of carrying out the witness.

Luther is aware of the necessary "No" answering this question. When the Pope supported the war against the Turks and approved the sale of indulgences in order to carry on that war, Luther wrote: "It is against Christ's doctrine, because he says that Christians shall not resist evil, shall not fight or quarrel nor take revenge or insist on rights. . . . [The Pope

[3] *Whether Soldiers, Too, Can Be Saved.* Works of Martin Luther, V. Philadelphia, 1931. Page 34f.

and the bishops] are called to fight against the devil with the Word of God and with prayer, and would be deserting their calling and office by fighting with the sword against flesh and blood. This they are not commanded, but forbidden to do."[4]

Luther states clearly that it cannot be the specific task of any Christian to fight a war since it is not the will of Christ. But Luther does not imply that pacifism is the adequate attitude of a Christian. He distinguishes between the two swords and the two realms, and thus he gets free space to state that the soldier, too, can be saved. It may be asked, however, whether this was actually a theological inference due exclusively to theological considerations. Since that refutation of pacifism was written after the peasants' war (1526), we may be reminded that Luther started differently when he wrote in his first thesis: "When our Lord and Master Jesus Christ said 'Repent' he willed the entire life of the believers to be one of repentance" (1517). We have only to extend Luther's reference to Mark 1:15 to Acts 1:8, and it is evident that Christian pacifism is the necessary consequence of Luther's preaching too: "When our Lord and Master Jesus Christ said: You shall be my witnesses, he willed the entire life of the believers to be a witness." It is the necessary consequence of any understanding of the Christian message which understands it as encompassing the whole of life and Jesus Christ as Lord of the whole world.

It is therefore not just speculation to assume that Luther's turning toward a dichotomy of life by the doctrine of the two realms is due to the growing establishment of his churches by affiliation with the princes. The understanding of the life of the Christian as a witness to the love of God leads necessarily to a very simple answer to the question of war and peace. With the birth of Christ, "peace on earth" was proclaimed, and God reconciled the world to himself in Christ (2 Corinthians 5:19). Peace is that which Christ brought us (the numerous passages of the Gospels need not be recounted). And therefore we have to understand the bene-

[4] *Op. cit.*, V, page 83f.

diction "Blessed are the peacemakers, for they shall be called sons of God" (Matthew 5:9) not as a negligible by-product of the gospel but as the clear statement that accepting the peace which Christ brought means making peace on earth. We have the peace which Christ brought to us only if we make peace on earth.

Thus, pacifism is not a kind of whimsical idea of over-idealistic Christians but is basic to faith as long as we understand faith as a way of life, an understanding of life which needs to be practiced. Contrary to this understanding would be a faith which is taken as an internal conviction. Such a spiritualistic understanding of faith is rejected by most Protestant theologians as inconsistent with the New Testament. So long as there is no evidence that waging war, killing as many people as possible, slaying, stabbing, robbing, and burning by military law can be understood as proclaiming the gospel, bearing witness to the love of God in Christ, pacifism is to be taken as the necessary basic attitude of Christians.

One has to be aware of the aim of such behavior, for the aim is by no means to be self-righteous or to keep one's hands clean. He will be the same after his witness, since he has at most reassured himself that he believes, but he will be scarcely aware of this. The aim is the one to whom the gospel is proclaimed, the enemy. Since the enemy is the neighbor when a war is imminent, he is the one to whom our witness is directed primarily. During such a time the words of Paul are valid, "Woe to me if I do not preach the gospel."

Therefore, the question whether waging a war against an enemy can be proclamation of the gospel to that enemy is the most urgent question for any Christian before and during a war. Only this question must determine his attitude. The answer should be unambiguous. Waging a war always means the threat of killing and exterminating the nation against whom the war is waged. There is not any possibility left to understand killing as an act of love. When we assume that killing is the only possibility of preventing the enemy from committing a crime, and we make killing an act of love, we seize the judgment of God in judging that the act of the enemy is to be condemned and that his crime is even greater than ours. The usurpation of God's authority will be the necessary presupposition of such a justification of a war.

But there is still another way to declare a war as an act of love although not toward the enemy. The neighbor to whom I show my love by waging a war is not the enemy but the people whom I protect from being slain, stabbed, or robbed by the enemy. Although according to the New Testament my neighbor is first the one against whom my weapon is directed, my people, my family, and my nation are also necessarily concerned, and hence they are my neighbors, too. Not because they are my family and my nation but because they are in danger and ask for support are they my neighbors, and the obligation to help them and to protect them as much as possible is obvious. The only question is whether I must do this at the risk of killing the enemy, knowing that this means denying the Christian witness.

The Quakers have given the answer to this question. One cannot love someone by killing a person for his sake. This argument is actually cogent if we do not look superficially at the given situation but ask for a more comprehensive understanding. If I kill a person for the sake of my friend, I necessarily load the burden of responsibility upon his shoulders. I am the murderer, but I shift the responsibility to my friend whether I want to or not, because I have done it for his sake. Hence, I feel myself justified. It may be true that my deed—participation in a war—has honorable reasons, but it can never be understood as an act of love. As love "does not insist on its own way" and "is not irritable or resentful" (1 Corinthians 13:5), love could not do anything wrong for the beloved either. Love can suffer until death for him, but love cannot kill for the beloved since it would hurt and soil him.

Generally, we refrain from recognizing that fact. The soldier is understood as a person who sacrifices himself for the nation. But actually he does not want to sacrifice himself; he wants only to sacrifice as many enemies as possible. The enemies who are killed are the real sacrifices of the war, which are offered deliberately to the god of war. The casualties on our own side are the necessary risk which we cannot avoid.

Emphasizing the casualties on our side and neglecting the enemies whom our soldiers really have killed is the same delusion as the businessman's pretension that he sells his goods only as a service to the state because he pays taxes. Actually he sells his goods because of the profit. Any war is waged in order to kill, slay, stab, rob, and burn as many of the enemies as may be necessary for our own gain.

In this context we can consider the question of a war which is waged because of a "just cause." The proponents of a just war refer to passages in the Old Testament which seem to indicate that God is willing to support a just cause as, *e.g.*, in Psalm 94:15: "For justice will return to the righteous, and all the upright . . . will follow it." The prayer of the righteous seems to justify the commitment to the just cause In Psalm 35:23: "Bestir thyself, and awake for my right, for my cause, my God and my Lord!"

But there are two criteria against the idea of waging war for a just cause. (1) The psalms put the just cause before God so that God himself will help if he judges that the cause is just. Therefore, this psalm does not favor man's helping himself. The prayer that God may justify a man's cause is a strict contradiction of man's assumption about carrying out his just cause by waging a war. If he prays that God establish justice, he may not do it himself. (2) Insisting upon one's own right would be contrary to the definition of love which Paul suggests in 1 Corinthians 13:5: "Love does not insist on its own way." Love is always more than "right" and "justice"; it transcends both. The Christian who tries to proclaim the Kingdom of God and his love—which is its justice (Matthew 6:33, NEB)—cannot insist upon his own right or upon the right of his nation, for he would deny his mission if he did.

However, this does not mean acquiescence to the other side. It does not mean to yield to injustice. It means real love which "does not rejoice at wrong" (1 Corinthians 13:6). The attitude of the Christian must proclaim a genuine love which is able to convince the enemy that his cause is unjust. War can never be a means to convince someone of his wrong, since arms used in this manner are the concrete denial of the faith that God will execute "justice for the oppressed" (Psalm

146:7). The responsible Christian has to take care that the just cause of his nation will never be at stake in an imminent war. He has to be on the alert before a war becomes the last resort.

It could be shown that the two World Wars were the last resort for helpless politicians because either they themselves as Christians or the Christians in their countries had disposed of the possibility that politics could be a field where the Christian witness has meaning. If the Christians in Germany had recognized in 1933 that the Communists and the Socialists who were imprisoned without any legal reason were their brothers for whom Jesus died, they could have stopped the following flood of injustice and atrocities. It is the main device of Christian pacifism to "restrain the evil in the very beginning," an application of the Latin motto, *principiis obsta*, to be aware of injustice in the world before it grows so great that war becomes the last resort.

According to the Christian mission this means awakening the conscience of one's own nation to the fact that the adversary also is a human being. The Christian witness must be directed against any propaganda which tries to label anybody as good or evil. For a Christian the main attribute of a human being is that God loved him so much that he gave his only Son (John 3:16). It is the positive attitude of Christian pacifism to intercede for any outcast whether he be Christian or non-Christian. The non-Christian is even more entitled to such intercession since we owe him this witness according to our Lord's Word. It must not be forgotten that the Japanese are right in calling the Hiroshima bomb the Christian bomb, not only because a chaplain spoke a blasphemous prayer before the plane which carried it took off but also because that bomb was rightly understood as an activity of Christians who were under the mission of their Lord.

It may be seen by this example how difficult the witness of Christian pacifism is after a war has already begun. How can a pacifist "make peace" under such circumstances? There is at best the possibility of trying to negotiate with the enemy. During World War II, Dietrich Bonhoeffer was probably the only one who tried to do this for theological reasons, as a

Christian. His example shows not only how difficult this is because of the suspicion on both sides, but also that such an attempt is misunderstood as deriving primarily from political motives.

Moreover, it is impossible to challenge one's own people with such an attempt, since it is confined to underground work. Actually such an attempt is the last resort for any pacifist, and he should make it clear to his government beforehand that just such an underground activity—that is, negotiations with the enemy at the risk of disloyalty to the government—is the necessary and final consequence in the case of a war. Thus the shadow of legalism and casuistry would be taken away from the pacifists, since they are not afraid to get their hands dirty, since they become despised and outcast themselves. They are able to sin courageously, too. The only difference will be that their sins do not make heroes out of them, since everybody will recognize their deeds as sins. Their aim becomes clear. They do not want to become heroes or even maintain their own righteousness; they want only to let the enemy know that the love of God is not yet lost in their own warring nation.

One last consideration may be added. Facing such a situation, the pacifist also can speak about an extreme case, but it is not the extreme case in which a sin is justified. It is, rather, the case where sin is so overwhelming that it is impossible to proclaim love without participating in sin. Such a case in which the Christian witness is extremely urgent is any war which a Christian nation—or a nation which is taken for being Christian—wages against non-Christians. And it may be that in such a war it is not enough to proclaim nonparticipation, to ask for negotiation, and to show solidarity with the non-Christians. It will not be believed when the war goes on without any change. Actions in favor of the enemy may be necessary even if such actions mean support of the enemies' war by making proclamations against one's own state and by sending food and medical supplies.

The pacifist who decides to support the enemy in such a way must be aware that this is actually transgression against God's holy commandment. He becomes responsible for the killing of his own brothers and kinfolk by strengthening the enemy. This shows that he did not do enough to bear witness before the war began. The real conflict is the case in which I am aware that I am committing a transgression against God's commandment but I cannot help doing so. If the possibility of bearing witness to the love of Christ is given only by transgression against the holy commandments of God, the conflict cannot be solved. We may ask, then, where our guilt originated when we omitted bearing witness to the love of God. We may submit to God's judgment, but we must not dispense once again with our mission.

Thus Christian pacifism is motivated in the fact that the Christian witness cannot be carried to anybody with a gun in the hand. Christian pacifism is not an end in itself but is the presupposition of the Christian witness. Its foundation is the love of God which is shed upon us through Jesus Christ and which cannot be accepted by participating in a war. Its foundation is the understanding of the eschatological deed of God in regard to all mankind and the whole life without any exception. Its foundation is the first thesis of Martin Luther that our Lord and Master Jesus Christ willed the whole life of his believers to be one of witness.

The meaning of Christian pacifism is therefore not to become righteous, to carry out a principle; it is, rather, to be disciples of our Lord. It is not necessary to insist on a principle. Karl Barth is then right when he states, "According to the sense of the New Testament we cannot be pacifist in principle, only in practice. But we have to consider very closely whether, if we are called to discipleship, we can avoid being practical pacifists, or fail to be so."[5]

I am afraid, however, that our interpretation of this statement differs from the interpretation which Karl Barth himself suggests. He assumes certain exceptions in extreme cases so that his rather pragmatic pacifism is a less strict attitude applicable only to the present situation but not to be generalized. Since we understand pacifism as the attitude which is the fundamental presupposition of Christian witness, we

[5] *Church Dogmatics*, IV, page 550.

cannot look to any situation in the past which either did not require this presupposition or entitled the Christian to dispense with his main task of preaching the gospel. And we cannot imagine such a situation in the future either. Therefore, the distinction can mean only that the pacifistic attitude is neither our own achievement which renders ourselves righteous nor a human device, a principle. It is to be understood as part of the human answer to God's gift, the gospel. Insofar as any human answer is incomplete, we are hesitant to call it a principle. But we do not know any answer to God's gift which does not require that we definitely dispense with preparing and waging a war and that we make peace wherever and whenever the decision is up to us.

Revolutionary Faithfulness

R. W. Tucker

R. W. Tucker's essay—which in correspondence with the editors he has described as "an agitational tract written in the theological mode"—testifies to the fact that one can adhere to the Quaker maxim "Speak the truth in love" and still employ forthright, unsettling, ungentle language. Challenging his fellow Friends to recover the revolutionary vision and discipline of their forebears, Tucker debunks much that contemporary Quakerism has come to signify, and he comes down especially hard on what he sees as its bondage to class-blindness and bourgeois conventions, admixed with a cultish, narrow kind of pacifism. What is needed, he says, is a return to Quakerism's central principle—"faithfulness, private and corporate, and its corollary, an openness to the unexpected." Needless to say, much of Tucker's indictment of the Friends has application to other religious groups. Author of the widely circulated pamphlet *The Case for Socialized Medicine*, Tucker was for several years deeply involved in the effort to enact Medicare. Now an editor in the trade journal field, he is a member of the Friends Meeting in Springfield, Pennsylvania. A slightly shorter version of his "tract" appeared in the Winter 1967–68 issue of *Quaker Religious Thought*,[*] the publication of the Quaker Theological Discussion Group.

REVOLUTION has become the world's most important social fact. In the advanced nations, revolutionary change is imposed upon us by technology, and we are profoundly unsettled. In the backward nations, the Marxists have taught millions to think of revolution as their only hope for material gain within their lifetimes. In Vietnam as in our city

* Rio Grande College, Rio Grande, Ohio 45674.

slums, dissent hardens into resistance, apocalypse is in the air. This is the environment in which official Quaker thinkers are so busily asking themselves if our faith can be made "relevant." What they really ask is whether Quakerism can be relevant to revolution.

We Quakers were born during an earlier revolution, and we were born relevant to it. That is, we were part of it.

Every great religious awakening works by revolutionizing men's hearts. But Quakerism, along with its Puritan antecedents, belonged to a more select category. Theology and exterior events were such as to turn inward energies outward and apply them to the social fabric.

The first Friends were changed men who were ardently concerned to change their world in fundamental ways. The social and doctrinal causes they thought up were extraordinarily advanced; many of them are still far from victory. Because we are loyal to one and another inherited cause, we rank today as first-rate reformers. The founders of our faith were not reformers. They were revolutionists in the sense in which that term is commonly used today. Like today's political revolutionists, they possessed revolutionary vision, revolutionary program, revolutionary discipline, and revolutionary organization.

Yet, unlike today's political revolutionists, they were not primarily political people. Their fervor was not for social change, but for faithfulness. What was revolutionary about them was their understanding of the obligations of faithfulness.

That is, it is clear what early Quaker social radicalism was not. It was not an admixture of Christian belief and radical ideology. This makes it sharply different from most current forms of Christian social radicalism.

Earlier in this century, the socialist movement in America produced revolutionists who tried to rethink their native Protestantism in the light of their Marxism. On one level this produced a rather engaging cult of "Comrade Jesus." On another level it produced the social gospel movement, which has attracted many modern Friends. Social gospel theology occupied itself in adapting Christian tradition to humanist social goals; it is being revived today within many Christian groups as they, too, look for relevance. They are right in seeing that Christians must come to terms with contemporary revolutionary ideologies. But Friends can approach this task with an enormous initial advantage, because we can start from an authentic revolutionary dynamic of our own.

This assumes, of course, that we thoroughly understand what our own tradition is. Happily, original Quaker viewpoints are again available to us through the work of Lewis Benson and other reconstructionist Quaker scholars. These men have proclaimed that early Quakerism was "prophetic, catholic, and revolutionary." They have spelled out in detail just how it was prophetic and catholic. Now let us ask just how it was revolutionary, and whether it can be revolutionary again in any way derived from the original.

It is not easy to focus upon the revolutionary aspects of early Quakerism. Because George Fox was relatively successful in his ecclesiastical and theological aims, and unsuccessful in his social aims, we naturally tend to see his program in the former terms. Lewis Benson, as a natural concomitant to knowing more about Fox than anybody, has been passionately concerned for the present-day social order throughout his adult life, to the point of initiating experiments in revolutionary Christian community. But as a writer and agitator, he is kept so busy defending his theological position that he has never had time to give adequate attention to his social position. History more largely is clouded for us, too: Friends represented, historically, a new quickening of revolutionary life within the Puritan revolution, and "Puritanism" to most of us is merely a bad word describing attitudes which were, at most, a minor element in authentic Puritanism.

Let us begin, then, by reminding ourselves that the Puritans were the bolsheviks of their time. They fought and won a long and bloody civil war. They cut off the head of a king, after holding what C. V. Wedgwood calls "history's first great show trial." They established a viable regime. They instituted new social and political and economic patterns. They worked hard to export their revolution and subvert neighboring governments. The religious historians produce long studies that barely mention these facts; likewise the political historians pay little attention to Puritan theology. But to the Puritans, politics and religion were one.

They had, like all revolutionists, an opposition on the left —people who felt they had not gone far enough in either social or ecclesiastical change; people who dissented from their subordination of means to ends. The Society of Friends arose among these opponents.

The first revolutionizing element in Puritanism was its understanding of the Christian's function in history. In those pre-Wesleyan times, Christians laid less stress on the notion that "Christ came to save sinners"; they *did* emphasize that Christ came "because God so loved the world." That meant what it said—the world as a social entity; institutions as well as individuals. Like medieval Catholics, and unlike modern American Protestants, they assumed that government should reflect religion and serve its purposes.

The great theological discovery of Puritanism, "the marrow of Puritan divinity" (as Perry Miller has labelled it), was covenant theology. God is concerned to save the world. He elects to do this by gathering a people to Himself through which to do His work of salvation. The Old Testament records his covenant with the Jews, in which He promised to be their God and they agreed to be His people. According to His grand design for human history, the old covenant with the Jews paved the way for, and was a model for, the new covenant through Christ, which superseded it. The Puritans thought of themselves as the exclusive people of God, expressly gathered for the purpose of doing His work in history.

The Puritans came out of the first generation of Englishmen to be biblically literate. They discovered covenant theology by reading Scripture in the light of Calvin's *Institutes*; it was, they insisted, plainly the theology of the writers of the New Testament, the one viewpoint that makes the entire Bible into an understandable whole. They discovered in the Bible a total blueprint for organizing church and state. They also discovered, or thought they discovered, a directive to themselves to go forth and rearrange church and state in accordance with that blueprint.

For early Friends, the revolutionary break with Puritanism came in their rejection of Calvinism. But it did not involve a rejection of covenant theology, certainly not of its political applications. If they rarely wrote about it, this is because they didn't have to; it was in the air they breathed; anyway, they were too busy writing about the things they *did* reject. One way of explaining Quakerism is to say that in the context of Puritan covenantism, the first Friends were teaching a radically new and deeper understanding of the nature of the new covenant. Christ had come to lead His people Himself. The new covenant was a living "dialogic" *relationship*.

The people of God were to be gathered into communities of discipleship; the model for any Christian community was the twelve original disciples. Like the original disciples, the community of discipleship engaged itself continually in hearing and obeying its divine leader; Christ sat at the head of Meeting. Leadership in the new covenant was prophetic, as it had been in the old covenant.

Exactly how did this set of beliefs produce revolutionary social purpose? It is instructive to make a list of specific revolutionary ingredients in original Quakerism:

1. Early Friends knew that what they were doing really mattered in world history. God does not gather a people to Himself just to have a people; history *is* God-in-history. To early Friends, *they* were the whole point of history. A belief in the importance of one's role in history is a key part of any revolutionist's make-up; it is a major ingredient in Marxism.

2. They possessed a revolutionary vision. For any revolutionary movement, the revolutionary vision is its explicit and detailed understanding of how the world could and should work. It continually produces criticisms of the existing social order. People who take up these criticisms for their own sake, however militantly they do it, are merely reformers; the revolutionist sees immediate social reform as a step toward a new order. We must take care not to see the first Friends as reformers. They started with the general Puritan vision of a new world, and drastically improved upon it; they envisioned a

Christian world radically different from the actual world; this was the source of their social creativity. Early American socialism was socially creative for a similar reason; it compares closely with early Quakerism, as a minority movement whose revolutionary vision evolved into other people's reforms.

3. Early Friends were not class-bound. They were not comfortable in their environment; they felt alienated from their society; they were outsiders. Revolutions are always made by people who at least inwardly are outsiders. After Friends became prosperous and comfortable, through some left-over revolutionary impulse, for generations we artificially maintained our sense of outsideness by practices of deliberate peculiarity. Have we abandoned plainness for the positive reasons we like to cite, or because we no longer have a sense of ourselves as creatively different?

4. Early Friends understood that revolutionists need the support of revolutionary communities. When today we read the accounts of men like James Naylor or Marmaduke Stevenson, we are struck first by their total faithfulness, second by their readiness to abandon family duties in the cause of faithfulness. These were people over 30 who yet could be trusted, because they had behind them Meetings which, in endorsing their concerns, automatically took over their private responsibilities for them.

We still produce our Stevensons, but nowadays they are highly unusual and cause controversy among us. In the beginning it was their Meetings that made them what they were. The original Friends Meeting was a community of revolutionary faithfulness, revolutionary in a collective sense even more than in its individuals. The intense corporateness of early Quakerism is its most alien characteristic to us today, yet the one perhaps most needed by Friends, because it offers so much to a world afflicted by the dissipation of community.

5. Early Friends had a revolutionary discipline, summarized in the word "faithfulness." They had a divine Leader; the whole work of their lives was to be faithful to Him; members helped one another in the task of learning and doing the things faithfulness required; corporate faithfulness made pri-

vate faithfulness easier. Discipline, that is, was understood dynamically in terms of loyalty to a leader, rather than statically in terms of obeying rules. The indiscipline so rampant among modern Friends, painful though it often is, in part represents an effort to smash outdated norms and clear the way to get back to the original sense of discipline.

6. Finally, early Friends built a revolutionary apparatus through which to do the work of overturning the old and instituting the new. Of this, more later. But it is worth noting that Quaker organization even to this day succeeds, surprisingly often, in producing and following prophetic leadership; the community is wiser and holier than the sum of its parts. Revisionist versions of Quakerism have inherited a revolutionary organizational structure that tends to push them toward stances more radical than most members want.

A sense of historical role; revolutionary vision; estrangement from the status quo; revolutionary corporateness; revolutionary apparatus and discipline—these are the ingredients that make any revolutionary movement work, whether Gandhi's in India or Castro's in Cuba. Revolutionary ideologies—violent or nonviolent, religious or secular—produce much the same sociology. This list shows that early Quakerism had a great deal in common with every other revolutionary movement. We should not fail to see it that way.

For all that, there is a fundamental difference between religiously motivated revolution, and revolution in terms of a secular ideology. This, too, we must not fail to see. The difference is eschatological. In the final analysis, Christians understand that the Kingdom comes as a gift from God, not at the end of a human struggle.

This insight has been misapplied by many Christian groups in a way that removes them from social struggle. Not so with Friends; our doctrine has always been, "the Kingdom of God is within." We are to practice "realized eschatology"— living *now* as though the Kingdom were already realized, because for us it is.

Among early Friends that meant a provocative innocency which was the life-style not only of individuals, but of Christian communities, Meetings. This was the immediate cause of their tension with the world around them. It also defines the methodological differences between early Friends and other revolutionists: They didn't just envision an ideal social order; so far as the world let them, they *lived* it. This was their mode of social confrontation. Marxists, like all politicians, are eternally calculating the effects of their actions. Early Friends were deeply interested in effects, but they sought first the Kingdom.

As we examine contemporary revolutionary ideologies, we must hold clearly in mind both the many points they have in common with early Quakerism, and this key point of difference.

The Lessons of Marxism

With contrite hearts we must acknowledge that Marxist successes are a measure of Christian failure. If the churches of Europe had been less committed, a century ago, to property and the status quo, they might have responded to the urgent need for distributive justice, and Marxism might never have arisen.

On this particular point Friends threw away their chance for relevance. "The trimmings of the vain world would clothe the naked one," said William Penn; and for generations, long before Thorstein Veblen, Friends wore plain dress first of all as a testimony against conspicuous consumption. We saw early that social and economic inequities are the wellspring of vanity. This is to our credit. But we applied this insight only in terms of private witness, when what was also needed was political organizing.

For Friends, of course, insights so advanced did not flow from rigorous development of ideological presuppositions, but from lives lived obediently, in the Power that brings the world under judgment. The fact remains that our insights were badly needed by the world, and after our first generation we treated them as private property. We retained our revolutionary vision, but we lost heart for the actual work of revolution.

There are many other Marxist insights that parallel Quaker thinking and condemn Quaker behavior. As a conspicuous current example, it is the Marxist intellectuals who worry themselves sick about mass culture and what it's doing to people. This corresponds to the traditional Friendly concern about worldliness. Revolutionary Quakerism should be busy updating its tradition on worldliness to a meaningful testimony on mass culture. Instead we are quietly abandoning our ancient witness to an inner-directed cultural life. We become indistinguishable from the world's people not only in our dress and speech, which hardly matters—but also in our television-watching and in our politics, which matters a lot.

This parallelism of social insight suggests a fascinating vision of what might have been. Rufus Jones and his successors "modernized" the Quaker social vision by making it coterminous with ideological pacifism, which was then in very primitive form. A generation or so earlier, they might just as readily, and just as legitimately, have turned instead to early Marxism. Had they done so, it would be the job of this essay to debunk Marxism, and to urge the lessons of pacifism, instead of vice versa.

Coming to terms with Marxism means coming to terms with humanism, since Marxism is humanism in revolutionary guise. "Man is the measure of all things" is a phrase the Marxists have borrowed from Protagoras. They interpret it to mean that the purpose of revolution is to put man in control of his own fate. It is impossible to overstate how basic this concept is to Marxist thinking.

An example may help. Marxism's labor theory of value starts as a moral assertion: The very economy can and should be organized around the belief that human ingenuity and human labor are the most valuable things there are; the value of every commodity is to be reckoned in terms of the human effort that went into its designing, its manufacture, its marketing. Thus man is to be the measure of all things in the most literal sense.

Christians must say "Yes, and no" to this sort of humanist concern. Man is *not* the measure of all things. *Sanctified* man is the measure of all things. That is, Christ is the measure. And it is Christ whom we seek to put in control of our fate.

But Christ said, "So far as ye have done it unto the least of these, ye have done it unto me." The second great commandment, to love one another, is, He said, "like unto" the first, to love God. Loving God entails loving people; inwardly it is the same process. So the Christian fully shares the humanist's concern for the condition of man. Indeed, his concern is more radical and his vision brighter, because it is Christ who defines his hope for all men.

In practice, Christianity has responded to humanism either with blind hostility, or, among Christian "liberals," by swallowing it whole. Social gospel Christianity, for instance, agrees with humanism in treating the human social struggle as an end in itself. Revolutionary Quakerism must respond instead with extensive agreement coupled with friendly criticism from the left. Our attitude must be, "You're right as far as you go, but you don't go far enough."

The real problem facing us all is not to oppose the humanist vision, in which man is the measure of all things, with the vision of a nobler world in which Christ is the measure of all things—but the prior difficulty of undoing a world in which things are the measure of man. Focussing on this, we are set free to put the so-called humanist challenge to Christianity in proper perspective, as a quarrel over theory among people who are allies in practice. It is an important quarrel, but in many ways it need not be a divisive one.

Few revolutionary movements have been as self-analytical as Marxism. What it has learned about itself may be applied broadly to Christianity viewed as a revolutionary movement.

Historically, Marxists have perverted their own principles in three different ways, which they label "utopianism," "reformism," and "bolshevism."

The utopian goes apart from the world to build his own revolutionary community. The reformist lowers his sights in the interest of immediate minor reform in his own lifetime, and lapses into liberalism. The bolshevik accepts any means to achieve his revolutionary end, so of course ends up with something quite different from the ideal social order originally envisioned. All three suffer from the same disease —impatience.

All three patterns may readily be found in Christian history. In fact, most Christians, like most Marxists, have ended up on one or another of these three sidetracks.

The problem is that people cannot readily reconcile themselves to a role of eternal struggle for goals eternally unreached. Yet this is precisely what is required. Even for the Marxist, a mature understanding must teach that perfection recedes infinitely—if you create the society you thought you wanted, by then you will see a need for still further change. For Christians the theoretical social goal is nothing less than universal sainthood and a social order that reflects, serves, and nurtures it. This goal is so lofty that it may never exist except in the Christian imagination as a standard by which to measure reality. It imposes upon Christianity a doctrine of permanent revolution.

The Christian, then, must reconcile himself to a revolutionary role that may bear no visible fruit at all in his lifetime. He must understand the need for constant revision of proximate goals. Somehow he must also maintain his revolutionary fervor. It is an extremely difficult balance to maintain.

Yet here is where the Christian revolutionist has an enormous advantage over the Marxist. He has already learned to live with receding perfection in his inward life; it is our common experience that the nearer we get to holiness, the more acute our awareness of how far we yet must go. And on the social plane, Christians are concerned for revolution as an aspect of their concern for inward spiritual revolution. Their inward satisfaction comes from being faithful, only secondarily from success in the outward goals that faithfulness directs them to labor for. The Marxist has only his outward success to sustain him; frustration in worldly goals is far more painful to him than to the Christian. No doubt revolutionary movements are inherently unstable, but the Christian revolution is markedly less so than the Marxist.

Most people do not think of history as something they need to have an attitude toward. Marxists do. They see history as process. Changes are taking place; they can be analyzed. The *method* of the revolutionist is to work in terms of historic trends, and bend them to his purpose.

Thus early Marxists saw labor unions as an instrument of the new class of industrial workers that history was bringing into being. The function of unions was to express the aspirations of the dispossessed. Therefore Marxists were active from the start in organizing unions and in bending them to explicit revolutionary purpose. Today the civil rights movement is seen as another potential vehicle for revolution, for the same reason. The Marxist, in short, studies history to find the motors that may get revolution moving.

Marxism is commonly misunderstood as seeking to collectivize mankind. It does not. Rather, Marxist analysis of economic history leads to the conclusion that collectivization is taking place willy-nilly, as a byproduct of an integrating economy. The Marxists then tackle the question of how to rationalize the process into community and brotherhood. Again, Marxism does not think of itself as favoring the bureaucratization of mankind. Rather, it concludes that huge bureaucracies are necessary for modern government and modern corporations and, indeed, for modern living standards. Then it tackles the question of how to return to people some measure of control over the decisions that affect our lives. Pacifists, Friends, and other well-intentioned people resist the assumption that collectivism and bureaucracy are inevitable, since both of these are rather unpleasant things; and therefore we are not equipped to influence their evolution, which is a principle reason why they are unpleasant things. The moral here is that relevance begins with the capacity to see reality as it is, even when we don't like it.

Reconstructionist Quaker thinkers stress the need for Friends to see history as drama, the eternal drama of God's way with man. God works constantly in history; He raises up prophets; He gathers a people to Himself.

What is hard to understand is the belief of some of these Friends that this view of history and the Marxist view are incompatible. Cannot the divine drama take place within a human history that is in process? The Marxist view of history is not necessarily a dogma; it is an analytical tool, a guide to action; anyone can use it. Granted, prophetic witness is motivated by inward urgency, not by analysis of social process. Granted, the Lord may use His prophets to produce changes that the Marxists can prove are not yet possible. Yet at the same time, an awareness of social process may help the witnessing Christian apply his witness more effectively. It may help him see the need for witness in the first place. We are not so rich in our understanding of the world we would be relevant to, as to be able to throw away any tool that may increase our understanding.

Finally, Friends need to understand something of the Marxist view of class.

A few years back, a Quaker committee rejected a manuscript on the dilemmas of middle-class pacifism, on grounds that "class" is an un-Friendly concept. One is obliged to reply (echoing Galileo): *Nevertheless, class exists.* It's even mentioned in the Seventh (Philadelphia) Query. High-minded religious people cannot wish it out of existence. The very desire to do so is itself a class phenomenon, as any Marxist can easily explain. People who are dispossessed do not need to be taught about class; only the comfortable and self-satisfied can ignore it.

Marxists define class economically; it is a function of one's relationship to the means of production. They have discovered that people who own a part of the economy, or have economic reason for identifying with the owning class, are inclined to see the world in a different way from those who are alienated from ownership. They see the world as manipulable, themselves as capable of individual influence. Nonowners see their world as hostile and themselves as impotent, except when they can be educated and led (by Marxists) to act collectively as a class.

Moreover, to justify their position, the upper classes are obliged to think of the lower classes as less than fully human. They end by making themselves unable to identify with the viewpoint of the dispossessed.

Christians, of course, have always understood hard-heartedness. They have always striven to open their hearts to the condition of all other men. This is the basic radicalizing element in Christianity.

But opening one's heart to the condition of others is not easy. Here is where the Marxist insights about class are helpful. They show us how our attitudes are hard-hearted, rooted in self-interest, where we may not be aware of it. Middle-class people grow up class-blind, but class-blindness is one of the few traits people can surmount by thinking about it. Marxism itself proves this; its leadership has come mainly from the upper classes.

Surmounting class-blindness is Quakerism's most urgent need today. Especially in Britain and the eastern United States, the Society of Friends is almost exclusively a middle-class organization, with disastrous effects upon its inner life and social potential.

Anarchic individualism, the characteristic that most separates us from our forefathers, is a class trait by Marxist analysis. The first Friends developed a tightly disciplined collective radicalism, but as we became more prosperous, we developed bourgeois beliefs in individual significance, until finally discipline collapsed and we started going off in all directions at once in both theological and social witness.

Working-class people just don't feel comfortable in most Friends Meetings, because of the kind of people we are. We export service to the slums, but, virtually alone among Christian bodies in America today, we offer no ministry there at all. Our Meetings there are declining Meetings, peopled by non-residents. Other Christian bodies have found new congregations when their neighborhoods ran down, deepening their vision and broadening their horizons along the way. We, to our shame, instead have developed subterranean elitist theories about ourselves.

Thus there is a widespread view that Quakerism is a "special" faith for "spiritual aristocrats," and not for the ordinary run of people. Yet original Quakerism was emphatically a movement of farmers, workingmen, and artisans. We honor the memory of martyrs who were employed as menial servants, whom we would not know how to welcome in our Meetings today.

Thus there is a general opinion that Quaker worship is too sophisticated for children, who should instead go to First-day schools. Yet children went to Meeting for 250 years; this was how they grew up to know about their faith. In one early Meeting, when all the adults were jailed, the children maintained public worship. In the unlikely event that any modern Meeting should be that faithful, could it possibly rely upon its children to keep things going? Children tend to be what we expect them to be—and we expect them to be something that makes us feel our worship is superior, something that excuses us from the need to widen our class basis.

The Cult of Nonviolence

The class character of Quakerism explains the peculiar nature of our pacifism these days. Our revolutionary inheritance, our truer instinct, leads us to seek out a revolutionary viewpoint. Yet we are estranged from our own revolutionary origin, even as we are influenced by it. Rampant individualism has reduced our sense of corporateness, leaving us free to look outside our own inheritance. So we discover a secular ideological system, pacifism, and make it one of our norms. Pacifism can be radical and sometimes revolutionary—but to a large extent we are capable of using it only in its nonrevolutionary and middle-class variant. That is, we use it cultishly.

Cultishness is the first and most conspicuous face of Quaker pacifism today. A prospective new Friend is likely to meet Quaker pacifism first in the shape of the dear old lady who rises in Meeting for Worship to speak to the children about why they ought to be pacifists. She tells homely little stories about pacifists who won through to victory in some worldly dilemma.

Such cult pacifism is pretty easy to debunk. It is false doctrine in obvious ways. It discounts the Cross, and the whole bloody history of martyrdom. Pacifist behavior may lead to great suffering and total worldly failure. Even when it does work as a tactic, religious people are not pacifists for that reason. Sophisticated pacifists are, of course, often the first to point this out. Still, there is a sense in which any ideology can be seen most clearly in caricature. Our old lady is interesting because her cultism is so evident.

The word "cult," when used pejoratively as it is here, is meant to suggest such grouplets as the Rosicrucians in religion, or the Trotskyists in politics—cliques of initiates, adhering to an esoteric doctrine which they are forever narrowing and defining, which they think gives them a special POWER. Just as the Rosicrucians claim they have special mental powers, so many pacifists believe they have special spiritual powers; pacifism makes them permanently one-up. Like the Trotskyists they think they are a vanguard, the experts to whom the world must someday turn.

There is a valid basis for such attitudes. The methodology of nonviolence often works by one-upping those who think more conventionally. And in a world in which violence has become impossibly dangerous, nonviolence may yet become the last resort of aggressors, as Nehru foreshadowed when he nonviolently invaded Goa. The point to be emphasized is that purely as a methodology, nonviolence need not necessarily have anything to do with religion, or even with peace-seeking. It can just as readily be used for power-seeking.

This is not to suggest that the methodology, or the so-called Philosophy of Nonviolence, which is its usual ideological companion, are without value for Christian revolutionists. It is extremely helpful to have available an arsenal of techniques which offer real hope in confronting and confounding violence. Pacifist insights can be as instructive to the religious radical as Marxist insights; perhaps more so. The trouble is that middle-class, respectable, very nonrevolutionary Friends have come to equate this modern methodology with their traditional Peace Testimony, with some very strange results.

What makes a cultist is not the truth discoverable in his position, but his vulgarizing of truth. Nonrevolutionary Friends vulgarize the Philosophy of Nonviolence when they religify it and try to make it inoffensive. Likewise, if the Philosophy of Nonviolence is to be equated with a Christian

principle of loving others, then it must be defined as a vul-
garization of Christian truth.

For one thing, there is a sense in which it is unseemly to
speak of a Christian "principle" of loving others. Rather,
there is an inward experience and growth to which Christ
summons us, one of whose consequences is that we find ourselves responding lovingly to others, or at least trying to.
Christian experience may very properly be summarized into
general rules; in some measure, Jesus did so Himself; but
Friends, above all others, have always emphasized that it is
the experience that lies at the heart of Christian faith and
practice, which alone can give spiritual validity to rule-fol-
lowing by individual or community.

The Philosophy of Nonviolence begins by assuming that
love can replace violence as a practical social force. Christian
experience impels one to live as though that assumption
were valid, but we are given no assurance at all that it really
is valid. On the contrary: "As they have hated me, so will
they hate you." Quaker commitment to love as a social principle was historically a matter of faith—faith held onto sometimes desperately, in the face of overwhelming evidence that
the world does not work that way.

A Christian, as Friends have understood the word, is someone who elects *now* to live as though the world were Christian. He will remain a committed person though the heavens
fall, because his inward condition demands it of him. He
ardently hopes to end war—a political change—but he would
continue a pacifist though certain his efforts would never bear
any fruit at all. The purely secular pacifist, if such a creature
exists, starts by being concerned with consequences. He is a
pacifist because he wants to end war. His motivation is pragmatic, teleological, and political.

What happens when an act of faith is turned into a political creed? Secular pacifist ideology, so far as it *is* secular,
cannot demand that its adherents remain faithful regardless
of whether it works. So the ideologues of pacifism are obliged
to figure out a methodology which they can say will probably
work, or at least work better in the long run than any other
method of social change. Where violence seems to work—

when race riots get anti-poverty funds for urban Negro ghettoes—pacifists have to assert that their way would have worked better. Possibly they are right. But along the way, they have to make certain assumptions about human nature and human motivation—and presto! a new theology.

When Friends begin to be pacifists not out of direct faithfulness to the Lord, but out of faithfulness to an ideological system, one effect is scrupulosity, the sin of the Pharisees. Scrupulosity consists in making up a code, an "ism," and living by it instead of living in the Life. Corporately, the effect is to take our most difficult social testimony, divorce it from our other beliefs, and make it a detailed system complete in itself, with its own burden of doctrinal assumptions. We give varying degrees of allegiance to it, while still thinking we give whole-hearted allegiance to our several kinds of Quakerism.

What are some of the narrower pacifist notions which are now so often taught as part of Quaker belief? Let us start with these two:

Nonviolent principles apply equally in personal and international relationships. Cultists of nonviolence do not simply oppose war and other forms of socially organized violence. They also eschew violence on a personal level. They teach that we ought not to spank our children, or permit schoolboy fights, or give a neighbor a piece of our mind, or *ever* admit to ourselves that we may not like someone. They assume that valid conscientious objection to war presupposes these attitudes.

And: *There is no significant moral difference between the violence of policy and the violence of passion.* There is the case of the man who cold-bloodedly, as an act of will, commits himself to a course of violence, for instance by going to war. Then there is the case of someone who loses his temper for a moment, in spite of his general desire to avoid violence and to treat lovingly with the world. By any standard of reason the first (moral error) is incomparably worse than the second (moral lapse). But in practice it is the second that shocks and upsets the cultists, because it happens in front of them and because it violates middle-class behavior norms.

In almost any Friends Meeting, the mild-mannered nonpacifist is likely to be weightier than the impatient, short-tempered Friend who tries and tries to be a pacifist.

Most people believe that "It's human nature to succumb to violence now and then." Pacifists could reply, "So what? We're talking about ending war. That's a social problem, not a problem of personal ethics." Instead, they urge that human nature should not be violent. This does profound disservice to their cause. Pacifism's failure as a popular movement in America, more than anything else, is because most people just do not believe that men are good enough to be pacifists.

Granted, a Christian hopes to respond lovingly to all who come his way. He has discovered that this has something to do with his ability to worship, with his capacity to love God. He knows that hatred stultifies inward growth, so he is determined not to let it take root in him. Granted, if we never got angry, if all men were tender at all times toward others, many evils would vanish. But, assuming everybody is not that good, we can still oppose social evils. The abolition of slavery certainly did not end man's exploitation of man, nor abolish our tendency toward the sin of using one another; it was nevertheless a cause worth working for, and Friends did work for it at great cost, both personal and corporate.

Quakerism is an "optimistic" faith, in that Friends have always insisted that man *can* be good. This was the great cry of early Friends against the Calvinists. But this is not to say that men *are* good. Early Friends knew, with Fox, that there is an ocean of darkness as well as an ocean of light. To come out of the darkness into the light is a work of total regeneration. It can occur in anyone, but few *will* it.

To the degree that we become regenerate, we see that we cannot take part in war, and that the ending of war is a political change we favor. But if we tie this political demand to the insistence that all who accept it become regenerate, we subvert the political aspect of our own cause. If on the other hand our real interest is in regeneration, why not foster it in terms of all the truth we know about the inward life, and let pacifism take care of itself? "Seek first the Kingdom."

And whether teaching politics or regeneration, let us beware of embodying our teaching within a specific view of human nature. The pacifist cultist's view of human nature is probably not true, but in any event, it excludes those who cannot accept it. By committing ourselves to it, we depart from the catholicity that ought to characterize any Christian body, and condemn ourselves to sectarianism.

A related cultist dogma is this: *Communication is a warm puppy.* Pacifists are hung up on communication, to the point of often resisting verbal confrontation. All problems can be solved, they tend to insist, if only people will communicate; and we can establish communication unilaterally if we are just pacifist enough. Offensive people with obnoxious doctrines will be our friends if only we will "understand" them. Behind this attitude is an assumption produced by class-blindness: *Anglo-American middle-class nice-guyism is a universal principle of behavior.*

George Fox was not a "nice guy." He could never have been hired as a Y.M.C.A. secretary. He said to a critic, "Thou art a dog," because that was what the man needed to have said to him. Gandhi, in the same spirit, said, "You are a fool," not to a heckler, but to an admirer. There was nothing genteel in "speaking to the condition" of others, and not much that was polite. Frequently the purpose of communicating was to disturb. As for "understanding" the people they were disturbing, "that of God" in early Friends really did respond to "that of God" in others, and so they understood all too well.

In the real world, some people *are* offensive and some doctrines *are* obnoxious, and the more one understands them, the more evident this becomes. Seeing such people as sick rather than evil, or as evil because they are sick, or because they had an unfortunate childhood environment, may help us not to hate them. It may also help us see how to shake them up. It is not much use in countering their influence, except as a debater's ploy. Some pacifists are like the girl in the *New Yorker* cartoon, tied to a railroad track by a mustachioed villain and saying to him earnestly, "You're sick, Murgatroyd, and I feel sorry for you," while the train approaches around a bend.

In the real world, some people who are not offensive, and whose doctrines are not obnoxious, may have good reasons for reacting to pacifists in hostile ways. The cultists who are so dismayed by verbal confrontation also seem able to conceal from themselves how extremely provocative of violence their tactics sometimes are.

A few years ago, some pacifists organized a sit-down in front of trucks at a missile construction site. After a while, an exasperated truck driver drove over one of them and all but killed him. A cry of protest went up from pacifists in all corners of the land, which was politically the thing to do—but the burden of their cry was "unfair!" How shocked they were! Yet surely the one thing they could not legitimately say was "unfair." Their sit-down was right and good—but they did ask for what they got.

Pacifist Friends are inclined to understand nonviolence as a gimmick for making the world respond to us in a genteel way. Our shock, when the world does not respond that way, is a measure of how sheltered our lives are.

American pacifists are not numbered among that segment of the population which has learned to expect to be pushed around. Yet we have the arrogance to go to American Negroes, for instance, and instruct them in nonviolence. How we grieve when they decide, after bitter experience, that it no longer fits their needs.

American pacifists cannot speak to the condition of lower-income working-class neighborhoods, where people are not hopeless but do live on the verge of hopelessness, and life is an unending struggle to maintain order in the face of chaos. For psychological reasons as well as because of outside pressures, these people exist in a highly authoritarian environment—in the education they get, in their families, in jobs and unions, in church life and all the other forms of community available to them. They can be led by indigenous, charismatic, authoritarian leaders into insurrectionary behavior over issues that seem close to them, i.e., violent labor struggles over bread-and-butter questions. Their young men detest the army and will play the corrupt system all they can to keep from being conscripted; those who cheat the medical examiners are regarded as lucky or clever. But confronting the system head-on seems idiotic to them at best, and may arouse extreme and irrational hostility. Pacifist attitudes and especially pacifist demonstrations are a threat to them on the deepest psychological level. These are an offense against order, and seem to them less than totally necessary. And the nonauthoritarian mode of middle-class pacifism is an attack against all the defenses working-class people have erected to preserve some measure of dignity in their lives.

American pacifists seem equally unable to feel the inwardness of life among the desperate poor, those who have no grasp on hope at all. With the rest of the middle classes, we were appalled by teen-age gang violence in New York City, and applauded when the gangs were broken up. It was then, and consequently, that teen-age drug addiction in the slums reached epidemic proportions. In an environment that was sick from past violence done to those who dwell in it, the gangs had provided an instrument for social cohesion that was desperately needed. In such an environment, perhaps no response is worse than a violent response.

At any rate, we don't know, because it is not our environment. Have we the right to assume that violence can never be chosen as a course of action by a person of conscience and intelligence? To weigh our personal commitment to refuse to accept a lesser evil, against someone's belief that involvement and participation is for him a more important value? Our tolerance is curiously one-sided—we easily tolerate nonpacifism among other Friends, who are our own kind and whose backsliding is in the direction of standard middle-class patriotism, while we condemn nonpacifism in the desperate poor.

If we are going to ask the world to accept pacifism as more than an occasional tactic, then we had better find a form of pacifism that is not tied to middle-class values. When we assume that humans are good, that evil is unreal, that with love we can get our adversaries to be nice, we cannot expect to be taken seriously by those whose whole life has taught them that men are always self-serving and often cruel, and that the haves will do anything to keep down the have-nots. A class-limited pacifism is incapable, by definition, of relevance in a time of revolution.

There are, of course, pacifists who understand all these things. Some of them have combined their pacifism with Marxist or anarchist insights. Some have made heroic efforts to get inside the life of the poor; the Catholic Worker movement, for example. The ideology of pacifism does offer useful insights from which Quakerism has benefited; individuals among us have adopted it in its revolutionary variant in ways that usefully force all of us to confront ourselves. But even if a secular ideology does hold the key to revolutionary relevance for the Society of Friends, it will not be this ideology, so long as its comfortable variant is so ready to hand.

The Lamb's War

According to the cultists of nonviolence, the secret of revolutionary relevance for the first Friends *was* pacifism. They teach, for instance, that the Quaker struggle for tolerance in Stuart England is a glowing early example of nonviolent tactics.

Like so many pacifist notions, this just isn't so. It assigns to early Friends an understanding of what they were doing that would not be invented for another 250 years. It puts them in a light that makes them seem attractive to twentieth-century middle-class American liberals. In fact, the first Friends were not engaged in a struggle for tolerance. They were engaged in what they called the "Lamb's War." When they filled the jails in London for openly violating the Conventicle Act, what they hoped for was the Quakerization of England. The live-and-let-live compromise of toleration was an accident, their acceptance of it a retreat.

According to Marxists, the Puritan revolution (including Quakerism) was a struggle between late feudalism and early capitalism. It succeeded because it was in tune, as its opponents were not, with the needs of its time. This may well be true as far as it goes, and it is suggestive to us in our present situation. But, equally with the pacifist view, it doesn't begin to touch the internal dynamic of early Quakerism.

The power to which the Bible and George Fox bear witness is not the power of a technique for getting people to do what we want them to do, nor is it the power of historical necessity. What they bear witness to is the power of the Cross. In very practical ways, the Cross is the most revolutionary fact in history. Relevance to it *is* relevance to revolution; this is the great lesson our forebears can teach us.

The lesson is almost inaccessible to us because we have let the Bible-thumpers spoil evangelical language for us. They use it individualistically, by teaching that the church is a by-product of personal faith. When early Friends spoke of Christ's saving grace and the need to respond to it, they meant not only that individuals should be reborn, but that Christian community should be reborn to perform a revolutionary function in history, through day-to-day immediate corporate faithfulness to its divine Leader. We cannot readily grasp this even when we try, some of us because we have adopted Protestant piety, others because we are rebelling against it.

Our problem is complicated by the fact that early Quaker thinking about community was aborted. It was not until our second generation, when ideas had already started changing, that Friends were free to come to Pennsylvania and build a social order from scratch. Even at this late date, and in spite of harassments, there were episodes that can be instructive. In the Welsh tract, for a time the Meeting organizational structure also performed judicial and governmental functions. The early Quaker vision of an ideal social order is, measurably, encysted within our organizational inheritance.

Today, with urbanization, mass culture, collectivization, bureaucratization, men become strangers to one another. The whole world longs for community. This is one of the great problems Marxism proposes to answer. Friends could make a contribution. A Meeting in the full spirit of authentic Quakerism would fully satisfy its members' need for community. It would also satisfy their need for an ideology that copes with change, and for an instrument to mold it.

Only, many of our Meetings are too large to be communities, if only for the mechanical reason that members are strangers to one another. Instead of subdividing, they turn into institutions and grow on that basis. Their unity is shallow, organizational rather than organic, founded at best on "love" in its more amorphous sense, at worst on burial-ground housekeeping. Even in small Meetings, where community is mechanically possible and often seems to exist, it is not overtly grounded in discipleship.

The Meeting structure was designed to be a flexible instrument in the hands of Christian revolutionists, and a new generation of revolutionary Friends can be expected to use it in exciting new ways. Can't a Meeting function as a housing co-op? Or a workers' co-op? A repertory theatre, perhaps? Job and neighborhood are the two areas where community is most natural, where its dissipation is most acutely felt. There is a gap here that could be filled by Meetings that are also semivoluntary communities performing an economic role. A few of our school Meetings already approximate this function.

Then there are Meetings that function as communities of concern. Jan de Hartog, in *The Hospital,* tells how the Houston Meeting for a while was organized totally around its corporate concern for a hospital, even holding its Meetings for Worship there. He also tells how this revived the Meeting and informed it with a new level of spirituality.

The number of possible concerns to serve as a focus for a Meeting is limitless. I can even envision a Meeting that is also a political club. Like a local in a radical political party, it would dispatch its members into neighborhood organizations, hold public meetings, arrange educational seminars, hire organizers, plan agitational activity. Bizarre? The original Meetings did all these things and more.

How do we get from here to there? The Marxist method is to look for tendencies toward the desired goal, and, finding them, to exacerbate them and inform them with revolutionary purpose. Are there trends within Quakerism today that potentially will free us to recover our revolutionary heritage?

Fortunately, there are. The Society of Friends is going

through a period when many of its non-basic beliefs are being shaken to their roots.

One cherished Quaker belief has been that we can bring holiness into our lives in the business world. Our prosperity and respectability as a people have been founded upon our discovery that it's good business to be a Christian businessman. Yet each year sees fewer and fewer young Friends seeking careers in the business world. There seems to be an unarticulated but growing conviction that in more and more areas of business life, it's no longer possible to be both a good Christian and a good businessman.

We have taught that the retailer must sell in a spirit of concern for his customer. But in a time of mass merchandising, the good salesman is the man who can move customers "up the line" from the advertised price leader to the higher-priced, more profitable merchandise. In many fields the retailer who scruples at victimizing the poor may shortly go out of business. We have maintained that the Christian businessman is "prompt in the payment of debts." But today in America the sharp businessman pays his debts as late as he can, so he can have the use of the money. Businessmen who refuse to play this game suffer competitively for their refusal. We have proclaimed the virtues of thrift and frugality, but most businessmen find it is bad business to practice either, and worse business if one's customers practice these ancient Protestant virtues. The small businessman, in short, must more and more weigh principle against competitive advantage. And of course, more and more of our commerce and manufacture is in the hands not of small businessmen, but of giant corporations; the Friend who works for them finds his ethical decisions have been made for him.

It is time we started generalizing from this situation. In the United States today, "affluence" depends on the manipulation of consent, the consent of human beings to pink telephones and electric manicures and other things commercially profitable, rather than to what is socially needed. We have created a new category of poor, people impoverished by lack of sales resistance; this is the proper significance of Cadillacs in Harlem. All these things the Marxists have been saying for some time. Can't the Quaker businessman say them with equal fervor?

It is leftists who have insisted that men are not things to be used by the hucksters, and have tried to organize consumer resistance. It is Marxists who have understood that advertising, as it is now generally practiced, is of itself an evil. And what have the Christians done? They have used huckster methods themselves, with ads about putting Christ back in Christmas, about how the family that prays together stays together. Friends, to our credit, instinctively avoid sloganistic religion (though partly for snob reasons). We believe "that of God" in one man can speak to "that of God" in another— can we adapt this principle to modern tasks of commercial and political persuasion? Have we really tried? We have a strong consumer testimony on funerals, but we have not expanded it into an understanding that one function of the Christian community is to act generally as an organizing center for consumer rebellion.

Here are major areas of life in which Friends have strong traditional positions, which events are asking us to reexamine. By doing so we may take a large step toward revolutionary relevance.

Another cherished Quaker belief is that the dissenter is the best citizen of all. This notion, too, is quietly fading. Quaker bodies recently have not felt it necessary to proclaim their patriotism in the process of declaring their dissent. We are not as sanctimonious these days in our conscientious objection as we used to be. Many of us have reached the point of advocating draft-dodging. That is, we maintain our ancient witness against war, but we also acknowledge that opposition to the Vietnam war in any form is preferable to non-opposition, and deserves our encouragement.

A number of Yearly Meetings are sending money through Canada illegally to help both sides in the Vietnam war. This is in our full tradition; we have always tried to act as neutrals and reconcilers. What is not at all traditional is the readiness of many Friends to admit that their attitudes are treasonable. We are so alienated from our government that increasingly we feel "treason" is an honorable word.

We seem to have concluded that we can no longer realistically hope to influence government by love and by Friendly persuasion. So in all types of dissent, many Friends turn more and more to civil disobedience. The theory here is that if social dislocation through protest can make the power structure uncomfortable enough, the power structure may make changes in order to regain its comfort. This is an outrightly revolutionary theory.

In short, events are more and more forcing us to think of ourselves as outsiders. Our social posture becomes steadily more radical. We lose members who are not ready to go along with this, but find a new constituency among concerned radical young people who feel a need for faith and religious fellowship. This change in membership makes it easier for us to assume a yet more radical posture, and so forth around again.

The favorable response to the "Back Benchers" is symptomatic. These young Friends issued their pamphlet in some trepidation. They carefully avoided all basic questions; they say nothing of theology or politics. They still ask very unsettling questions: Is it really appropriate for Friends to be in the business of running college prep schools for the upper classes? Isn't property-holding an albatross around the neck of most Meetings? Why not discipline? Their pamphlet uncovered an underground of discontent which few had imagined existed.

There is a real possibility that we will in fact become once more revolutionary, not of our own accord but because we are forced to. This raises a question: When most of our members are conscious revolutionists, will they be revolutionists in their capacity as Friends? Or will they be revolutionists in terms of secular ideologies, who just happen to be Friends? Will we find an organic corporate relevance to revolution, or will we just be swept along?

The attitudes that gave our forebears corporate relevance are available to us today if we want to use them. We can try to direct our own future, or we can let it happen to us. It is certain to happen anyway. Those of us who believe revolutionary faithfulness can make a contribution to it had better get busy contributing.

Our annals abound with tales of blind obedience and its surprising consequences, and we still have a few ministering Friends who will sit down in midsentence if they feel the Spirit leave them. We still have a few Meetings that are communities of concern, rather than umbrellas over private concerns. We still have a few nominating committees that may say to a reluctant Friend, "We've considered this prayerfully, and we believe it is the Lord's will that thee *should* accept this appointment." But for most of us this sort of unity is unthinkable. So the faithfulness for which we strive is faithfulness to an alien cult. This is not what we were first called apart to be faithful to.

Some of us have decided we are "Protestants"—whatever that means. Some of us have decided we are "mystics"—whatever that means. Some of us put a troika at the head of Meeting: Jesus and Gandhi and Buddha. Some of us are reduced to sensationalism. Thus, we are fond of a saccharine painting, "The Presence in the Midst," in which an effeminate and Aryan Christ in a nightgown appears in Meeting. Significantly, His portrayed function is not to lead Friends, but to bless them and make them feel good.

Once we offered the world a revolutionary vision. Now we offer it a tactic for solving one of its problems, a tactic that often doesn't work. Once we thought of ourselves as a people of God. Now, in Lewis Benson's phrase, "the rich suburban Friends Meeting has become merely a form of do-it-yourself Protestantism." Once we yearned to serve the Lord. Now we conform ourselves to a Philosophy of Nonviolence. Once our purpose was to be the sort of people who love other people. Now we aim to apply creative nonviolence to conflict situations.

The first Friends stormed the Kingdom as though it were the Bastille. New Christian behavioral patterns, new social and political and economic insights were spun off as a by-product. A new Quaker movement in the same spirit would of course be pacifist, but pacifism would not be the highest principle to which everything else had to be subordinated, any more than it was to our forebears. The central principle was and should be faithfulness, private and corporate, and its corollary, an openness to the unexpected.

The central *social* principle would be the principle of revolution: that is, a radical apprehension of how minimally Christian the present social order is, and how urgently it needs to be revised. Such an apprehension is fully available to us now, through many routes. We can learn that revolution is the most important social reality in the world today, and ponder the need for Quaker relevance. We can acknowledge that the original Quaker revolution has never been finished. We can perceive the glaring contrast between the world around us and the world a Christian vision makes imaginable.

All this will come readily to us as we learn that true discipleship means following Christ all the way to the Cross. It means inwardly shouldering all ills and all oppressions, as He did; getting under the weight of them, learning their agony—and acting accordingly. This is the only way of sensitizing ourselves to joy. Christ's Cross is Christ's path, and ours, to Christ's crown.

Under the revolutionary burden of the Cross, we may once again declare the Lamb's War, and set forth to wage it with all we are.

Vietnam: Crisis of Conscience

Robert McAfee Brown

Robert McAfee Brown has been in the forefront of the opposition to the war in Vietnam. Convinced that such opposition is a matter of utmost moral urgency, he has taken part
in peace demonstrations, he has counseled young draft
resisters, he has served as a leader in the organization known
as Clergy and Laymen Concerned About Vietnam, he has lent
his pen and his voice to the end-the-war cause. Yet strong
though his stand has been, it is notably devoid of ill temper
and self-righteousness. He does not hurl epithets at the policy
makers; he recognizes the complicity of us all. In particular
he believes that the churches and synagogues have been dere-
lict in their duty of sensitizing the nation's conscience, and
that they bear a heavy burden of responsibility for the
calamitous course of events. In this article—taken from a
talk given at St. Leo's Church (Roman Catholic) in St. Paul,
Minnesota, and later published in *The Catholic World* (October 1967)*—Dr. Brown spells out what he sees as the primary obligations of the religious communities in relation to
the Vietnam conflict. Well known as an ecumenical theologian, Dr. Brown is Professor of Religion at Stanford University. He is the author of such books as *The Ecumenical
Revolution, The Spirit of Protestantism,* and *Observer in
Rome: A Protestant Report on the Vatican Council.* And he
is joint author—with Abraham J. Heschel and Michael
Novak—of a book which bears the same title as his article
herein.

WE have just engaged in a number of liturgical
acts—singing, praying, listening to Scripture. The root meaning of liturgy is, of course, much wider. Coming from *laos*

* Harristown Rd., Glen Rock, N.J. 07452.

and *ergos*, it means "the people's work," whatever people do. With the passage of time, the word was narrowed in its meaning to come to mean mainly what people do in church, but that is not a full enough meaning of liturgy. Prayer is liturgy, but so is politics. Writing a congressman is a liturgical act. At this moment our act of liturgy is a consideration of Vietnam before the tribunal of conscience and before the throne of God.

On such issues as Vietnam, it is also very important that we act together and in concert with all men of goodwill; otherwise, our small voices will be both divided and frivolous. As Protestants, Catholics, Jews and men of goodwill, we disagree about many things. Jews and Christians differ in their assessment of Jesus of Nazareth, but we do not differ in our belief that all Vietnamese are children of God. Protestants and Catholics differ on the dogma of the Assumption, but they do not differ on the dogma that it is wrong to kill civilians.

It is a particular source of gratification to me to be speaking here in the Archdiocese of Saint Paul, and I regret particularly that Bishop Shannon is not here today, for as some of you may know, he and I have recently become what might be called pen-pals. We have disagreed about style, but not about concern. In a time when relatively few voices from the Roman Catholic hierarchy have spoken directly on Vietnam, he has. When Christians and Jews gathered from all over the country a few years ago for the memorial service for James Reeb in Selma, Alabama, Bishop Shannon was there. He represents the type of concern with which I hope all of us in the religious communities can align ourselves.

We do not have a very good record on that type of concern. I am haunted by the realization that as later generations look back on the late 1960's, they are going to ask, "As the war was escalating, as civilian casualties were mounting, as the right of dissent was being stifled, as the world was moving perilously close to World War III, where was your voice, why did you not speak up?" I see the very fearful parallels to the situation in the fact that in Germany, in the thirties, the churches did not speak up until it was too late, that in the United States in the late fifties and early sixties, the churches did not speak up on civil rights until the eleventh hour. The question is not, what right have we to be speaking, but what right have we to be silent.

There have been, then, three paramount evils in our day—totalitarianism, racism, and war. And we are in danger of being judged for not having come to terms adequately with any of them. Many of us, I am sure, have been confused. We have not felt that we knew enough to take a stand, and we have found other issues to occupy our attention so that we could avoid the issue of Vietnam. I, myself, felt this way for a long time. The issue seemed too perplexing, too difficult to fathom. There was too much one had to learn to have a judgment. For me the tipping point came in the first Fulbright hearings over a year ago, when I, who had been content to leave the matter to experts, discovered that the experts disagreed, that one could have all the expertise imaginable about Southeast Asia, and still dissent vigorously from our administration policy. I saw that those who had the facts could come to very different conclusions about them, and that it was the job of all of us to become as informed as we could and add our voices to the public discussion, insisting that those who were expert enlighten us where we were wrong, and reinforce us in our concerns where we were right. This is the kind of debate and discussion that must now continue at an infinitely accelerated pace.

Let me make one more introductory but basic comment. It is not my intention to suggest that our government is engaged in a massive conspiracy to involve us ever more deeply in Vietnam. I see nothing to be gained in the public debate by the kind of stridency that merely calls our policy makers evil men. I think it is clear that we have stumbled into this war step by step; we have made, over the course of a number of years, small mistakes, small miscalculations, that have gradually trapped us in a situation that is increasingly difficult to justify—politically, tactically, morally, and even militarily. In this situation we are now, in fact, doing many evil things. We are not excused from that fact because the other side is doing evil things as well, unless we succumb to the proposition that we are entitled to be exactly like the enemy from whom we claim we are liberating the Vietnamese. For example, it is clear that there has been torture of prisoners on *both* sides. That this has been done by the Vietcong, however, does not justify our doing it. We must insist that our nation is morally accountable, and morally concerned people must say so. And we must speak and do something about our concern, even at the risk of unpopularity.

It is against this background that I will highlight what seem to me issues that make Vietnam a crisis of conscience, particularly for those of us in the churches and synagogues.

I

First, I think the churches and synagogues have an un-equivocal obligation to maintain the right to dissent. A few weeks ago, I would have assumed that this right was pretty well built into the fabric of American life—but now I think it must be an immediate concern. We are living in the wake of General Westmoreland's speech to the effect that those who object to our policy in Vietnam must bear the responsibility for lengthening the war, aiding the enemy, costing the lives of Americans, and following a pro-Communist line. It seems to me that the only conclusion to be drawn from this line of reasoning is that we must be silent and give our support to anything our country decides to do.

We must emphatically reject this conclusion and the premise upon which it is based. For, whether spoken or merely implied, it is finally an act of idolatry. It is what in biblical terms is called the worship of a false god. Its most blatant expression is the phrase "My country, right or wrong." To the Jewish and Christian community, such a statement, whether on the lips of a churchman or a statesman, is a blasphemy. But it expresses a sentiment that seems to be growing in this country. One detects it on the lips of those in the highest places in our government and finds it most tragically after the sentence which always begins, "I believe in the right to dissent, but. . . ." And what follows the "but" increasingly obliterates what precedes it.

Simply from the point of view of the meaning of democracy, this is a travesty of the democratic process. Dissent is the lifeblood of democracy, and the attempt to stifle it is the most important step on the road to totalitarianism. But we of the churches and synagogues have a further responsibility, for we affirm the right of dissent not merely in terms of a belief in the democratic process, but in terms of the God we worship. The point is put with utter clarity and succinctness in the Old Testament in the first commandment, when Yaweh says, "You shall have no other gods before me," and in our day the "god" that most threatens to usurp the loyalty of the one true God is the god of the nation. In terms of the Jewish heritage we all share and from which we all come, we are never entitled to put anything finally above our loyalty to God. It cannot be country, it cannot be political party, it cannot be ideology. The New Testament makes the point with the same succinctness and clarity. The disciples are told that they are to stop preaching all this nonsense that has galvanized them into action in the early Christian community. And when they are told that they must keep silent, Peter, speaking for the disciples, responds, "We must obey God rather than men." Hopefully, most of the things we do as citizens, our obedience to men, our obedience to the state, can also be obedience to God. But if a time comes in the life of the individual Jew or Christian when there is a conflict between these two loyalties, the choice he must make is crystal clear. Our ultimate loyalty can never be to nation—it must be to God. And for many of us, the more the moral horror of the war increases, the more imperative it will be to speak the word of dissent.

II

There is a second area in which the churches and synagogues have a particular obligation. It is to defend the right of conscientious objection to this war. We in the religious community are those who over the centuries have tried to instill in men the recognition that they are ultimately accountable before God and must be willing to pay the price of that accountability. It is not appropriate for us to begin to modify this imperative to say to people, "Follow your conscience except when it goes against majority opinion." Indeed, conscience is most important, most sacred, precisely when it represents a minority viewpoint, precisely when it is being used as a leavening action by God in the life of the community to force uncomfortable questions. So, we in the churches and synagogues are called upon not only to defend the expression of conscience, the right of dissent, but also to see to it that our country protects the rights of conscience.

There are two important obligations in this area that we must make our special responsibilities. The first is to take more seriously our obligation to provide legal and moral and spiritual support for the young man facing military service who has decided that in conscience he cannot kill his fellowman. If his objection is genuine, there are procedures to protect that right, and we must always see that it is protected, whether we agree with his particular expression of conscientious concern or not. We must see that he is given the alternative of serving his country in a way that is conscientiously acceptable to him and to his draft board.

But I think that the time has come to go beyond that into a second area of support of conscientious objection. There is arising in our land a group of young men who are not able in good conscience to answer affirmatively the question on the draft board statement: "Are you opposed to participation in war in any form?" They are committed to the fact that they cannot participate in this particular war. But they cannot in conscience say that they might not at some time in the future participate in another war, or that they might not in conscience have participated in some war in the past. The issue they face is not war in general; it is the war in Vietnam. At the moment those who take this position in integrity really have only three choices: perjury, Canada, or jail. The present law discriminates against all but the absolute pacifist, and the Jewish and Christian heritage in the field of ethical teaching has always dealt not just with generalities or principles, but with specifics. There has been for at least fifteen hundred years in Roman Catholic moral teaching what has been called the theory of the just war. Certain wars have been held to meet the criteria of just wars—others have not. In other words, there has been a principle of discrimination, of selectivity, in Roman Catholic teaching on this point. Furthermore, in terms of what has happened since the beginning of the atomic era, it is very hard in terms of traditional criteria to justify many of the things we are doing in Vietnam. The Holy Father himself has shown this kind of concern. In an encyclical issued last fall, he made it clear that he was dealing not with war in general, but with this particular war, the war that is being waged in Southeast Asia, and he urged men to bring this particular war to an end. "In the name of the Lord," he said, "we cry out to them to stop. Men must come together and get down to sincere negotiations. Things must be settled now even at the cost of some loss or inconvenience, for later they may have to be settled at the cost of intense harm and enormous slaughter that cannot even now be imagined."

III

A third area in which the churches and synagogues have a particular obligation is to continue to point out what the war is doing to us. We are all familiar with the overt horrors of what is happening to people in Vietnamese jungles. But along with that is the more covert and subtle horror of what is happening to us at home. There is an increasing insensitivity to the fact that as a nation, even as individuals, we are losing any sense of constraint in the way in which this war is being waged. And I think it is a point about which we as the religious community must increasingly try to disturb the nation. Until rather recently we talked about a negotiated peace —we seem now to be talking almost exclusively about military victory. Our policy is now, in the words of one of our generals, to keep bleeding the enemy until they are forced to their knees.

Let me give a couple of other examples of this escalation

of moral numbness. The first one is susceptible to misinterpretation, and I want to make clear what I do and do not mean. In World War II we learned that the Nazis had attacked civilian strongholds, killed civilians, leveled towns to the ground, deported civilians, and destroyed fields in what was called a "scorched earth" policy. Many will remember the sense of moral repulsion with which we learned about these things. They will remember that in the Nuremburg trials we condemned individual leaders for their part in such crimes. And yet, when we look at Vietnam, we find the same kinds of things being done there. We are attacking civilian strongholds, killing civilians, leveling civilian towns, deporting inhabitants, and destroying the fields around the villages. We do not call it a scorched earth policy—we call it Operation Cedar Falls. I am *not* saying that our soldiers are like Nazi soldiers. I *am* saying that twenty years ago there was activity that repulsed us morally when it was done by someone else, but does not repulse us now when it is being done by us. It is a frightening experience to read even the criteria by which judgments were made at the Nuremburg trials, and discover that this is the kind of thing for which individual Germans were held to account by us: "The following acts or any of them are crimes coming within the jurisdiction of the tribunal for which there shall be individual responsibility—ill treatment of civilian populations, murder or ill treatment of prisoners of war, wanton destruction of cities, towns or villages, inhuman acts committed against any civilian population." One trembles to think what would be the judgment against our nation if those criteria were to be applied against us at some time after the end of the Vietnam war.

Another area where we seem to be increasingly numb is the growing rate of civilian deaths. A recent issue of the *Saturday Evening Post*, which I cite because it can hardly be written off as a radical left-wing journal, reported that at least a million children had been injured since this war began, and that 250,000 children had been killed. Now suppose one were to say that is a tremendous exaggeration. Suppose the figures were ten times too high, and one could take comfort in the fact that instead of 250,000 children killed, there had only been 25,000. The fact that one can even conceive of saying "only 25,000 children killed" is an indication that we have come to take for granted things that should shock us almost beyond belief. There is a need in this kind of situation then—when things are happening which are destroying our capacity to make moral judgments—for reiteration of what in the calmest terms can be called the principle of constraint. And it is surely a task of the religious communities to keep pressing this point. We cannot allow ourselves to keep drifting in a direction in which we are more and more willing to say that anything goes in this situation—whatever will end the war is all right. From this perspective, human life becomes cheaper and cheaper, as the stakes in victory get higher and higher.

This principle of constraint cannot be abandoned by our nation without our becoming so brutalized in the process that there will be nothing worth salvaging from a war won in such a dehumanizing fashion. There are many lines on which one can try to clarify certain types of actions within this war. Let me just quote from a letter that was sent over the names of 8,000 Roman Catholic laymen and clergymen, among whom Bishop Shannon was one of the signers. In addition to other matters the letter specifically stated: "We ask you to join us in condemning emphatically and unambiguously at least the following aspects of American intervention in Vietnam: (1) indiscriminate bombing which grossly destroys any sufficient distinction between combatant and civilian; (2) the use of napalm and fragmentation bombs; (3) defoliation tactics and crop destruction which leave the countryside a ravaged wasteland; (4) the torture of prisoners in any form whatsoever." This is the kind of thing where at least certain lines must be drawn.

IV

Fourthly, the churches and synagogues have a particular responsibility to press the questions we want to avoid thinking about, and to do this in the name of fidelity to truth. Many areas in the prosecution of the war and in the official justification of our presence in Vietnam must be continually called up for reexamination. To illustrate this point I pick out an area we would rather not think about—one that I think is most sensitive and most explosive—our attitude toward communism. It is a particular task of churches and synagogues to raise this question for reexamination, because over the years we have done a tremendous amount to create a kind of hysterical anti-communism. I stress the adjective. There are many reasons why Christians and Jews should be concerned about communism, but we have contributed a note of hysteria which makes it almost impossible to talk about the problem with any semblance of a sense of reality, of dealing with facts and not simply with emotions. The presupposition we seem to accept unquestioningly is that there is a monolithic structure of worldwide communism, which is the same everywhere, and which must be opposed no matter where it crops up and with whatever means necessary. I think it is very hard to defend that thesis when one looks at the state of the world today. For in recent years this communist monolith has been crumbling into fragments. It is not a communist ideology that is holding many of these nations together—it is their sense of nationalism and their passionate commitment to their own independence. This nationalistic spirit in Vietnam makes the Vietnamese very eager to be free from dependence upon China. Recent border disputes between China and Russia make it clear that the tension between those two communist countries is close to the breaking point. Yugoslavia's freedom from a total domination by Russia is a fact that our own foreign policy has long recognized. And it is ironic that at precisely the moment when we are saying we must halt communism in Vietnam, we are forcing this crumbling monolith back into a new kind of alliance.

Now this kind of comment, of course, makes most Americans uneasy. It implies that in some parts of the world a form of communism is going to be the political and economic structure under which people will live and, indeed, will choose to live. If we are really willing to allow free elections in South Vietnam, the chances are very high that South Vietnam will go communist. If we are really willing to let the Vietcong participate in its own right in peace negotiations, it is clear that the peace treaty will contain elements favorable to that ideology. Elsewhere in the world we have come to terms with this fact, and we must be prepared for this eventuality in Vietnam or face the alternative that by sheer force of arms we are determined to impose our will upon that nation and indeed upon all that part of the world, committing ourselves to defend by force of arms, reactionary governments that have only in their favor the fact that they declare themselves to be anti-communist. If to be anti-communist means to support dictatorships and oppressive minorities whether in Southeast Asia, South America or elsewhere, then we must see that we are setting ourselves up as those who will choose the government that other people will have. And we are forgetting what I think is a tragically important fact about our world today, that the primary enemy we must contend with is not communism, but poverty.

I am saying nothing new in saying this. This is a theme found in the Vatican Council document on *The Church in the Modern World*, in the central deliberations of the World Council meetings last summer in Geneva on "The Christian and the Social and Technical Revolutions of Our Time." The real split in our world is not between communist and non-communist nations—it is between rich nations and poor nations. And as long as we throw all our energy simply into hysterical anti-communism, we increase this poverty gap and bring about with greater inevitability the sort of world revolution in which the cause of justice will be against us. So in this whole area of such fundamental questions as our attitude toward communism and the ways in which we are to deal with the needs of men in the world today, churches and synagogues have a particular responsibility to raise some of the uncomfortable questions.

V

A fifth concern that must especially weigh on the religious communities is the responsibility of forcing discussion of alternatives to our present policy. We have the obligation as citizens to be politically involved. We must avoid the notion that we can somehow provide a panacea, but we must insist that to continue to escalate does not exhaust the possibilities open to us. Here, too, I see two kinds of concerns to be faced. We must try to inject into our national discussion a willingness to follow through the consequences of our present policy of escalation. We have moved step by step from the presence of technical advisers in the south to token military presence in the south, to increasing military presence in the south without bombing the north, to increasing presence in the south combined with bombing of the north, to massive military presence in the south with increased bombing of the north, to massive military presence in the south with not only the bombing of the north but the mining of harbors and the shelling from the shore of cities and towns. We are proceeding in a direction which can only lead us day by day, stage by stage, to the point where the logic of the position will force us not only to bomb supply routes from China, but to go over the border into China to bomb nearer the source of supplies, to bomb Peking, and so forth, and somewhere along the line to decide that we must make the shift from conventional to atomic weapons. We must insist that if this policy seems only to be leading to disaster, it is imperative that discussion not cease, and that other alternatives be explored.

That, of course, is the second part of the point I am now making. There must be continued discussion of alternatives. We must not be persuaded that the only alternative is to pull out tomorrow. There are many other specific proposals in the public discussion with which we have an obligation to acquaint ourselves and force our statesmen to consider. Whatever the details, and at this point we in the churches must acknowledge our need to consult with the experts, it seems to me such things as the following must come through loudly and clearly to the rest of the world.

First, that we will take the initiative, at some risk, to give evidence of our willingness to shift from exclusively military to diplomatic action. Whether by stopping the bombing by deescalation, or other means, we must gain credibility for the notion that we are seeking other than a military victory. At the moment the rest of the world has little cause to accept that as a conviction on our part. A second assurance we must try to give is that we do not intend to use the conference table to win a victory that we have been unable to win on the battlefield. And, thirdly, we must give the world firmer reasons to believe that we will treat with utmost seriousness any attempt by agencies other than ourselves to bring about the beginnings of negotiation. There is instance after instance in which such people as U Thant have gotten preliminary discussions going and our response has been to escalate, start bombing again or mine the harbor of Haiphong, causing negotiations to be broken off. We have a very delicate and important job here convincing the rest of the world that we are genuinely willing to respond to negotiation maneuvers coming from others.

In this kind of situation, though we do not have expertise, we must insist that alternatives be explored. And we have a clear responsibility to support those who have taken stands and have really risked something to bring about a change in policy. Our task, then, within the churches and synagogues, is to create the kind of ground swell of middle opinion that must be taken seriously in Washington. Our policy makers seem to be able to write off quite easily anti-war sentiment among the far, far left, among certain pacifist groups, among the beatnik and hippie crowd. But we represent (let's face it) the American middle class. It is here that the voters are found, and it is from here that must come the kind of pressure that can make a difference.

VI

Sixthly, we of the religious communities must now be making massive preparations for the rebuilding and rehabilitation of war-ravaged areas, for years of helping to recreate where we have destroyed. It is not enough to act on the political struggle and say we prepare to rebuild when the war is over. We must be preparing to do it now. We must be gathering together the resources of our Catholic, Protestant and Jewish agencies, recruiting manpower in colleges and universities, people who will be prepared to go to Vietnam not to promote the American way of life, but simply to be available for what use they can be to the Vietnamese in whatever tasks are needed in repairing some of the damage we have done. I repeat, this must never be a substitute for current political involvement, but it must be something that goes along with it.

Finally, I want to suggest a point that I hope will not sound too hysterical. I think we must begin to face the fact that in our American life it may become increasingly difficult to speak. All the things I have suggested so far may, if the intensity and bitterness of the war increase, become avenues of expression that are cut off from us. If that day should come, what then? Do we throw in the towel and quit, do we go into hiding? No, in that situation more than ever the words must still be spoken, the body must be placed on the line of witness. Then, more than ever, we will have to say we must obey God rather than men; then, more than ever, we will have to trust that God can use even our apparent failures in the fulfillment of his purposes; then, more than ever, we must be prepared if need be to suffer and die, trusting in the God whom the Jew hears on Sinai and whom the Christian sees on Calvary, affirming that nothing can separate us from his love or release us from his demands. There is a final verse of a wonderful hymn that Roman Catholics have been helping Protestants rediscover. It describes where, if all else crumbles, we must finally be prepared to stand: "Let goods and kindred go, This mortal life also, The body they may kill, God's truth abideth still, His Kingdom is forever. Amen."

Gospel and Revolution

16 Bishops of the 3rd World[1]

Time was when bishops all too often disdained to concern themselves with social ills, and either directly or indirectly aligned themselves with the exploiters rather than with the exploited, with the privileged few rather than with the impoverished masses. Happily, that day is rapidly passing—a development to which this statement issued by a group of "Third World" bishops bears laudable witness. Declare the bishops: "Christians and their pastors should know how to recognize the hand of the Almighty in those events that from time to time put down the mighty from their thrones and raise up the humble, send away the rich empty-handed, and fill the hungry with good things." The document constitutes an impressive plea for distributive justice—a plea voiced by churchmen who live in lands where such justice is scandalously lacking. Originally published in the French journal *Témoignage Chrétien*, the document was translated by Mr.

[1] The original signatories numbered 15, but one more bishop has since signified his wish to be associated with the document. They are therefore as follows: Helder Camara, Archbishop of Récife, Brazil; John-Baptist Da Mota e Albuquerque, Archbishop of Victoria, Brazil; Luis Gonzaga Fernandes, Auxiliary of Victoria, Brazil; Georges Mercier, Bishop of Laghouat, Sahara, Algeria; Michel Darmancier, Bishop of Wallis and Futuna, Oceania; Amand Hubert, Vicar Apostolic, Heliopolis, Egypt; Angelo Cuniberti, Vicar Apostolic of Florencia, Colombia; Severino Mariano de Aguiar, Bishop of Pesqueira, Brazil; Frank Franic, Bishop of Split, Jugoslavia; Francisco Austregesilio de Mesquita, Bishop of Afogados de Ingazeira, Brazil; Gregory Haddad, Melchite Auxiliary of Beirut, Lebanon; Manuel Pereira Da Costa, Bishop of Campina Grande, Brazil; Charles Van Melckebeke, Bishop of Ning Hsia (China), Apostolic Visitor to Singapore; Antonio Batista Fragoso, Bishop of Crateus, Brazil; Stephen Loosdregt, Bishop of Vientiane, Laos; Waldyr Calheiros de Novais, Bishop of Volta Redonda, Brazil.

James Gordon for the December 1967 issue of *The New Blackfriars.**

1.   As bishops of some of the peoples who are striving to develop, we endorse the anxious appeal of Pope Paul VI in his letter *Populorum Progressio*, so as to define their duties for our priests and faithful, and to send words of encouragement to all our brothers in the Third World.

2.   As they are in this Third World, our Churches are caught up in a confrontation no longer simply of East and West, but of three great groups: the western powers which grew rich in the last century, the two Communist countries that have also become great powers, and finally the Third World, still seeking an escape from the domination of the great powers, and the freedom to develop in their own way. Within even the developed countries there are still classes, races and peoples that have not yet received their rights to a full human life. An irresistible urge is working these poorer elements towards their betterment by liberating them from all oppressive forces. Although most countries may have gained their political freedom, economic freedom is still a rarity. Few also are countries where social equality prevails, an essential condition of true brotherhood, for peace cannot exist without justice. The peoples of the Third World are the proletariat of existing humanity, exploited by the great, their very survival threatened by ones who, because they are stronger, arrogate to themselves the sole right to judge and police peoples less rich in material terms. In fact our peoples are no less wise or just than the great powers.

I. Independence in the Face of Political, Social and Economic Systems

3.   Revolutions are and have been part of the evolution of the world. Nor is this surprising. All the constitutions in force

* St. Dominic's Priory, Southhampton Rd., London N.W. 5, England.

today originated at a time more or less distant from a revolution, that is to say from a break with some system that no longer ensured the common good, and the establishment of a new order more likely to bring it about. All revolutions are not necessarily good. Some are only palace coups d'etat, and result only in a change of oppressor. Some do more harm than good "engendering new injustices . . ." (*Populorum Progressio*). Atheism and collectivism, to which some social movements have thought it necessary to commit themselves, are serious dangers to humanity. Yet history shows that some revolutions have been necessary, that they have abandoned their original opposition to religion, and have produced good fruits. There is no longer any dispute about the French Revolution of 1789, which made possible the declaration of human rights (cf. *Pacem in Terris*, 11–27). Several of our countries have had to bring about these radical reforms, and are still having to. What should the attitude of Christians and Churches be to this? Paul VI has already shown us the way in his encyclical on the progress of peoples (*Populorum Progressio*, 30–32).

4.   From the doctrinal point of view the Church knows that the Gospel demands that first fundamental revolution which is called "conversion," a complete return from sin to grace, from selfishness to love, from pride to a humble willingness to serve. This conversion is not merely internal and spiritual, it affects the whole man, his physical and social as well as his spiritual and personal being. It has a communal aspect laden with implications for all society, not only for life on earth, but more for the eternal life in Christ who, Himself raised from the earth, draws all humanity to Him. Such in the eyes of a Christian is the integral flowering of man. Besides, for twenty centuries, visibly or invisibly, within or outside the Church, the Gospel has always been the most potent ferment of deep social change.

5.   Nevertheless, throughout her historical pilgrimage on earth, the Church is in practice always tied to the political, social and economic system that in a given period ensures the common good, or at least an ordered society. So much so that sometimes the Churches may seem to be fused with

such a system, united as if in wedlock. But the Church has only one bridegroom, and that is Christ. She is in no way wedded to any system, least of all to the "international imperialism of money" (*Populorum Progressio*), any more than she once was to the monarchy and feudalism of the Ancien Régime, any more than she will be in the future to some form of socialism. A glance at history is enough to show that the Church has survived the ruin of systems that thought they had to protect her interests, or that they could make use of her. Today the social doctrine of the Church, reaffirmed at Vatican II, is already dissociating her from this imperialism of money, one of the forces to which she was for a time tied.

6. Since the Council, voices have been raised, forcefully demanding an end to this temporary collusion between the Church and money which is condemned from so many sides. Some bishops have already set the example.[2] We ourselves have a serious duty to examine our position on this question, and to free our Churches of all trace of dependence on great international finance. "You cannot serve both God and Mammon."

7. In face of the recent development of this imperialism of money, we must remind ourselves and the faithful of the warning given by the seer of Patmos to the Christians in Rome, when its fall was imminent, a great prostituted city, living in a luxury earned by the oppression of peoples and by slave traffic: "Go out from her, my people; that you be not partakers of her sins, and that you receive not of her plagues" (Apoc. 18, 4).

8. In what is permanent and essential, namely her faithfulness to and communion with Christ in the Gospel, the Church is never in the pay of political, economic or social systems. As soon as a system ceases to ensure the common good to the profit of some party involved, the Church must not merely condemn such injustice, but dissociate herself from the system of privilege, ready to collaborate with another that is better adapted to the needs of the time, and more just.

[2] Cf. *Populorum Progressio* gives the example of the late Bishop of Talca (Chili), Manuel Larrain.

II. Faithfulness to the People

9.   All of this applies to Christians as well as their leaders in the hierarchy and the Churches. We have not here abiding cities—Christ our leader willed to suffer outside the town (Heb. 13, 12, 14). Let none of us cling to our privileges and our riches, but let each stand prepared to "share what he has, for such sacrifices are pleasing to God" (Heb. 13, 16). Even if we have not succeeded in acting with goodwill and love, let us at least be able to recognize the hand of God correcting us as a father might a son in situations where this sacrifice is forced upon us (Heb. 12, 5).

10.   We do not judge or condemn any of those who believe conscientiously that they must go into exile to preserve the faith in themselves and their children. The only ones who should be strongly condemned are those who evict populations by material or spiritual oppression, or by the appropriation of their lands.

Christians and their pastors are dedicated to remaining among the people in their own country. History shows that it is seldom a good thing in the long run for a people to take refuge in exile far from their native land. It must either defend itself effectively against the alien aggressor, or else accept such reforms as are necessary. It is a mistake for Christians to cut themselves off from their country and people in the hour of trial, particularly if they are rich, and would only flee to preserve their affluence and their privileges. It is true that a family or an individual may have to emigrate to find work, in accordance with the right of emigration (cf. *Pacem in Terris*). Yet a large scale exodus of Christians could lead to crisis. It is on their own soil and among their own people that Christians are normally called to live, in solidarity with their brothers, of whatever religion, that they may be living witnesses among them to the love Christ has for all.

11.   As for us priests and bishops, our duty to remain where we are is even more pressing; for we are the representatives of the Good Shepherd who, far from fleeing like a mercenary

in the hour of danger, remains in the midst of his flock, ready to give up His life for His own (John 10, 11–18). Jesus does tell the apostles to go from town to town (Matt. 10, 23), but this is strictly in a case of personal persecution for the faith; during a war or revolution involving the people with whom the pastor feels solidarity the case is quite different. If the people itself decided to go into exile, the pastor might follow his flock. But he cannot consider only his own safety, nor seek it in the company of a few profiteers or cowards.

12. Furthermore, Christians and their pastors should know how to recognize the hand of the Almighty in those events that from time to time put down the mighty from their thrones and raise up the humble, send away the rich empty-handed, and fill the hungry with good things. Today "the world persistently and urgently demands recognition of human dignity in all its fullness, and social equality for all classes."[3] Christians and all men of goodwill cannot do otherwise than ally themselves with this movement, even if it means renouncing privilege and fortune for the good of the human community, in a greater conception of society. The Church is by no means the protectress of great properties. She insists, with John XXIII, on the sharing of property, since property has primarily a social purpose.[4] Recently Paul VI recalled St John's words: "But if any one has the world's goods and sees his brother in need, yet closes his heart against him, how does God's love abide in him?" (1 John 3, 17), and those of St Ambrose: "The earth is given to everyone, and not only to the rich" (*Populorum Progressio*, no. 23).

13. All the Fathers, of the East as well as of the West, repeat the words of the Gospel: "Share out your harvest with your brothers. Share ye our crops, which tomorrow will have rotted away. What shocking avarice for a man to leave all to mildew sooner than leave part of it to the needy! 'Whom am I wronging,' says the miser, 'in keeping what belongs to me?' Alright, but tell me, what are these goods that belong to you? Where have you got them from? You are like a person who,

[3] Patriarch Maximus at the Council, 27th October, 1964.
[4] Mater et Magistra, No. 389–391.

taking his place at the theatre, would like to stop others coming in, meaning to enjoy by himself the spectacle to which all have an equal right. This is what rich people are like: proclaiming themselves sole masters of common goods that they have monopolized, merely because they were the first to possess them. If each kept only what is required for his current needs, and left the surplus for the need, wealth and poverty would be abolished. . . . The bread you keep belongs to another who is starving, the coat that lies stolen in your chest to the naked, the shoes that rot in your house to the man who goes unshod, the money you have laid aside to the poverty-stricken. In this way you are the oppressor of as many people as you could help. . . . No, it is not your rapaciousness that is here condemned, but your refusal to share" (St. Basil, 6th Homily against wealth).

14. Taking into account certain necessities for certain material progress, the Church has for a century tolerated capitalism with its legalization of lending at interest and other practices that so little conform to the moral teaching of the prophets and the Gospels. She cannot but rejoice to see another social system appearing that is less far from that teaching. It will be the task of tomorrow's Christians to follow the initiative of Paul VI, and channel back to their true sources, which are Christian, these currents of moral strength, solidarity and brotherhood (cf. *Ecclesiam Suam*). Christians have the duty to demonstrate "that true socialism is a full Christian life that involves a just sharing of goods, and fundamental equality."[5] Far from sulking about it, let us be sure to embrace it gladly, as a form of social life better adapted to our times, more in keeping with the spirit of the Gospel. In this way we shall stop people confusing God and religion with the oppressors of the poor and of the workers, which is what the feudal, capitalist, and imperialist systems are. These inhuman systems have engendered others which, intended to liberate the peoples, in fact oppress the individual if they fall into totalitarian collectivism and religious persecution. But God and the true religion have nothing in common with the

[5] Patriarch Maximus IV at the Council, 28th September 1965.

various forms of the Mammon of Iniquity. On the contrary, they are always on the side of any who wish to promote a more equitable and fraternal society involving all God's sons in this human family.

15. The Church greets with joy and pride a new mankind that respects not money concentrated in a few hands, but the workers, the labourers, and the peasants. The Church is nothing without Him who never ceases to endow her with the power to thrive and so act, Jesus of Nazareth, who for so many years chose to work with his hands in order to reveal the outstanding dignity of workmen. "The worker is infinitely superior to any amount of money," as a bishop of the Council reminded us.[6] Another bishop from a socialist country declared: "If the workers do not achieve some measure of control of their industries, all constitutional reform will be useless. Even if the workers sometimes receive better wages under some economic system, these increases alone will not satisfy them. In fact they want to own rather than sell their labour. Today the workers are increasingly aware that work is a part of being human. But a human being cannot be bought and sold. Any trading of labour is a form of slavery. . . . This is the direction in which human society is progressing, even in a system reputedly less concerned with individual dignity than we are, namely Marxism" (F. Francic, Split, Jugoslavia, October 4th, 1965).

16. This is to say that the Church rejoices to see developing in humanity forms of social life where work finds its proper place of predominance. As arch-priest Borovoi noted at a meeting of the World Council of Churches, we have made the mistake of adapting ourselves to the pagan juridical principles inherited from ancient Rome, but alas, in this sphere the West has sinned no less than the East. "Of all the Christian cultures, the Byzantine has done most to sanction social ills. It adopted uncritically all the social heritage of the pagan world and consecrated it. The civil law of the pagan Roman Empire was preserved under a cloak of ecclesiastical tradition for many more than a thousand years at Constanti-

[6] Mgr. G. Hakim, Archbishop of Galilee, at the Council, 10th November 1964.

ople and in Medieval Europe, and in Russia in the centuries
since the period (sixteenth century) when our country began
to think of herself as the heir of Byzantium. Yet it is utterly
opposed to the social traditions of primitive Christianity and
of the Greek Fathers, to the missionary preaching of our
Saviour, and all the teaching of the Old Testament prophets
who never grow old." (World Council of Churches. July 12th,
1966. Church and Society Conference, Geneva.)

II. Faithfulness to God's Word

7.   There is no political aim of any kind behind our words.
Our only source is the Word of Him who spoke through His
prophets and apostles. The Bible, particularly the Gospels,
denounces any attack on man created in God's image as a
sin against him. Atheists today unite with believers in fulfilling this requirement of respect for the human being, working together in a common service of mankind in its search
for justice and peace. Thus we can confidently address these
words of encouragement to all men, for we all need courage
and strength if we are to perform successfully the huge and
urgent task of saving the Third World from poverty and hunger, and of freeing mankind from the catastrophe of a nuclear
war: "Never again war, away with weapons."[7]
    The poverty-stricken populations, in the midst of which the
All-merciful has placed us as pastors of a small flock, know
by experience that they can rely on themselves and their
own efforts more than on help from the rich. Some rich nations or some rich people among the nations do indeed offer a
fair measure of help to our peoples, but we should be living
in a delusion if we were to wait passively for a spontaneous
conversion of all about whom our father Abraham warns us:
"neither will they be convinced if some one should rise from
the dead" (Luke 16, 31).
    It is for the poor peoples and the poor among them to
strive for their own advancement first of all. Let them regain

[7] Paul VI at the U.N.

confidence, let them educate themselves out of illiteracy, let them persevere in building their own destiny, let them develop, using all the methods that modern society puts at their disposal, schools, transistors, newspapers: let them hear the people who can waken and form the awareness of the masses above all the words of their pastors, and let the latter give them in entirety the Word of Truth and the Gospel of Justice. Let the apostolic movements of militant laymen put into practice the exhortation of Pope Paul VI: ". . . It is for lay folk, by their free initiative, without waiting for orders and directives, to instil the Christian spirit into the mind, the customs, the laws, and the constitutions of the community they live in. Changes are necessary, deep reforms are indispensable: they must work with determination to breathe into them the evangelic spirit . . ." (*Populorum Progressio*, No 81). Finally, let the poor and those who are working for them unite, for union is the only strength of the poor, to insist on and promote justice in Truth.

18. It is indeed truth and justice for which the people are above all hungry, and all who are responsible for instructing and educating them must busy themselves about it zealously. Some false conceptions must at once be removed: it is not true that God wishes there to be rich men enjoying the good things of this world by exploiting the poor: it is not true that God wishes there to be poor people always wretched. Religion is not the opium of the people. Religion is a force that exalts the humble and casts down the mighty from their seats, that gives bread to the hungry and reduces to hunger the overeaters. Jesus certainly forewarned us that the poor would always be with us, but this is because there will always be the rich to amass the goods of this world, and also there will always be some inequalities due to varying capabilities and other unavoidable factors. But Jesus teaches us that the second commandment is equal to the first, for a man cannot love God without loving men his brothers. He warns us that all of us will be judged according to a single text: "I was hungry, and you gave me to eat . . . it was I who was hungry" (Matthew 25, 31, 46). All the great religions, all mankind's systems of wisdom echo this text. The Koran

declares the final test to which men are subject at the moment of God's Judgment: "What is this test? It is to buy back captives, to feed orphans at a time of famine . . . or the poor man sleeping on the hard ground . . . and to make for oneself a law of pity" (Sour. 90, 11–18).

19. It is our duty to share our bread and all our goods. If some claim the right to amass for themselves what is needed for others, then it becomes a duty for public authorities to enforce sharing which has not been done voluntarily. Pope Paul VI reminds us of it in his latest encyclical: "The common good, then, sometimes calls for the expropriation of certain properties that on account of their size, their small development or complete lack of it, the poverty inflicted on the population, or the considerable damage done to their country's interests, constitute an obstacle to collective prosperity. Stating it clearly, the Council reminded us no less forcibly that the available funds are not to be left to the careless whims of the individual, and that egotistical speculation must be banned. Consequently, citizens blessed with copious incomes arising from the national resources and effort cannot be allowed to transfer a large part of it abroad solely for their personal profit, careless of the manifest wrong they are inflicting on their country" (*Populorum Progressio*). Nor can rich foreigners be allowed to come for the purpose of exploiting our poverty-stricken peoples under the pretext of business or industry any more than a few rich people can be suffered to exploit their own peoples. This is what causes bitter nationalism, which is always to be deplored and which is the opposite of real collaboration between peoples.

20. What is true of individuals is also true of nations. Unfortunately, there is today no effectual world government able to enforce justice between peoples and to distribute goods justly. The economic system now in force permits rich nations to grow even richer, even when they are giving a little help to poor nations, which are growing proportionately poorer. The poor nations must, therefore, insist, using every legitimate means within their power, on establishing a world government in which all peoples without exception are represented and which can ask for, even enforce, a just sharing of

goods, a state of affairs essential for peace. (Cf. *Pacem in Terris*, No. 137; *Populorum Progressio*, 78.)

21. Even within every nation, the workers have the right and duty of forming real trade unions to insist upon and to defend their rights: fair wages, paid holidays, social security, family allowances, co-ownership . . . it is not enough for rights to be acknowledged on paper through laws. The laws must be implemented and governments must exercise their powers in this respect in the service of the workers and the poor. Governments must labour to bring to an end the class war which, contrary to what is usually maintained, has been unleashed, only too often, by the rich, who continue to wage it against the workers by exploiting them with inadequate wages and inhuman working conditions. Money has for a long time cynically waged a subversive war throughout the world, destroying entire peoples. It is high time that the poor peoples, upheld and guided by their lawful governments, should effectively defend their right to life. God did after all reveal himself to Moses, saying: "I have seen the affliction of my people who are in Egypt, and have heard their cry because of their task masters . . . and I have come down to deliver them" (Exodus 3, 7–8). Jesus in fact took upon Himself all mankind to lead it to eternal life, for which the earthly preparation is social justice, first form of brotherly love. When Christ frees mankind from death by His resurrection, He leads all human freedoms to their eternal fulfilment.

22. Thus we address to all men the Gospel words which some of us[8] addressed last year to their peoples who were subject to the same anxieties and spurred by the same hope as all the peoples of the Third World: "We urge you to remain constant and dauntless, as evangelical leaven in the workers' world, relying on the words of Christ: 'Look up and raise your heads, because your redemption is drawing near' " (Luke 21, 28).

[8] Manifesto of bishops of the North-eastern region of Brazil. Récife, 14th July 1966.

England's Troubles and the Catholic Left

Desmond Fennell

It is Desmond Fennell's contention that there are two common misconceptions about the English Catholic Left: that it is attempting an intellectual synthesis merely between Marxism and Christianity, and that it is engaged in politics as a Marxist and revolutionary force. In fact, says Fennell, its essays in intellectual synthesis have a much wider scope, and it has failed to become politically effective because of its dependence on the New Left, its defective Marxism and a Catholic inferiority complex. Fennell's piece originally appeared as an unsigned contribution to the January 1968 *Herder Correspondence.** Formerly the editor of that monthly review, Fennell is engaged in writing a book on the Irish Revolution. His published books are *Mainly in Wonder, The British Problem,* and *The Changing Face of Catholic Ireland.*

THAT the English Catholic Left is a synthesizing intellectual movement is fairly generally known. Because, however, of the stress laid by the Slant group on Marxism and the wide publicity which they achieved over a year ago as "Catholic Marxists," there is a common misconception that the intellectual synthesis being attempted by the movement as a whole is merely between Christian ideas and Marxism.

That this is far from true is made clear in a foreword by Laurence Bright of Slant to one of the latest Catholic Left books, *Man, Culture and Christianity* (London: Sheed and Ward) by a fellow Dominican, Giles Hibbert, who does not belong to Slant. Referring to the decline of empiricist philosophy, Fr. Bright says that it has been replaced in the last

* Herder and Herder, 232 Madison Ave., New York, N.Y. 10016.

few decades "by the philosophy of language (deriving from Wittgenstein) in England, and by existentialism in German and France." He then adds:

The two streams of thought have in fact much in common yet little has been done to relate them, less still to apply thei related insights in the study of theology. Interestingly, it i among Catholic theologians in England, for so long negligi ble contributors to the Christian renewal, that the work o synthesis has begun. Brian Wicker's recent *Culture and The ology* (London 1966) approached these questions from standpoint that was mainly, though not exclusively, linguistic in the present book Giles Hibbert has a more phenomeno logical and existentialist approach. The two books comple ment each other in an important sense, and furthermore i each the social-political ideas deriving from Marx and th insights given by a critical study of literary texts are also es sential elements in the synthesis.

The principal currents flowing into Catholic Left thinking ar named in these sentences. One would have to add, howeve that the "critical study of literary texts" derives a large meas ure of its method and inspiration from Prof. Leavis and tha the general approach both to Marx and to the problems o culture is very much influenced by Raymond Williams an other British New Left prototypes such as Richard Hoggar and Stuart Hall.

Obviously, such a wide field provides room for a book—o for many books—touching only in a marginal way on Marx ist theory or on the business of politics. Hibbert's is such book, and the fact is that the best work of the Catholic Lef so far has been done in the field where theology, various con temporary philosophies, liturgy and sociocultural studies con verge.

Hibbert's concern is to use the resources of experience an of various intellectual methods to achieve, and point the wa to, a Christian man's grasp on his actuality in the given cir cumstances of contemporary England and the contemporar Church. Rejecting the abstraction and fragmentation throug which modern European man, whether Christian or not, ha been led aside from a living hold on reality, he also reject

any idea of speculative synthesis, regarding it as a poor substitute for the "integration" of "diverse manifestations of
man's general sensibility" in "actual living." In this respect,
Man, Culture and Christianity is a pioneering book—in sympathy with the Catholic Left but leaving the merely synthetic
stage of the movement behind it. The author's concern for
community and spontaneity in a realized, corporeal actuality
of life is directly spurred by his consciousness of how life in
England, under the aegis of the dominant culture of Oxbridge
and London, has been starved of these elements in modern
times.

But the Catholic Left also has, in the Slant group, a front
that proclaims itself predominantly political in concern and
intent. This fact, along with its attendant publicity and propaganda, has led to a second common misunderstanding about
the English Catholic Left: it is thought to consist of, or at least
to include, a group of English Catholics actually involved in
contemporary *politics* as *revolutionaries* and as *Marxists*. On
the evidence of their writings, the Slant group would seem to
share this view, at least in regard to themselves. So the misconception, which is triple in nature, derives from a public
image (which is partly a publicity image) and from a self-deception on the part of the Slant writers—the latter feeding
the former.

It is easy enough to see how the public image has arisen
among that broad class of contemporaries who are both susceptible to image-making publicity and unable to distinguish
between "right feelings" about politics and actual involvement
in politics. Take the title and cover of Brian Wicker's latest
book, *First the Political Kingdom* (London: Sheed and
Ward).

The title, we learn from a prefatory quotation to the text,
derives from Kwame Nkrumah's dictum: "Seek ye first the
political kingdom." A subtitle reads: "A personal appraisal of
the Catholic Left in Britain." The cover picture shows a young
semitic-looking (Algerian?) guerilla carrying a gun on his
shoulder. On closer inspection, he is seen to be an Orthodox
Jew, presumably one of the irregulars who conquered the
home territory of the present state of Israel. While this iden-

tification introduces an element of moral ambiguity—for the gain perhaps of a subliminal reference to the chosen people of the Bible—the overall message of title and cover picture combined is "third-world," "violently militant," "revolutionary" and suggests both Catholic involvement in politics generally and, specifically, in the rise of foreign oppressed peoples in former colonial territories.

Now the text of the book is in fact a useful, critically committed account of the nature, genesis and development up to the present of the English Catholic Left, in which the political struggles of Africa and Asia are mentioned only once or twice in passing. Moreover, as early as p. 25, Wicker comments:

The fundamental uncertainty about immediate political policies that much New Left writing exhibits is one of the characteristic elements in the New Left that has been carried over into the thinking of the Catholic Left.

Absence from Politics

Lack of policies means absence from politics in any real meaning of the word. The fact is that an unresolved tension exists between what Wicker's text has to say and the "image" presented by title and cover picture. If this is understood, the book as a whole can be seen as a remarkably complete presentation of the Catholic Left; for the tension it materializes is the tension within the movement itself between wish and fulfilment, between dream and performance, between the desire to be effective in the concrete world-as-it-is and the sense of impotence which both prevents this and drives the desirers to seek compensation in daring scholastic word games and in lyrical descriptions of heaven; that is to say, in very traditional exercises of Catholics not really in this world.

The publicity orientation of Wicker's book was not an eccentric deviation on the publisher's part. Feeling references to Vietnam, Zambia, Algeria and the ex-colonial nations in general occur regularly in the writings and public lectures of the Slant people and their sympathizers. Some of them also give favourable mention to the Soviet Union and the East European countries, saying that, given the choice (which they have!), they would prefer to live under such regimes than in the fundamentally less free conditions of contemporary Britain. Then again, some of these Catholics quote the information offices and official publications of countries ruled by Communists, or by postcolonial regimes of the Left, with a lack of critical sense which is in fact a lack of common political sense oddly akin to the manner in which loyal Catholics before the Council regarded the Roman Curia. If Wicker's account of the Catholic Left shows scant awareness of all this, it is probably due to the sober good sense of the author who tried to keep to what he regarded as essential and real in the movement.

For clarity's sake, however, it is useful to point out that there is no parallel between the Slant commitment to anticolonial revolutions and the commitment of the intellectual Left to the Republican side in the Spanish civil war. No Catholic Leftists have gone to fight in anticolonial revolutions (as none of them has gone to live in Eastern Europe), nor do they suggest that English Catholics should take part in these wars. They are not engaged, not publicly at least, in organizing supplies of arms. For themselves, they are averse to guns, holding that, while Britain needs revolution, a shooting revolution would be "irrelevant" (Wicker, p. 67). In short, they see their function in the anticolonial wars as that of cheering for the men who use the guns "out there."

Viewed objectively in this context of inaction, the gun-carrying guerilla on the cover of Wicker's book, and the cheers for anticolonial guerillas and revolutions generally, assume a familiar contemporary significance. They relate not to politics, Marxist or otherwise, or to revolution, but to that liberal, literary and vicarious cult of violence, felt as a symbol of virility, spontaneity and negation, which dates from the period before the First World War and which has of late been finding its chief expression—a literary expression—in New York. It is not irrelevant that just as Raymond Williams, the father-figure of the New Left, is a lecturer in English at Cambridge, the basic academic interest of several of the prominent figures in the Catholic Left (including Brian Wicker and the principal founders of *Slant*) is in the field of modern literature. Small wonder, in a romantic age where poetry has its wings clipped and politics presses all life to its shapes, that modes proper to romantic literature should squeeze themselves into political disguises, even turning the tables, as it were, by transforming *politics* and *revolution* into graphic metaphors for private parties.

Slant and English Politics

Whatever about distant places, it stands to reason that the primary involvement of a group declaring itself politically committed would be in its own nation's politics at home. The principal issues of contemporary English politics are not only widely known, but have become to a large degree the world's concern. An empire has been lost, a moral lethargy and sense of purposelessness (the English "malaise" or "sickness" it is generally called) affects all areas of the nation's life. There have been eight major balance-of-payments crises in the past 20 years. Entry to the European Common Market has been effectively blocked for an indefinite period. In short, the readjustments necessary to find a new form for the national life after the end of the imperial period have not been made and it is evident that no mere tinkerings with the sterling exchange rate or with the economy as a whole will suffice to do this. It seems likely that a constitutional transformation at least as far-reaching as that effected in France under De Gaulle will be required.

We have seen, with Wicker, that the Catholic Left, including Slant, suffer from a "fundamental uncertainty about immediate political policies." It is thus not surprising that they have nothing of importance to propose in regard to these pressing concerns of the nation, that they are, in other words, absent from the nation's essential politics. What might be surprising, however, if one has not yet grasped the utterly a-political nature of Slant, is that these major concerns of the nation are not even ordinary topics of discussion in their writings and lectures.

A glance through the 140 pages of Wicker's book will disclose no treatment of any of the above-mentioned issues, no discussion of England's present plight—much less any proposals for overcoming it. That England now finds herself in what by the evidence of political history is a typically revolutionary situation, namely, the situation following on the loss of an empire, is not noticed in these pages. What one will find are analyses of analyses of such concepts as "total redemption," "revolution" (conceived of in the abstract in an unspecified time and place), "tragedy" ("modern" and otherwise), "the revolutionary aspect of the double stance," and so on. In this, Wicker is of course, as chronicler of the Catholic Left, not always to be blamed; he does say repeatedly that there is "a great deal of detailed work to be done."

English Catholics and Politics

The fact that the Catholic Left is not involved in English politics does not, of course, mean that this is true of English Catholics in general. They are involved with their fellow citizens on both the national and the local level and very much in the trade unions. Traditionally most of them have voted and worked politically on the left, that is to say, for Labour and for kindred groups. This is another of the ordinary features of the British political scene of which the self-styled "Catholic Left" seem oblivious; used by them, it might have given them an entrée into politics, if they had really wanted one.

The title "Catholic Left," as used here and in Wicker's book, does not even indicate that the Catholics in question are "further left" than other Catholics. The "Catholic Left" are distinguished from other Catholics not by their leftism—which is impossible to assess politically while they are not involved in politics—but by their conscious attempt to relate a political stance to Catholic theology. In this they depart from a traditional norm of Catholic political thought and action in Britain, Ireland and the other English-speaking countries.

However, even if Catholic involvement in politics is not dependent on the Catholic Left writers, the Catholic contribution to politics is impoverished by the lack of relationship between this bunch of alert, widely read minds with their potentially fertile ideas and the mass of Catholic voters and politicians. This impoverishment is especially regrettable at a time when England's political needs are unusually acute and when there might have been an opportunity for a specifically Catholic service to the nation. As things stand, it seems likely that the solution which England will find for her present crisis will be one in which English Catholics will play no important, certainly no creative, role for lack of ideas and of intellectual leadership.

However, what has worked as impoverishment in one direction has worked as frustration in the other. The basic reason why the Catholic Left has failed to be political is that it has failed to establish a growing working relationship with the Catholic people. Transforming political action needs a substantial body of people sharing like ideas which set them consciously apart from others. Since they came from the Catholic people and were determined to bring their Catholic theology to bear on their politics, the Slant group could hope to find the people they needed only among their own.

In fact, however, by the language which they used and by the language which they did not use, they signalled that they sought no political fellowship with the Catholic people or with any representative cross-section of them. Their political language was a more or less theologized dialogue with the secularist and academic New Left movement, which was not only unrelated to the Catholic people but considerably less related to real English political life than the mass of English Catholics. The concrete circumstances and history, the special needs and political potentialities, of the Catholic population of England have found no place in the writings and public lectures of the Catholic Left.

Defective Marxism

The avoidance of the people offered to them by their own circumstances—by their own place in history—was not only a refusal of politics, but a negation of their professed Marxism. As "Marxists" it made them akin to those whom Stalin described in his *Marxism and Linguistics* as "scribes and talmudists of Marxism" who "see only the letter of Marxism and not its essential nature." The Slant group have manipulated some of the "letters" and ideas of Marxism in the belief that this makes them Marxists; whereas Marxism under capitalism is primarily a collective endeavour of thought and action by a proletariat and its leaders. The application of Marxist method in political action is a more essential part of being a Marxist than the use of Marxist jargon.

In *The Holy Family* Karl Marx wrote:

Ideas never lead beyond the established situation, they only lead beyond the ideas of the established situation. In fact, ideas cannot realize anything. The realization of ideas requires men who apply a practical force.

It is through the "men who apply a practical force" that ideas enter politics and become politics, while themselves being remade and defined. But the "practical force" can be provided only by a body of "men" who have the dimensions, the cohesion and the self-consciousness of a "class" or a "people." The Catholic Left have evolved ideas, but, lacking a people, these ideas have accomplished nothing real, have not become politics.

As is well known, Marx saw the proletariat, conceived of as a mass of alienated and radically dehumanized workers, as the people pre-eminently predisposed for the realization of revolutionary ideas. It is remarkable that this central Marxist concept has played no role in Catholic Left thinking and is absent from Wicker's discussion of the movement in his latest book. Nor has any explanation been offered for avoiding the topic. Any serious Marxist analysis of their own reality by

English Catholics would certainly have included not only the concept of the proletariat, but the realization that the Catholic masses of England, seen in historical perspective, formed the subproletariat until very recent times and still have proletarian qualities.[1]

(It would be tedious and, in the circumstances, irrelevant to detail all that a truly Marxist-revolutionary analysis by the Catholic Left *might* have concerned itself with. Suffice to mention that the Catholic population of England, through its largely Irish and labouring-class origins, has had a certain experience of revolutionary activity and is connected with the only living revolutionary tradition in the British Isles; further, that the Irish revolution, which occurred within the United Kingdom within living memory—and thus has an obvious relevance and can be easily studied—was made by Catholics, was partly inspired by Marxist and partly by theological ideas, and was an anticolonial revolution which set a pattern of tactics for many others, including some now going on. But though close at hand, relevant, and containing many lessons which beginners need to learn, the Slantists, who are themselves partly of Irish origin, have ignored it along with much else close at hand, preferring to find their examples thousands of miles away.)

Wicker rightly sees the lack of policies of the Catholic Left as a legacy from the New Left's political agnosticism. Its scholastic and otherworldly preoccupations, as well as its self-deception in regard to its Marxist and revolutionary role, derive in large measure from the same quarter. If the Slant people, in joining the New Left, thought they were turning from a Church out of touch with worldly and political realities to a laboratory where tough-minded men matched living facts to forge the nation's future, they were deceived; insofar as it was the Church in an English-speaking country that was involved in the comparison, their latter plight was considerably worse than their first. There was, indeed, more than a touch of the pot calling the kettle black when Raymond Williams (in *New Blackfriars*, Nov. 1966) charged the "New

[1] Cf. John Hickey in *Urban Catholics*, London: Chapman, 1967.

Left Catholics" with being "engaged in a search for rhetorical solutions to tensions of an understandable, perhaps, intolerable, but certainly idiosyncratic kind."

Probably a lot of the confusion goes back to the title and ambiguous contents of *The Long Revolution* by the Welshman Raymond Williams (published 1961). Both title and contents met a need among the new university generation, so there was little critical confrontation of one with the other, little doubting of the implicit, very welcome message. But a critical reading of *The Long Revolution* might have revealed the author as a reformist bound to lose rather than as the revolutionary destined to win—sometime or other and without fisticuffs— which many new-fledged *literati*, eager to enjoy the don's life plus the revolutionary's kicks, took him to be.

After all, Williams' "Long Revolution," as chronicled by him through the nineteenth and early twentieth centuries, was a whole series of "mere reforms"; their posthumous, collective elevation to revolutionary dignity did not really alter this fact. By failing to show that the modern British revolution had been building up before 1914, and that it was frustrated and betrayed, the author made his own thesis into a suave rejection of the historic revolutionary tradition in Britain. But even Williams' watered-down version of "revolution" was exposed, in his final chapter, as a loser, not a winner.

Writing there on "Britain in the 1960s," he showed how the advance of "the collective idea," the extension of democratic control, the cultural progress of the people as a whole —all essential components of his "long revolution"—had in fact been outpaced by powerful "counter-revolutionary" forces (though he did not use this adjective). As remedies he suggested certain very reasonable reforms. That they would be sufficient to swing the scales seemed most unlikely; how, if they were sufficient, the force necessary to implement them could be applied in the teeth of the status quo, he did not say.

Another title, say, *The Abandoned Revolution*, might have made Williams' book, despite its laborious prose, into a tonic of erudite realism. Instead there was born a comforting myth for radicals—but not only for radicals. A new, extremely gentle meaning for revolution, that would bring reassurance to any capitalist, bourgeois or old-time Catholic heart, passed into currency. One could now serve the good, doomed cause by talking about it and by calling it revolutionary, while the politicians and the parties got on with the nation's business— or failed to get on. "Out there," in history, politics would continue to mean first and foremost the pressing affairs of the nation. Revolution would mean a movement of thought and action climaxing in a point where some men found the existing state of affairs so intolerable that they saw human life, beginning with their own, as justifiably expendable for the common good. But "inside," in books and little journals and at high table, these things would be seen differently.

Inferiority Complex

Perhaps the ultimate cause of the sterility of Catholic Left attempts to enter politics was a Catholic inferiority complex. Such a complex is reflected in the banners which the movement has used—"Catholic Left," "Catholic Marxists." It is reflected in the oft-reiterated statements that "Catholics must be committed to the Left," "must be socialists." The implication is that Catholics urgently need to be something which certain other men are, and which is not included in being a Catholic Christian, in order to be adequate men and citizens and to serve the cause of man. More, that the "left" or "Marxist" or "socialist" content of the resulting amalgam is what gives it real force in terms of actual life.

Conversely, the Catholic Left did not come forward as "Left Catholics" or as "Marxist Catholics," with the stress on the Catholic Christian content as the element that makes the man. Obviously, this feeling of *intrinsic Catholic insufficiency* has much to do with the already-mentioned failure of the Catholic Left to address its political front to the historic Catholic people.

Both *socialism* and *the Left* have been devalued as political terms by their history in Britain and by the multiplicity of contradictory and negative meanings that have been given to them in recent decades—from Sweden's monopoly capitalism to Stalin's collectivization, from Berlin border guards to African tribal dictatorships. In *The Long Revolution* Raymond Williams several times bears testimony to the fact that the word *socialism* has no real meaning in contemporary Britain. The same is even more true of *the Left*, which has never really come to life as a term in English politics—not surprisingly, given the pragmatism of Englishmen. The fact is that in the actual political arena in Britain today socialism and the Left are nothing to commit oneself to. In the universities, it is true, both are OK words, supplying brave feelings and giving alienation a cause; but in national politics they are linguistic debris.

Since this is the case, any fresh decision on the part of a new group to use these terms must, if the use is to be effective, be a freely taken and rationally founded decision. It must be accompanied by awareness of their factual hollowness and by a public display of this awareness in the form of critical sifting, *distinguos*, rejection of most of what the terms have actually come to mean, and pointedly refurbished definitions. But such a free, critical approach to the terms in question is possible only where there is inner freedom. If, as has been the case with the Catholic Left, the Left and socialism are felt to represent essential saving elements for essential Catholic insufficiency, such inner freedom is not present—the relationship to the words is mystical. As a consequence, the use of these words by the Catholic Left has struck many people as naïve and uncritical, not to say loose.

In line with the general tone of critical realism which pervades Giles Hibbert's book, he at least, in his brief incursion into such matters, affixes an adjective—"genuine"—to the socialism he recommends and refers briefly to the word's sorry history. But the general practice of the Catholic Left has been to use *left* and *socialist* much as pious books use *good* and *holy*, with the implication all the time that it is somehow "radical" for an English Catholic to describe himself in terms which, as of this moment in Britain, stand for politics that have failed.

"Socialism, revolution and England need the Church to succeed." This true statement is virtually the obverse of what the Catholic Left have been saying. It is a statement which, if accompanied by adequate exposition and by the living evidence of a dynamically humanizing, politically radical Catholic community, would have made England, and not only England, at least curious to hear and see more. Instead of telling (merely) Catholics that they need to acquire what certain others have, it would be telling all conditions of men that they need to share somehow in the life that Catholics have, if their hopes for a better life are to be fulfilled.

This statement, and the support of it by adequate exposition and by a transformed church life, have all along been within the reach of the group calling themselves the Catholic Left. With all the talent they comprise, with the valuable work already done by Wicker, Eagleton, McCabe, Kerr and Hibbert to build on, with their attention turned not merely to the culture and worship but to the major concerns and urgent needs of the nation—that is to say, with a dose of more active patriotism than they have hitherto displayed—this could have been the means of creative entry into the nation's politics, at their very centre, for the English Catholic community. But it would have been possible only for Catholics who believed from the start in the potential sufficiency of the Catholic Christian life—that is to say, for Catholics not suffering from a Catholic inferiority complex.

The Free Church Movement in Contemporary Catholicism

Rosemary Ruether

The hope for conciliar reform of the Roman Catholic Church that was generated by the Second Vatican Council has not been realized, declares Rosemary Ruether, and now that Church is spiritually and existentially, though not formally, in schism. As conservatives hold fast to their triumphalist, hierarchical view of the church and moderates contend for reform from within, more and more progressives "are withdrawing from hierarchical jurisdiction and setting up para-institutional organizations, communities, and forums by which their own voices can be heard." Many of the latter group are satisfying their hunger for human community through participation in house churches, nonterritorial parishes, etc.—the various forms of Christian life and celebration that make up the "underground church," or what Miss Ruether calls a "free" or "believer's" church. Such voluntary association is the church's authentic form, says Miss Ruether —though this does not mean that the institutional church should be dispensed with altogether. The two forms are actually "interdependent polarities within the total dialectic of the church's existence"—but man being what he is, the dialectic has never worked quite the way it should. The author of *The Church Against Itself*, Miss Ruether is visiting lecturer in Historical Theology at Howard University. Her essay is from the Spring 1968 *Continuum*,* of which she is an associate editor.

IN THE euphoria which followed immediately after the II Vatican Council, it appeared that the Roman Catholic Church was actually accomplishing the near impos-

* Saint Xavier College, Chicago, Ill. 60655.

sible: namely, an established institution renewing itself through the channels of constituted authority. It appeared that, after centuries of fear and stagnation, a revolutionary renewal was taking place that was to catapult the Roman Church into dialogue with modern times. There was to be balanced assimilation of the best of contemporary thought, but without loss of historical continuity, without schism or breaking of ranks on any side. Some of the Protestant observers at the Council, such as McAfee Brown and Albert Outler, expressed considerable awe at this achievement and felt that, for them, this was the most extraordinary aspect of the Council: the phenomenon of an institution renewing itself from within established channels, maintaining its unity and the whole moving forward in one orderly progression.

As the impact of the Council has had an opportunity to develop, and many of the theories of the Council, enunciated at that time with such balanced assurance, are now in process of being lived through and made concrete in the life of the church, this optimistic judgment is by no means so certain. It is one thing to define a noble theory of episcopal collegiality, we discover, but quite another to put this into practice when it implies a concrete challenge to the old power structures and lines of authority which heretofore have prevailed. It is one thing to outline a beautiful concept of the church as a community and its liturgy as the celebration of its life together, but quite another to begin to scrutinize the present structure of the parish in the light of these ideas. In retrospect it becomes apparent that much of the image of unity and orderly self-renewal given by the conciliar decrees was possible only because these decrees were sailed across the surface of the episcopal minds in an almost Platonic state of abstract discussion. But the liberal theologians who promoted these theories and sold them to the bishops did not fully anticipate and face up to the revolutionary implications of translating these theories into practice. A good example of this kind of non-existential thinking in the framework of conciliar theology is provided by George Tavard's recent book on the ecclesiology of the Council, *The Pilgrim Church*. The tone of this book was so airily complacent, so oblivious to the existential tensions involved in translating conciliar theology into practice, indeed so oblivious to the dimension of actuality altogether that it was dubbed by one reviewer as an example of the "theology of Middle Earth" (see *The Critic*, Dec.–Jan. 1967–68, pp. 81–82). In this respect the objections of the conservatives, while unenlightened theologically and historically, were perhaps more realistic. They, at least, were not fooled as to the real implications of translating theories of collegiality, ecumenism, community, liturgical and theological relevance into practice.

But today this honeymoon is over, and the problems of living through a difficult marriage of past and present, a past and present which are not a little incompatible, has begun. We are engaged in a confrontation between two entirely different forms of thought about Christianity. The old mould of thought: formal, legal, triumphalist, defining all power as operating from the apex of the hierarchy down; this mould of thought is so far removed from the communal and secular orientation that characterizes modern Christian thought that the two points of view not only differ in their conclusions, but in their interpretation of practically all the premises as well. They have virtually no common principle of coexistence, because, even when they use the same symbols, they mean very different things by these symbols. It is not unfair to say that probably never in the history of Christianity has there existed, within the formal boundaries of a single ecclesiastical institution, poles of opinion which share so little of what we might call "a common faith." What is more, as liberals press for further reforms, and conservatives retreat and harden the lines of their traditional positions, the chasm between the old and the new church threatens to become increasingly broad until today it is practically unbridgeable. A good example of this is the recent flap between Archbishop Lucey of Texas and John L. McKenzie. Father McKenzie's book, *Authority in the Church*, expresses attitudes broadly accepted by Catholic liberals, and yet the judgments expressed therein concerning the authentic nature of Christian authority were so radically foreign and unknown to the official Catholicism which rules the American Church that when a group of priests in Archbishop Lucey's diocese used excerpts from the book in the statement of policy handed to the Archbishop, he almost went into a state of apoplexy. He was dumbfounded by ideas such as "love as the guiding principle of authority," insisting that love has nothing to do with church authority, that authority is founded on power delegated by Christ to the hierarchy, and Father McKenzie's ideas were confused, heretical, and completely without foundation.[1] This incident in which an archbishop accidentally came across ideas which are current and generally accepted among liberals and found them completely unheard of and offensive well illustrates the almost total breakdown of communication that presently exists.

We Catholics today may not yet have any formal institutional schism, but that is more an inherited bit of cultural lag than an expression of inward unity. Spiritually we are already in schism. Those open to the spirit of change pursue their own conversations through their own media of communication and amidst their own communities of thought, while those determined to resist what they regard as the total oblivion of the church as they define it gather off in their own communities with their structures of power and increasingly their own press. The two sides seldom meet or converse; or rather, I should say, the liberal camp is passingly and somewhat humorously acquainted with what they regard as the obtuseness of traditionalist thought, while the traditionalists are in a state of rage over certain obvious outcroppings of change in the church, but without being in the least acquainted with the thinking that is going on in liberal Catholic circles. The two sides seldom if ever really come into any kind of dialogue, and when they are forced into a confrontation, as for example the exchanges between Archbishop Lucey and John McKenzie, or the symposium on the church sponsored by the *National Catholic Reporter* which included such liberals as Dan Callahan, as well as representatives of Catholic Traditionalism such as Archbishop Dwyer and Brent Bozell, the editor of *Triumph* magazine, the result turns out

[1] See December 1967 issues of the *National Catholic Reporter*.

to be double monologues which lack even the most elementary consensus that would make real communication possible.

Yet, although we in the Roman Catholic Church are in an existential schism, we still supposedly continue to operate within the same formal institutional structures. We still presumably go to the same parishes and send our children to the same parochial schools. The power structures of the church are still hierarchical and all lines of authority still proceed from the top down almost without modification. So, despite all the verbiage about community and collegiality, there are still no institutional structures which really express the collegiality of the bishops with the Pope, of priests with bishop, and of people with the hierarchy. To be sure we have an episcopal synod that met recently in Rome, but its powerlessness to effect anything by itself and apart from Papal command was all too clear. In practice, the powers in Rome have no intention of letting this synod operate as a body that can really make policy, with the Pope acting merely as presiding officer. Rather they intend to keep, as much as possible, an unmodified hierarchical relationship between Rome and the national episcopacies.

In the same way, on the diocesan level, we have movements for priests' senates, but these are either paper councils which act as mere rubber stamps for the bishops, or else they are revolutionary and partly underground operations, which, in effect, are engaged in a power struggle with the bishop. By the same token, the so-called layman's voice in the church, insofar as it is voluntarily taken into the clerical councils, is expected to be the docile, obedient voice which says only what it is told to say. Insofar as there is an independent voice of the laity, it is found in underground or para-institutional organizations like the National Layman's organization which operates and meets without official sanction or status. So the theories of collegiality on all levels of the church, when put into practice, produce, as might be expected, not voluntary sharing of power, but a revolutionary power struggle, with those below increasingly setting up their own unauthorized organizations with a view to breaking the present power structure. It is becoming increasingly evident that if any real sharing of decisions and modification of the hierarchical, one-way line of communication is to be made, with few exceptions, it will not be done voluntarily by the hierarchy, but forced upon them in some way by the organizing of those groups which are presently excluded from these councils. The difficulty, of course, is that within the present canonical theory, those below have no legitimate power base from which to operate vis-à-vis the hierarchy. Therefore, they have to fall back on methods which border on sabotage, such as withholding funds, withdrawing from the parish and school, using the popular press to embarrass the hierarchy and to reveal its secret orders and decrees and, finally, massing together in unauthorized organizations which can present a threat of sheer numbers to the hierarchy and which cannot be destroyed by individual reprisals. That is to say, when sixty percent of the priests in the diocese are organized, the bishop cannot very well suspend them all as he could a DuBay or a Hefner. When hundreds of thousands of lay people organize in a network through the country, their combined financial power becomes sufficient to make the bishops sit up and take notice, while a petition sent by a mere hundred or even a thousand lay people might be ignored.

This hierarchical intransigence toward any real change that touches on their powers as magistrate, font of sacramental power, and arbiter of doctrine has virtually forced the emergence of a widespread phenomenon which I have chosen to call "The Free Church Movement in Roman Catholicism." By the "free church" I mean essentially all the various ways and means of expression by which Catholics are withdrawing from hierarchical jurisdiction and setting up para-institutional organizations, communities, and forums by which their own voices can be heard; voices which really express their own positions and needs and are not simply the echo of the power structure above them, whether this be the Pope vis-à-vis the bishops, the bishops vis-à-vis the priests, or the clerical power structure as a whole in relation to the laity. Para-institutional organizations have become necessary because it has become obvious to each group that the power structure above them, in fact, does not intend to enter into any real dialogue or shared decisions, but will only allow that voice to be heard which is an echo of its own.

Let us survey some of the ways in which this development of non-juridical or free church structures is happening on different levels of the church and in relation to different spheres of control. In each case we shall note common characteristics. First of all a refusal of a one-way top-downward mode of communication and authority. This entails, in practice, a partial withdrawal from the jurisdiction of the power structure in some way, either moving off the territory it can control to operate in some independent organization or a kind of seizure of power, often somewhat covert and with specious accolades to the power structure which barely conceal the fact that the new organization is seeking to usurp a part of its power. The Chicago priests' senate has become a master of this technique. Here there seems to be emerging a divergence between moderate and radical Catholics. The moderates are still hoping to officially integrate the present power structure, and so they are inclined to plan and make petitions, but are reluctant to engage in any decisive action without permission, but to wait for concessions from the hierarchy before they act, even if this appears slow in coming or confined to various forms of tokenism. The more radical opinion leans toward a frank departure from the present power structure. This group tends to regard the whole present hierarchical structure as irrelevant and probably irreformable, and they are engaged in setting up new organizations and communities which implicitly, if not explicitly, suggest the view that the present hierarchy is not to be reformed and democratized by slow stages, but rather is to be overthrown and replaced. This divergence between moderates and radicals also corresponds, to some extent, with the kind of Catholics who are more church-directed in contrast to the Catholics who are more world-oriented. The "Church Catholics" still assume the church institution as the fixed point of reference, and cannot imagine renewal in any other form except reforming and up-dating the church institution, while the kind of people who are more interested in being Christians than in being Roman Catholics, more interested in social witness than in churchmanship, tend to regard the up-dating of the institution as futile and the institution itself as irrelevant to Christian life.

In surveying this conflict in the church, let us look first at its most conservative manifestations, namely in a power struggle within the hierarchy itself, and then move on to its more radical manifestations. Within the hierarchy there is a very real although not yet fully surfaced struggle between Rome and the national episcopacies. In certain quarters we find an increasing insistence of the national episcopacies on running their own house and taking fraternal advice but not commands from Rome. The most publicized and perhaps most advanced example of this is the national episcopacy of Holland which, more and more, is operating as an autonomous national Catholic Church, treating the Pope as a brother bishop with whom they wish to stay in communication, to be sure, but refusing to be treated as a subordinate tool of the papacy through which orders can be passed without consultation. The Dutch church is not uniformly liberal, by any means. It has its conflicts between liberals and traditionalists too, but the difference between Holland and the United States lies precisely in the determination of the Dutch hierarchy to keep in center stream and play a meaningful mediating and leadership role. But this very effort to keep in dialogue with the whole spectrum of Catholic thought within their church means that the Dutch hierarchy has been forced to close ranks against the meddling of Rome which would like to strike down the Dutch liberals from outside. Thus the jurisdictional struggle in Holland is taking place more between the national episcopacy and Rome than between bishops and people. There are some highly advanced theological opinions and experimental communities in Holland, and the Dutch bishops are not completely enthusiastic about everything that is happening, but they want to keep in touch with it, precisely to keep it within the bounds of the church. And they realize that in order to keep these left-wing groups, to some extent, under their supervision, they have to allow a reasonable amount of freedom and diversity. But in this effort to keep control over their own house, the Dutch bishops have had to exercise a certain autonomy from Rome in a number of important instances, and thus the Dutch church as a whole emerges with something of the character of an autonomous national church in relation to the jurisdictional claims of the Papacy.

This kind of independence on the national episcopal level is exceptional, however. By and large Roman Catholic bishops are not yet ready to dispute the subordination of the national episcopacy to the Papacy. The continued acceptance of the Papal nuncio stands as a potent symbol of this continued imposition of a hierarchical rather than collegiate relation of the episcopacy to Rome. More important, most of the bishops are sufficiently traditionalist in their leanings and unsympathetic toward freedom of thought and experimentation in community life that they welcome the heavy hand of Rome as a way of cutting off such liberal experimentation within their own churches. This is particularly true in America where most of the bishops are conservative, ecclesiastical capitalists by training and are culturally unequipped to deal with the new thinking. Thus the jurisdictional struggle in America is taking place between bishops and their communities rather than between the national church and Rome.

Some of the most striking developments of the free church principle have actually taken place among religious communities. The Benedictine monastery in Cuernavaca and the Glenmary Sisters in the midwestern United States were recent examples of contests between authority and religious communities which ended with the religious communities' defining themselves outside the jurisdiction of the hierarchy and continuing their previous work as a free community. A crucial issue here is the question of the property of the community, since it is difficult to continue its work without some of these resources. Thus it is important to realize that some of these communities are not leaving their property behind, but are secularizing it and taking it with them when they depart from the jurisdiction of the hierarchy. Moreover none of these groups regard themselves as having left the Roman Catholic Church, but rather simply to have left a certain power structure, which, by implication, was regarded as non-essential to the meaning of Catholicism. Indeed one might almost say that among liberal Catholics today, the idea of leaving the church has become almost an archaic gesture, and when persons like Charles Davis make highly publicized exits from the church they are likely to be criticized by the liberal Catholic press, not as renegades, but as persons whose views were not sufficiently advanced to be able to make the distinction between the church and the ecclesiastical organization.

In addition to the examples given above there is a widespread struggle between traditionalists and reformers within the religious orders which is leading to the departure of many religious who regard such structures as outdated and untenable contexts within which to fulfill their own Christian vocation. This too is a new note. In times past religious often left the orders, but they left singly and as discredited Christians. Today, however, many religious are leaving with the insistence that they do so, not to abandon, but to fulfill their religious vocation. Some of these religious go into secular witness as individuals, but others are living together in small communities in which they still bind themselves to each other by their same religious vows. They thus constitute themselves as free nonjuridical religious communities. They thus hope to create new, voluntary forms of covenanted community life which can be relevant for our times, freed from the institutional apparatus which has accumulated around the old religious communities and prevented them from adapting to the new situations. The Immaculate Heart Sisters in Los Angeles, on the other hand, are an example of a religious order that has tried to update its organization as a whole and in so doing have come very close to declaring their autonomy from their Cardinal Archbishop. If they could find some more ready sources of independent cash, they would probably go even farther in this direction.

Parallel to the development of the free religious community, we have among laymen and secular priests the development of what is called "the underground church." The term "underground" indicates the ambiguity of the present situation. Small assemblies are popping up in all sorts of semi-secret places, acting in place of the local parish without the knowledge or authorization of the Ordinary, but without consistently departing from his province. They are free churches more by subterfuge than by open revolt. The phenomenon of underground Catholicism springs, of course, from a tremendous hunger for authentic community. The present impersonal, territorial parishes are geared to an individualistic spirituality at best. They express no real community, either in terms of shared decisions, meaningful community action, or even a sense of real joy and celebration together. They are drab, incredibly dull, insultingly mediocre sacramental service stations, where people come to fulfill some obligation and carry away as quickly as possible some imaginary deposit of grace. Those who have a vision of the church as a real Christian community in which communion with God is expressed in interpersonal concern, friendship, and joint action find the typical parish untenable. Thus a considerable number of the more educated and sensitive Catholics are sitting loose or pulling out of the territorial parish and looking for some other alternative. This quest for a gathered Christian community may take several forms. Existing nonterritorial communities may provide an outlet for some people. In Los Angeles the oblates of the Benedictine Monastery in Valyermo were, for a while, a vehicle for the creation of a voluntary community by some of the most active Catholics in the area. The lay members of the Grail in the Cincinnati area are a similar group. A lively Newman club, like the one at the University of Chicago, provides an outlet for Catholic intelligentsia in the area, many of whom have no official connection with the University. Emmaus House in New York provides such an experience of celebration in community for some of the Catholic community there. Such places are technically under some official authority, but they are being used as nonterritorial local churches in a way which is certainly not intended by the diocesan officials.

A more frank expression of the underground is found in many small communities which meet rather regularly for worship in their own homes. This is a widespread phenomenon and a continual contest is being waged between episcopal authority and such house churches. Some dioceses have approved house Masses with an effort to keep them under their control and let them be used as an occasional weekday supplement which in no way alters the obligation to the parish. Other dioceses have tried to outlaw them altogether. In either case, however, the house Mass has a strong tendency not merely to supplement but to replace the parish community and become an autonomous conventicle, and this is why it is regarded with such suspicion. In most cases such house churches exist by subterfuge rather than open revolt. They skirt authority and fulfill some aspects of the letter of the law. They get most of their spiritual nourishment from unauthorized assemblies, without consistently turning their back on the official institutional structure. Here the more timorous Catholic is aided by the large impersonal nature of the typical Catholic parish which makes it possible for him to keep a foot in the door while seldom if ever attending its services. He may be regularly attending some house church or nonterritorial community without his official pastor even being aware of his absence or the diocese aware of the existence of such gatherings. Even if the pastor or the bishop becomes aware of these, there is little or nothing that can be done to make a layman conform to the territorial parish. Such groups can be attacked only by trying to remove or suspend its celebrants, and if such a community gets to the point where it no longer cares if its celebrants are suspended or even ordained, then the last tie is cut. Even excommunication would now be irrelevant to the life of such a group.

Recently the contest between the underground church and authority has been engaged in more openly, either because such a group decided to seek some official recognition of its existence or because their numbers had grown to such an extent that they could no longer be overlooked. An example of the former situation occurred recently in Trenton, New Jersey, where an underground community asked its bishop to authorize them as a nonterritorial parish. Their leader, a young priest named Father Hefner, quit his post as curate at a parish in order to be the regular leader of the group. The bishop refused to recognize the group and suspended the priest, even threatening him with excommunication if he persisted. But he and the group declared that they would continue to operate without authorization and were not intimidated by suspension or excommunication. At the time of this writing the community was still in operation. A similar community engaged in a somewhat less dramatic confrontation with Bishop Sheen in Rochester about the same time. A somewhat different situation was created by the development of a large floating community in Washington, D.C., that called themselves the "People," and for about a year operated large celebrations called "The Action Mass." This group was, in large part, the brain child of Mr. Landon Dowdy, who is a prominent civil rights lawyer in Washington. Dowdy was antipathetic to the small house church community which he saw as a narrow in-group. He conceived of the Action Mass more as a mass movement than a gathered, covenanted community with regular membership. Dowdy envisioned the creation of what he called "the People school" which would be a cadre of musicians, artists, poets, speakers, and so forth who would develop techniques for creating liturgical happenings. Dowdy saw this group as moving around, creating happenings in various situations and contexts, and gathering spontaneous communities on the scene that would bring together people who might otherwise have no connection with each other: rich and poor, black and white, Catholics, Protestants, Jews, and non-believers. As the Action Mass developed, the format of the Roman Mass appeared as more and more of a handicap in this idea. Meanwhile the Action Mass grew ever more popular until thousands were attending it every Sunday, and the leadership group had to organize several masses in different parts of the city. Cardinal O'Boyle became increasingly alarmed by this phenomenon and began to try to lean on rubrical regulations and to close off the jurisdictional loopholes which the people were employing for the operation of this Action Mass: namely, the large number of non-diocesan institutions and clergy in the Washington area. Finally, when the group began to get widespread publicity, the Cardinal fell upon them with the full force of his powers, ordering them to disband and trying to close off the participation of all priests, religious institutions and seminarians. However, this crisis created by the Cardinal actually coincided with an internal crisis within the group itself between the more conventional Catholics who envisioned the Action Mass as a nonterritorial parish, and those like Dowdy who were moving in the direction of secular, non-denominational spontaneous celebrations, which assumed no institutional base. The result was that the leadership was split. Dowdy pulled out altogether to work on completely free non-institutional modes of celebration along the lines of the hippie Be-in and the liturgical happenings which are being developed by people like Sister Corita. A more conservative group then carried the Action Mass into a protest phase in which they fought and petitioned the Cardinal and finally won a sort of grudging recognition as a charitable organization, with permission to hold official Masses four times a year. This group keeps in touch on other weeks by some kind of free agape or celebration of the Word, and is presently engaged in various community action projects.

The break-up of the Action Mass, however, revealed a significant thrust of opinion among the liturgical radicals toward a completely non-ecclesiastical mode of Christian community, action, and celebration. It is difficult to know how widespread this phenomenon is, or how many are really acting it out in a consistent manner, but there is no question in my mind that it is a growing edge of opinion. This group simply deems the official institution, with the apparatus of sacramental power and authority, completely irrelevant to real Christian life and worship today. This group sees the church as a floating spirit of renewal abroad in the world, and the call of the Christian to assembly is essentially a call to go where the action is. Sometimes this may entail a group covenanting together for some period of time to do some specific work. Sometimes it may mean celebrations which arise momentarily around a particular occasion or event. The celebrants of such communities are charismatic. They arise as the natural leadership of the group, and are designated, not by institutional authority, but by popular acclaim. They are the true gurus of the community, and their authority can be acclaimed because it is a charismatic authority which is created in and creates freedom, and no longer has any connection to institutional subservience.

Thus we see that the Catholic quest for authentic community and celebration of its life together is carrying the more avant garde out beyond institutional Catholicism or even institutional Christianity altogether into relation to a much more widespread hunger for spiritual experience among people of our time. There are increasing signs of this spiritual hunger as a very potent new religious force abroad in the land, and it is equally evident that organized Christianity is proving almost completely inadequate to meet this challenge. This does not mean that the new groups are necessarily anti-clerical. They are beyond that kind of thinking, since the clerical structure is completely irrelevant to them, and they welcome the few clerics and religious like Dan Berrigan and Sister Corita who know how to speak their language. But by and large they are turning from the churches, or rather not even approaching them because no nourishment for their hunger is to be found in these places, and they are turning to new kinds of outlets. The hippie communities which, more and more, are turning from drugs to the authentic traditions of mysticism and contemplation; little meditation and yoga groups that are springing up all over the place; a new influx of gurus from the mystical past; not to mention the social activists and the peaceniks—all these form a broad and somewhat interlocking wave of spiritual unrest that is finding and developing its own methods of community, contemplation, and celebration. Some parishes sponsored by the traditional denominations and a few recognized Christian thinkers are relating themselves to this arena and serving its needs, adapting forms of Christian preaching and celebration to its spirit, but in so doing they find themselves forced to the boundaries of conventional Christianity and are likely to be considered out of bounds by their fellow religionists. The overwhelming majority of organized Christianity is unable to relate to this new hunger at all, and so is simply being left behind, serving an older generation, but deserted by those who are thinking with a new age.

These then are some of the movements and tensions which I see at work in present day Catholicism. Now I would like very briefly to analyze these phenomena in a way that may serve to put them in an overall ecclesiological perspective. We have here really several kinds of renewal operating with different goals and understandings of the church. First of all, we have a form of renewal that is striving, essentially, for a democratization of the institutional church. Councils of bishops, priests' senates, laymen's councils; all these belong to the drive for an overall democratization of the church organization. This kind of movement is not actually free church in its view of the church. If it wears somewhat of a rebel face at times now, this is simply because it has not yet succeeded in its goal. It is free church by default rather than by desire, in much the same way (although, I trust, not with the same fate) as Presbyterianism in the English Reformation became free church, not because this was its own polity, but because it failed in its actual goal which was to take over and become the new organization. This institutional movement would find satisfactory completion at that point at which it succeeds in remodeling the balance of power in the Roman Church along the lines which presently prevail in other modern denominations, such as the American Episcopal Church; i.e., when it achieves a situation in which the pastor is called to the parish through a cooperative effort of the bishop and an elected council of laymen who represent the congregation; when the parishes furnish elected lay as well as clerical representatives to make up a diocesan council which would have legislative powers as well as the power to elect the bishop; when a similar representative body with similar functions would also operate on the level of the national church and finally on the level of the international church, meeting in regular council to pass decrees and with the power to elect the Pope and to appoint the working committees of the international church. This kind of drive to democratize the church would not alter its hierarchical structure, but it would de-

cisively shift the balance of power, so that this power, instead
of emanating from the top downward, would really be seen as
emanating from the community upward and forming standing
administrative bodies and ministries on every level to do the
work which the community cannot do directly itself. This is
the elective representative principle that everywhere operates
as the modern political style of life. This movement for
thoroughgoing democratization is quite legitimate and I believe is the necessary minimum for the organizational survival
of the Roman Catholic Church. The present tensions will be
absorbed into constructive action and will be prevented from
passing into schism only when groups on every level actually
have a share in the making of the decisions which affect their
life and work in the church.

However, out beyond this institutional redress of the balance of power, there is a movement which is not yet fully
born, but which has implicitly and ever more explicitly what
I would call the genuinely free church ecclesiology: that is to
say, the ecclesiology of the Radical Reformation. Here we
have to distinguish the question of the establishment of the
church within the state which is presently disappearing for
everyone, thus dictating a certain voluntarism of the church
vis-à-vis society as the church situation which is becoming
general for everyone; and the question of the freedom of the
community to gather, form, and order its own life. It is
this second aspect of the free church position to which
I am now referring since the question of disestablishment
is now largely an obsolete issue, at least here in America.
The free church, in the sense that I am using it, is the
free community within historical Christianity. It is founded
on a view of the church which denies that hierarchical institu-
tionalization belongs to the essence of the church. The church
is seen essentially as the gathered community of explicit
believers in which sacramental distinctions between clergy
and laity are abolished, priestly roles become purely contex-
tual and functional; the whole community arising by joint
covenant entered into by the existential analogue of believer's
baptism; that is to say, by voluntary adult decision. This
concept of the believer's church is, I believe, the authentic

church, and it is the understanding of the church which ever reappears in the avant garde at the moments of real church renewal. It is the avant garde and full expression of the church of renewal.

However, this does not mean that it can simply replace the institutional church. The institutional church represents the historical dimension of the church's existence. As such it is a necessary, albeit secondary expression of the church. It is necessary precisely for that dimension of historical perpetuation of the church's message as tradition which continually makes the gospel available to a new generation. By contrast the gathered church of explicit believers cannot perpetuate itself. If it tries to do so, it simply loses itself and becomes another institution. The two are really interdependent polarities within the total dialectic of the church's existence. The charismatic community can be free to be itself when it can resign the work of transmission to the institution and allow itself to form its life and let go of its life only so long as the vital spirit lasts within it. The historical church, in turn, remains vital and is constantly renewed through its ability to take in and absorb the insights of the believer's church. But in order to receive the fruits of the believer's church, it must be willing to accept whatever freedom the believer's church feels is necessary for the flowering of its own experimental spirit. It must be willing to let communities arise autonomously and without any specific kinds of institutional ties to work out their own gifts, and yet still to remain in the kind of open communication with these free communities which will allow their fruits to be given to the church as a whole. Only in this way does the whole dialectic of historical Christianity work as it should. But, of course, it does not and never has worked completely as it should in this way because the church is fallen man and hence is selfish and grasping, lacking in freedom and anxious about its security and vested interests. Hence we constantly block the free movement of the dialectic of renewal in the church and fall into alienation and schism. Much of the work of the Holy Spirit flees outside the bounds of historical Christianity and takes up its work elsewhere.

When we know the church after her true nature we must ever remain hopeful of the church's transparency to the Spirit. When we know its historical actuality, we cannot but be doubtful of its capacity for the Holy Spirit. In actuality, those most perceptive in understanding and most active in exercising a witness to Christ are found on the fringes of the institutional church, even outside its formal boundaries. Only in faith, hope, and charity is it possible to exist in the church in such a manner that we are, at the same time, both dedicated to it and disinterested in it, both really concerned about its failures and yet not ultimately concerned about them, knowing that it is what it is and cannot escape the judgment of its calling, yet God is not limited to it, but shall raise up a people to do his will wherever he pleases.[2]

[2] Rosemary Ruether, *The Church Against Itself* (New York, 1967), p. 65.